Democracy Promotion in t Neighbourhood

C000232434

EU external democracy promotion has traditionally been based on 'linkage', i.e. bottom-up support for democratic forces in third countries, and 'leverage', i.e. the top-down inducement of political elites towards democratic reforms through political conditionality. The advent of the European Neighbourhood Policy and new forms of association have introduced a new, third model of democracy promotion which rests in functional cooperation between administrations. This volume comparatively defines and assesses these three models of external democracy promotion in the EU's relations with its eastern and southern neighbours. It argues that while 'linkage' has hitherto failed to produce tangible outcomes, and the success of 'leverage' has basically been tied to an EU membership perspective, the 'governance' model of democracy promotion bears greater potential beyond the circle of candidate countries. This third approach, while not tackling the core institutions of the political system as such, but rather promoting transparency, accountability, and participation at the level of state administration, may turn out to remain the EU's most tangible form of democratic governance promotion in the future.

This book was originally published as a special issue of *Democratization*.

Sandra Lavenex is Professor of International Politics at the University of Lucerne, Switzerland and is also Visiting Professor at the College of Europe.

Frank Schimmelfennig is Professor of European Politics at ETH Zürich, Switzerland.

Democracy Promotion in the EU's Neighbourhood

From Leverage to Governance?

Edited by
Sandra Lavenex
and Frank Schimmelfennig

Routledge
Taylor & Francis Group

LONDON AND NEW YORK

First published 2013
by Routledge

2 Park Square, Milton Park, Abingdon, Oxon OX14 4RN
711 Third Avenue, New York, NY 10017, USA

Routledge is an imprint of the Taylor & Francis Group, an informa business

First issued in paperback 2017

British Library Cataloguing in Publication Data
A catalogue record for this book is available from the British Library

ISBN13: 978-0-415-52311-0 (hbk)
ISBN13: 978-1-138-10986-5 (pbk)

Typeset in Times New Roman
by Taylor & Francis Books

Publisher's Note
The publisher would like to make readers aware that the chapters in this book may be referred to as articles as they are identical to the articles published in the special issue. The publisher accepts responsibility for any inconsistencies that may have arisen in the course of preparing this volume for print.

Contents

EU democracy promotion in the neighbourhood: from leverage to governance?

Sandra Lavenex[a] and Frank Schimmelfennig[b]

[a]*Institute of Political Science, University of Lucerne, Hirschmattstrasse 25, 6000 Luzern 7, Switzerland;* [b]*Centre for Comparative and International Studies, Eidgenössische Technische Hochschule (ETH) Zürich, European Politics, Haldeneggsteig 4, 8092 Zurich, Switzerland*

EU external democracy promotion has traditionally been based on 'linkage', i.e. bottom-up support for democratic forces in third countries, and 'leverage', i.e. the top-down inducement of political elites towards democratic reforms through political conditionality. The advent of the European Neighbourhood Policy and new forms of association have introduced a new, third model of democracy promotion which rests in functional cooperation between administrations. This article comparatively defines and explicates these three models of external democracy promotion. It argues that while 'linkage' has hitherto failed to produce tangible outcomes, and the success of 'leverage' has basically been tied to an EU membership perspective, the 'governance' model of democracy promotion bears greater potential beyond the circle of candidate countries. In contrast to the two traditional models, however, the governance approach does not tackle the core institutions of the political system as such, but promotes transparency, accountability, and participation at the level of state administration.

Introduction

During the past two decades, the European Union (EU) has developed into an agent of international democracy promotion in its neighbourhood. The EU had long conceived of itself as a community of democracies and recognized the need to strengthen its own democratic credentials. Some of its external policies – most prominently, its Southern enlargement to Greece, Portugal, and Spain – had also been regarded implicitly and informally as a contribution to democratization. However, most of its external relations – above all trade agreements and development cooperation – had been notable for their apolitical content and the principle

1

of not interfering with the domestic systems of third countries. It was only in the early 1990s that external democracy promotion became an explicit, formal, and general aim of the EU. In the Treaty of Maastricht (1992), the EU declared the development and consolidation of democracy as a goal of development cooperation (Art. 130u) and its Common Foreign and Security Policy (Art. J.1), and the principle of democracy was introduced in all its external trade and aid agreements.

From its beginnings, EU democracy promotion has been a multifaceted policy. We distinguish three models, two that reflect main approaches to external democracy promotion and a third model that is more germane to the EU as a framework for regional integration.[1] The first model is linkage. It consists of activities that tackle the societal preconditions for democracy and give support to the democratic opposition and other civil society actors in the target countries. The second model of democracy promotion is leverage. This approach induces democratic reforms via political conditionality. Finally, the EU also promotes democratic principles through policy-specific, functional cooperation with third countries. We refer to this third approach as the governance model of democracy promotion. Whereas the linkage approach has been a constant in EU external policies since the early support to democratic transitions in Latin America in the 1980s,[2] the leverage model then became dominant in the 1990s after the end of the Cold War. The governance model started becoming more prominent in the early 2000s in the context of the European neighbourhood policy (ENP) which seeks to promote neighbouring countries' approximation to the EU's system of rules below the threshold of membership.[3]

In the early 1990s, the political integration symbolized in the creation of the EU coincided with the transformation of many Eastern European countries and these countries' gradual rapprochement with the EU. While the EU continued to give support to democratic transition in Central and Eastern European countries through economic aid and targeted action towards civil society, it also embraced a more explicit and direct approach to democracy promotion by making aid, market access, and deepened institutional relations from association to membership conditional on a third state's progress in institutional democracy. In the relations with candidate countries, political conditionality or leverage came to epitomize the EU's democracy promotion efforts. Most notably, the Copenhagen Criteria agreed by the European Council in 1993 made the consolidation of liberal democracy the principal condition for starting accession negotiations. From the first round of Eastern enlargement negotiations, opening in 1998 and excluding Slovakia because of its democracy deficits, to the discussions about the membership prospects of Turkey and the Western Balkans, political conditions related to the state of democracy have been of central relevance. Whereas linkage continued to be the preferred approach to democracy promotion in Africa, Asia and Latin America, democracy, human rights and the rule of law became 'essential elements' in almost all EU agreements with third countries as both an objective and a condition of the institutionalized relationship. In the case of violation, the EU introduced the (theoretical) possibility to suspend or terminate the agreement.[4]

The relative success of EU leverage in Central and Eastern European countries through political conditionality in triggering democratic change was mainly attributed to the attractiveness of membership.[5] Although political conditionality remains an important declaratory policy in the EU's external relations, its practical relevance has always been limited outside the enlargement context. Inconsistency and ineffectiveness is the general picture.[6] The marked slowdown of EU enlargement and the failure to implement conditionality consistently beyond the circle of candidate countries have therefore partly shifted the attention of academics and practitioners away from leverage as a model for EU democracy promotion.

In recent years, the implementation of new association policies below the threshold of membership has yielded attention to a third approach to democracy promotion that has come to complement the two traditional channels and strategies of external democratization. This third approach consists in the promotion of democratic governance norms through third countries' approximation to EU sectoral policies, i.e. functional cooperation. Less top-down than leverage and less bottom-up than linkage, this functional approach operates at the level of democratic principles embedded in the governance of individual policy fields and unfolds through the deepening of transgovernmental, horizontal ties between the EU and third countries' public administrations. The ENP, which the EU designed as an institutional framework for managing relations and developing cooperation with the non-candidate countries of Eastern Europe, Northern Africa, and the Middle East, is a case in point. It proclaims shared values (including democracy, human rights, and the rule of law) to be the basis of neighbourhood cooperation and links the intensity of cooperation to the adoption of shared values by the neighbourhood countries.[7] In practice, however, it is up to the neighbouring countries to decide to what extent they would like to cooperate with the EU on democracy, human rights, or the rule of law, and non-cooperation does not prevent intense cooperation in other sectoral policies, such as the environment, trade, or migration. Considering the constraints on democracy promotion outside an enlargement framework, the European Commission suggested refocusing the EU's efforts from the promotion of democratic regimes to the promotion of democratic governance, that is more transparent, accountable, and participatory administrative practice within the limits of autocratic regimes. It outlined that '[d]emocratic governance is to be approached holistically, taking account of all its dimensions (political, economic, social, cultural, environmental, etc.). [. . .] Accordingly, the concept of democratic governance has to be integrated into each and every sectoral programme' in the relations with third countries.[8]

This special issue seeks to reflect and assess EU democracy promotion in the regions covered by the ENP and Turkey at a critical juncture when the past successes of leverage in Central and Eastern Europe are unlikely to be repeated in the future and the conditions and impact of alternative models of democracy promotion are still insufficiently researched. Some of the contributions explore the potential and limits of leverage in the European neighbourhood in such pivotal countries as Turkey and Ukraine. Others focus on the prospects of the governance model of promoting democratic rules and attitudes in Northern African and Eastern European countries through transgovernmental, sector-specific cooperation – a model that seems to be especially suited to the EU's relations with neighbouring non-candidate countries. The special issue goes beyond the existing literature by broadening our understanding of EU democracy promotion conceptually and theoretically and by providing a comparative assessment of effects and effectiveness of different models of democracy promotion in the EU's neighbourhood.

In this introductory contribution to the special issue, we comparatively define and explicate the different models of democracy promotion. We then move on to describe the current context of EU democracy promotion in the European neighbourhood, the decreasing relevance of leverage and the need to explore other models. In the two final sections, we give an overview of the contributions and draw general conclusions.

Models of EU democracy promotion

Democracy promotion comprises all direct, non-violent activities by a state or international organization that are intended to bring about, strengthen, and support democracy in a third country. This definition excludes the use of physical coercion as well as indirect and unintended effects such as the international demonstration effects of successful democratic transitions or the potentially positive effects of general international interconnections on democracy. 'Democracy' is understood in a very general and simple way as the accountability of public authorities to the people. Accountability mechanisms comprise, inter alia, the accountability of officials to the electorate through free and fair elections, the accountability of governments to parliaments, or the accountability of agencies to public scrutiny. Any activities designed to strengthen accountability, and hence also responsiveness to the citizens, qualify as democracy promotion. The concrete contents of democracy promotion activities vary across targets, envisaged outcomes, channels and instruments. For the purpose of this special issue, they are a matter of empirical analysis, not definition. We focus on democracy-promoting activities of the EU as an international organization rather than on the activities of its member states. Moreover, we further focus on strategies and behaviours rather than on the motivations of the EU. In other words, we are not interested in explaining why the EU promotes democracy and whether it is normatively desirable.

There is an extensive literature exploring the nature of the EU as an international actor but at a level that is too general and abstract for the purposes of this special issue. Whereas this literature discusses the 'actorness' of the EU, its peculiar organizational characteristics and capabilities as a non-state foreign policy actor in general,[9] we prefer to describe the assumed organizational features and capabilities at the level of individual strategies. Another important strand of the literature seeks to describe the EU as a distinctive kind of 'power' in the inter-national system. 'Civilian power'[10] and 'normative power'[11] are the two best-known labels, though neither of them is sufficiently specific for the study of democracy promotion. For one, the promotion of democracy as defined above fits with both characterizations. Given the correlation of democracy with peace, international institutions, and trade, the promotion of democracy is a relevant activity for a civilian power engaged in civilizing an international system based on military self-help and the balance of power (see Note 10). Democracy pro-motion also matches well with the 'normative power' perspective according to which the EU projects its fundamental norms globally. In addition, both con-ceptions of EU power do not distinguish between different models of democracy promotion.

We propose three ideal-typical models of democracy promotion: linkge, lever-age, and governance. These models can be distinguished on four main dimensions: the target system of democracy promotion, the envisaged outcome, the main chan-nels, and the typical instruments.

- *Target systems of democracy promotion*. Democracy promotion can be tar-geted at the *polity* as such, including the electoral regime, the division of powers between state organs, and respect for individual rights and civil liber-ties. On the other hand, it may operate at the level of *society* and target the socio-economic preconditions for democratization, including economic growth, education, the spread of liberal values, and the organization of civil society and the public sphere. Finally, democracy promotion may also target *sectors*: the policy-specific governance regimes – such as environ-mental policy, market regulation, welfare regimes, or internal security.
- *Envisaged outcome of democracy promotion* Depending on the target, the outcome of successful democracy promotion differs. If it is targeted at the polity level, the typical outcome should be democratic institutions guaran-teeing vertical (electoral) and horizontal accountability as well as the rule of law. When the target is society, the envisaged result is a democratic, 'civic' culture and meso-level institutions such as civic associations, parties, and a democratic public sphere. In the case of sectoral democracy promotion, the goal should be 'democratic governance', i.e. procedural prin-ciples of democratically legitimate political-administrative behaviour, including sectoral transparency, accountability, and societal participation.
- *Channels of democracy promotion*. The actors primarily addressed by inter-national democracy promotion can be governments, societal actors, or administrations/agencies. Correspondingly, we speak of an intergovern-mental, transnational, and transgovernmental channel of democracy pro-motion and of a top-down, a bottom-up, and a horizontal direction of external democracy promotion.
- *Instruments of democracy promotion* The most basic distinction regarding the instruments or mechanisms of international democracy promotion is

Table 1.   Three models of democracy promotion.

	Linkage	Leverage	Governance
Target	Society	Polity	Sector
Outcome	Democratic culture	Democratic institutions	Democratic governance
Channel	Transnational	Intergovernmental	Transgovernmental
Instruments	Socialization	Conditionality	Socialization

'conditionality vs. socialization'.[12] Conditionality implies a bargaining process in which an international actor uses selective incentives in order to change the behaviour of actors in the target country. These target actors are assumed to weigh the benefits they derive from democratic change against the costs and to comply with international conditions if the benefits exceed the costs. By contrast, socialization is a learning process in which an international actor teaches domestic actors democratic norms and practices in order to persuade them of their superiority. Democratic change then results from a change in normative and causal beliefs.

In principle, democracy promotion may be conceived to vary independently across these dimensions. Conditional incentives may be targeted at changing electoral regimes as well as improving civil society organizations and they may work top-down as well as bottom-up. The same is true of international socialization efforts, to take just a few of the possible combinations. However, both theory and practice have tended to concentrate on the three ideal-typical combinations summarized in Table 1.

Although this introduction presents all three models of democracy promotion, overall the contributions to this special issue focus especially on the leverage and governance approaches. While recognizing the enduring relevance of the linkage model of democracy promotion, our main interest is in the question to what extent there has been a shift from the leverage to the governance approach in EU external relations, and under which conditions each of these approaches is effective. This focus is corroborated by the fact that whereas new foreign policy initiatives reflect a move away from accession conditionality towards forms of association below the threshold of membership, levels of EU external aid and support for civil society have remained relatively constant over time.

Linkage

The transnational linkage model is based on two pillars: 'direct' democracy promotion through support for democratic civil society and political opposition groups, on the one hand, and 'indirect' democracy promotion through intensified transnational exchanges with democratic countries, on the other. In both cases, the role of the external actor (in this case the EU) consists in enabling and empowering societal, non-governmental actors to work for the democratization of their home country from below.

Direct support can be material or educational. The EU may, for instance, give money to pro-democratic civil society organizations or parties or provide them with infrastructure such as computers, mobile phones, or photocopying machines. It may also organize meetings, seminars, and conferences that help these societal organizations to improve their political strategies and their cooperation. This leads us to the general expectation that the *effectiveness of linkage increases with the intensity of direct EU support to pro-democratic societal organizations*.

The *indirect channel of linkage* is broadly related to the modernization account of democratization.[13] According to modernization theory, democracy is a function of the level of social and economic development of a country. In his pioneering work, Seymour Martin Lipset studied the social conditions or 'requisites' that support democracy and identified 'economic development' – broadly understood as a syndrome of wealth, industrialization, urbanization and education – as the most important one. Economic development goes together with better education, less poverty, the creation of a large middle class and a competent civil service. It thereby mitigates the class struggle and promotes cross-cutting cleavages. In addition, it nurtures a belief in tolerance and gradualism and reduces commitment to extremist ideologies. In sum: 'The more well-to-do a nation, the greater the chances that it will sustain democracy'.[14] More recent contributions to the modernization theory of democracy complement Lipset's socio-economic 'requisites' of democracy. While Boix and Acemoglu and Robinson[15] emphasize income equality and the mobility of elite assets as democracy-promoting structural factors, Inglehart and Welzel[16] highlight change towards emancipative and self-expression values in post-industrial societies as a source of demand for democracy.

How can the presence or specific activities of the EU contribute to such socio-economic development? First of all, any indirect linkage impact of the EU is necessarily of a longer-term nature. Rather than affecting the short-term calculations and power resources of governments and non-governmental organizations, it helps to transform the environment and socio-economic structures of third countries. Furthermore, some of these activities and impacts may be unintended side-effects of general EU–third country relations. We can further distinguish economic development, education, and contacts as indirect linkage mechanisms.

First, the EU may promote the *economic development* of target countries. By increasing trade relations, investment and development aid, it can contribute to democracy-conducive wealth in general.

The positive effects of trade, aid, and investment may increase with diversification in two respects. On the one hand, they are most helpful if they do not simply benefit small economic elites but if their benefits are spread out as broadly and evenly as possible across the population thus contributing to general wealth and higher income equality. On the other hand, they are most likely to promote democratization if they strengthen mobile against immobile assets. Rather than nurturing the agricultural or primary resources sectors, the EU would therefore have to focus its trade and investment on the industrial and services sectors. We thus hypothesize that *the effectiveness of EU linkages increases with EU trade, aid and investment, in particular if the benefits reach society at large and are concentrated in the secondary and tertiary sector of the economy.*

Second, the *effectiveness of linkage increases with EU support for education in the target societies* By helping to raise the levels of literacy and education in the target societies – i.e. through building schools and universities, funding educational programmes, further educating teachers, welcoming students – the EU can prepare the ground for successful democratization in the future.

Finally, the *contact hypothesis* predicts that the *effectiveness of democracy promotion increases with the frequency and intensity of contacts between the EU and the target society.* Through business contacts, work or study abroad, tourism, longer-term migration, and media exposure, target societies may come into contact with democratic ideas and practices. To the extent that these contacts convey an attractive social and political alternative, they may contribute to value change and inspire more demand for freedom and political rights in the target countries.

In sum, we hypothesize that the more the EU directly supports pro-democratic civil society organizations and indirectly supports the modernization of target societies through contacts, diversified trade, aid, and investment as well as educational programmes, the more the linkage model of democracy promotion will be effective. However, in order to be possible, and to produce demand for (more) democracy from below, these contact, exchange, and support activities require a modicum of transnational openness on the part of the target country and of autonomy for the civil society. Linkage efforts will not reach civil society if a country is isolated from the outside world and civil society has no freedom of manoeuvre. Thus, the *effectiveness of linkage* also *increases with the external accessibility and domestic autonomy of civil society.*

Leverage

According to the leverage model, the EU targets third-country governments with the aim of inducing them to introduce democratic change in state institutions and behaviour. It constitutes a top-down strategy of democracy promotion that does little to foster a civic culture or strengthen intermediary institutions such as civic associations or the public sphere. Even if it is successful, leverage might thus contribute to a formally functioning democracy that is, however, not necessarily underpinned by democratic culture and civil society.

In order to produce institutional reform through leverage, the EU uses political conditionality. Conditionality is best conceived as a bargaining process between the democracy promoting agency and a target state.[17] In a bargaining process, actors exchange information, threats and promises in order to maximize their utility. The outcome of the bargaining process depends on the relative bargaining power of the actors. Informational asymmetries aside, bargaining power is a result of the asymmetrical distribution of the benefits of a specific agreement (compared to those of alternative outcomes or 'outside options'). Generally, those actors who are least in need of a specific agreement are best able to threaten the others with non-cooperation and thereby force them to make concessions.

In using conditionality, the EU sets the adoption of democratic institutions and practices as conditions that the target countries have to fulfil in order to receive rewards from the EU – such as financial aid, technical assistance, trade agreements, association treaties and, ultimately, membership. States that fail to meet the conditions are not coerced to introduce democratic reforms but simply left behind in the 'regatta' to assistance and membership. The analytical starting point of the bargaining process is the domestic *status quo*, which differs to some extent from the EU's standards of democracy. The status quo is conceived as a 'domestic equilibrium' reflecting the current distribution of preferences and bargaining power in domestic society. EU leverage may upset this domestic equilibrium by introducing (additional) incentives for compliance with democratic rules into the game.[18]

The most general proposition for the effectiveness of EU leverage therefore is: *A government introduces democratic changes in state institutions and behaviour according to EU conditions if the benefits of EU rewards exceed the domestic adoption costs* The more detailed conditions then specify the size of the benefits as well as the size of the costs. In addition, credibility is an intervening variable. With a given size of benefits and costs, the effectiveness of leverage increases with the credibility of conditionality.

In a first step, we can differentiate between tangible (material and political) and intangible (social or symbolic) rewards.[19] The former include financial assistance, market access, and voting rights in the EU, the latter international recognition and praise. In general, democracy means a loss of autonomy and power for the target governments. These governments have to respect, *inter alia*, the outcome of free and fair elections, the competences of courts and parliaments, the rights of the opposition and national minorities, and the freedom of the media. Lest a target government blocks democratic change, these political disincentives need to be balanced in kind by political incentives such as military protection or economic assistance to improve the security and the welfare of the state – and the reelection prospects of the government. We therefore hypothesize, first, that *tangible rewards are a necessary condition of effective leverage*. This hypothesis is corroborated by Kelley who shows that socialization efforts by international organizations have not been sufficient for the reform of ethnic politics in Central and Eastern Europe and by Schimmelfennig, Engert, and Knobel who find that international organizations unable to provide material incentives have generally been unable to produce democratic change in the region.[20]

Second, *the effectiveness of tangible rewards increases with their size*. Accordingly, the promise of enlargement should be more powerful than the promise of association or assistance, and the impact of the EU on candidates for membership should be stronger than on outside states not considered potential EU members. Only the highest international rewards – those associated with EU membership – can be expected to balance substantial domestic power costs. Comparative empirical studies concur on the finding that the conditional promise of membership in the EU has been a requirement for effective EU democracy promotion[21] or has produced the strongest effect on democratization in Europe's neighbourhood.[22]

Third, *the effectiveness of sizable material and political rewards increases with their credibility.* In a conditionality setting, credibility refers to the EU's threat to withhold rewards in case of non-compliance with EU conditions and the EU's promise to deliver the reward in case of compliance. On the one hand, the EU must be able to withhold the rewards at no or low costs to itself, and it has to be less interested in giving the reward than the target government is in getting it. If a target government knows that the EU prefers unconditional assistance to no assistance or unconditional enlargement to no enlargement, then conditionality will not work. Therefore, *the effectiveness of leverage increases with the asymmetry of international interdependence in favour of the EU.* On the other hand, the EU must be capable and willing to pay the rewards. Promises lose credibility if they go beyond the EU's capabilities, strain its resources, or produce internal divisions among the member states. The credibility of the promise is also weakened when the payment of the reward is distant: target governments tend to fulfil costly conditions when are rewarded instantly. Hence, *the effectiveness of leverage decreases as the EU's costs of rewarding, internal disagreements, and the time until the payment of the reward increase.* On the basis of this reasoning, assistance and association have been more credible rewards than accession, which is not only costly and divisive but also requires several years of negotiation – the more so, the poorer, the bigger, and the more culturally distant the target states of democracy promotion are. The strongly contested candidacy of Turkey corroborates this correlation.

Fourth, *the effectiveness of EU leverage increases with the strength and determinacy of its conditions.* Most fundamentally, given the domestic equilibrium in the target state, rules are unlikely to be adopted if they are not set up as conditions for rewards. In addition, we can distinguish between strong and weak conditionality depending on how consistently and explicitly the organization links rewards to the fulfilment of conditions. The stronger the conditionality, the more likely it will be effective. In addition, the determinacy of the conditions, and the determinacy of the rules from which they are derived, enhances the likelihood of adoption. Determinacy refers both to the clarity and formality of a rule. The clearer the behavioral implications of a rule are, and the more 'legalized' and binding its status, the higher is its determinacy. Determinacy matters in two respects. First, it has an informational value. It helps the target governments to know exactly what they have to do to get the rewards. Second, determinacy enhances the credibility of conditionality. It is a signal to the target countries that they cannot manipulate the rule to their advantage or avoid adopting it at all. At the same time, however, it binds the EU. If a condition is determinate, it becomes more difficult for the EU to claim unjustly that it has not been fulfilled and to withhold the reward. Empirical research on EU conditionality in Central and Eastern Europe shows that the strength of conditionality has had an impact on how quickly candidate countries adopted EU rules, whereas formality did not matter as long as the conditions were clear and clearly communicated.[23] However, a lack of determinacy, e.g. in the area of minority rights, may well lead to inconsistent conditions and outcomes across the target countries.[24]

Last but not least, *the effectiveness of EU leverage depends on the political costs of democratic reform for the target governments.* Domestic costs are low if meeting the EU's political conditions engenders no or low power costs for the target government. This is the case if compliance is not perceived to endanger the dominance of the ethnic core group, threaten the integrity of the state, or to undermine the target government's practices of power preservation and its institutional power in the state apparatus. By contrast, domestic political costs are prohibitively high if the EU's demands are seen as threats to the security and integrity of the state or as tantamount to regime change. Research shows that EU conditionality is generally ineffective vis-à-vis autocratic regimes[25] but also if meeting EU conditions risks the survival of a democratic governing coalition – unless the reward of membership or accession negotiations is very close.[26]

In sum, on the basis of theoretical and empirical research, we hypothesize for the leverage model of EU democracy promotion that it is likely to be most effective if the EU sets strong and determinate conditions for quick and credible accession to full membership, if interdependence between the EU and the target state is asymmetrically favouring the EU, and if the domestic power costs of fulfilling these conditions are low for the target state government. This means that with increasing 'enlargement fatigue' and the diminution of countries subject to membership conditionality, the leverage model of EU democracy promotion becomes less relevant. Against this backdrop, alternative, less 'direct' forms of democracy promotion through linkage and governance may gain in prominence.

Governance

Like the linkage model, the governance model postulates mainly an indirect way of democratic governance promotion. We call it the 'governance model' for two reasons. First, rather than focusing on electoral democracy, it embeds elements of democratic *governance* in sectoral cooperation arrangements between the EU and public administrations in target countries. 'Democratic governance' locates the notion of democracy at the level of the principles that guide administrative rules and practices in the conduct of public policy. The focus is thus less on specific democratic institutions such as elections or parliaments but rather on the principles underlying democracy which are applicable to all situations in which collectively binding decisions are taken.[27] These principles include transparency, accountability, and participation. Transparency refers both to access to issue-specific data and to governmental provision of information about decision making. Accountability is about public officials' obligation to justify their decisions and actions, the possibility of appeal and sanctioning over misconduct. This can include both horizontal accountability between independent state agencies (such as investigating committees, or ombudsmen) and vertical accountability that emphasizes the obligation for public officials to justify their decisions. Finally, participation denotes non-electoral forms of participation such as involvement of non-state actors in administrative decision- and policy-making.[28]

Second, democracy promotion according to this model is embedded in the EU's 'external governance'.[29] External governance refers to institutionalized relationships with non-member (and non-candidate) countries such as the ENP countries, in which the partner countries commit themselves to approximate their domestic policies and legislation to the EU *acquis*.[30] These institutionalized relationships establish horizontal transgovernmental networks between public administrations in the EU and third countries in a specific field of public policy.[31] Democratic governance is promoted indirectly as part of the third countries' approximation to EU sectoral legislation such as environment, competition, immigration or any other policy field. Given that these EU policies were designed for liberal democracies, they often contain democratic governance principles related to transparency, participation or accountability. These could be, for example, rights of stakeholders in environmental policies to be consulted, to have free access to information, and take legal recourse against administrative measures.[32] This model of transgovernmental democratic governance promotion does not necessarily address civil society actors, nor does it directly affect the overarching institutional arrangements of the polity. Therefore, even if it is successful, democratic governance promotion may still occur within a generally semi-autocratic political system – although, as we shall argue, a certain level of political liberalization and of civil society empowerment is a necessary condition for its success.

In conceptualizing the conditions for effective democratic governance promotion, the model follows an institutionalist approach[33] that focuses on properties of the EU *acquis* and on the institutionalization of cooperation in explaining EU influence. In addition to these institutional variables, the approach needs, however, to pay attention to sector-specific factors as well as conditions of the third country. As illustrated in Table 1, the governance model is mainly based on socialization as a trigger of change, although it can also be linked to the use of conditionality. Accordingly, it stipulates that the transfer of democratic governance norms and rules is a function of institutionalized exposure of target countries to the EU. The conditions for socialization are the more favourable the more that these norms and rules are codified in EU institutions and the more intensely third country officials are in contact with EU institutions. At the same time, the governance model also assumes that sector-specific interdependence and costs can either promote or impede this socialization process.

Given the focus on EU *acquis*-transfer as an instrument of democracy promotion, the first hypothesis is that *the more that democratic governance elements are legally specified in the EU acquis, the more likely it is that these norms will be effectively transferred to the third country*. This effect should be even stronger when the respective principles are also included in sectorally relevant international treaties to which the third country abides.

The vehicle through which the EU *acquis* and hence democratic governance principles are transported are transgovernmental interactions between EU actors and their sectoral counterparts in a third country's administration. It is our second hypothesis, therefore, that *the more these interactions are institutionalized in transgovernmental networks, the more likely it is that the democratic governance norms will be effectively transferred to the third country* The reason is that transgovernmental networks between EU and Member State administrative officials and experts, on the one hand, and administrative officials of the partner countries, on the other, are expected to facilitate communication and, by engaging third countries in joint problem solving, facilitate rule transfer.[34] In so far as these networks are also concerned with the implementation of the respective policies, they can act as laboratories for the realization or relevant democratic governance norms.

The additional involvement of other international actors – mainly other international organizations – in the promotion of the same democratic governance norms should enhance the effectiveness of EU norm transfer. Hence our third hypothesis: *The more EU activities are supported by other international actors, the more likely it is that these norms will be effectively transferred to the third country.* As in the case of international treaties, the support for EU norms by international actors strengthens the legitimacy of the EU *acquis*.

The positive impact of cooperation in transgovernmental networks facilitating communication and engaging ENP states in joint problem solving with the EU, however, may be offset by some sector-specific factors, such as the costs of adaptation that a third country faces in the particular sector and the degree of interdependence with the EU in the respective policy. The fourth hypothesis is therefore that *the higher the expected adoption costs of the third country are and the less sectoral interdependence favours the EU, the less likely successful rule transfer is.*

As with linkage, external influence finally depends on the openness and autonomy of domestic administrations in the target countries. The horizontal transgovernmental ties that are at the heart of the governance model presuppose a certain degree of decentralization of administrative structures, empowerment of administrative officials, and openness towards contacts and cooperation with the administrations of international organizations and other countries. In other words, *the effectiveness of democratic governance promotion increases with the accessibility and autonomy of the administration of the target country* (fifth hypothesis). The autonomy of civil society also plays a (secondary) role in the governance model, in particular for the application or implementation of democratic governance norms: the functioning of transparency, accountability and in particular participation necessitates the existence of active civil society which demands access to the decision-making process. Table 2 summarizes the main conditions of effective democracy promotion stipulated by the three models.

On the part of the EU, the effectiveness of the linkage model depends on transnational support fostering civil society, pro-democratic parties, and modernization.

Table 2.   Conditions of effective democracy promotion.

	Linkage	Leverage	Governance
EU conditions	Support for civil society and socio-economic development Intensity of transnational contact	Kind, size, and credibility of EU incentives	Institutionalization of democratic governance and transgovernmental relations Sectoral interdependence
Domestic conditions	Accessibility and autonomy of civil society	Political adoption costs	Sectoral adoption costs Accessibility and autonomy of administration

As for leverage, effectiveness depends on the kind, size, and credibility of EU incentives: the credible prospect of membership holds the highest promise. The governance model of democracy promotion stipulates a high degree of EU and international institutionalization of democratic governance norms and of transgovernmental relations – as well as sectoral interdependence that is high and favours the EU. Domestic conditions relate to adoption costs and the structure of state and society. In the leverage model, the general political adoption costs of governments potentially stand in the way of effective democracy promotion, whereas the governance model focuses on sectoral, policy-specific adoption costs. The success of linkage crucially depends on the accessibility and autonomy of civil society, whereas democratic governance promotion primarily requires the accessibility and autonomy of the administration.

Democracy Promotion in the EU Neighbourhood

In the past decade, research on democracy promotion in the accession countries has focused on leverage, i.e. the EU's political accession conditionality. Several comparative studies have concurred on two main findings.[35] First, only the credible conditional promise of membership has proven a powerful tool in helping Central and Eastern European countries to consolidate democracy. Socialization strategies or the use of weaker incentives have generally not been sufficient to bring about democratic change. Second, even a highly credible membership perspective has not been effective if meeting the EU's conditions implied regime change or threatened the political survival of the third state government as it has been the case in Slovakia in the mid-1990s and in Yugoslavia under Milosevic until 2000.

Both conditions for successful EU leverage arguably are on the wane, however. First, the EU is currently unwilling to extend the perspective of membership to countries beyond the current candidates in the Western Balkans and Turkey. While membership is excluded for the Northern African and Middle Eastern neighbours, the EU has not been willing to commit itself to a conditional accession promise for the European transition countries of Moldova and Ukraine either.

For all these neighbouring countries, the EU has designed the ENP as an alternative to rather than a preparatory stage for membership. Even in the candidate countries, political accession conditionality has lost credibility (cf. Kubicek, 2011). At any rate, the potential accession date of most candidate countries will likely be so far in the future that the incentives of membership lack power in the present.

Second, the EU's political conditionality has proven highly inconsistent below the threshold of accession conditionality. On the one hand, political conditionality is strong at a declaratory and programmatic level. The ENP is based on the EU's commitment to promote core liberal values and norms beyond its borders and claims to use political conditionality as the main instrument of norm promotion. ENP strategy documents tie both participation in the ENP as such and the intensity and level of cooperation to the ENP partners' adherence to liberal values and norms.[36] In addition, the 'essential elements' clause features in almost all legal agreements between the EU and partner countries in the region.

Implementation is patchy, however. Comparisons of ENP Action Plans reveal an incoherent democracy promotion policy and the overriding importance of the EU's geostrategic and partner countries' political interests.[37] In a comparative analysis of EU responses to violations of democratic norms in the post-Soviet area, Alexander Warkotsch shows that, while the existence of a democracy clause in EU–third country agreements significantly increases the likelihood of an EU response to anti-democratic policies, it is not significantly correlated with responses that go beyond verbal denunciation.[38] Strong sanctions are more likely to be used against geographically proximate states and less likely against resource-rich countries. Studies of EU democracy promotion in the Mediterranean confirm this picture. The EU's application of political conditionality in this region is undermined by its efforts to build a multilateral partnership in the Southern Mediterranean and to promote peace in the Middle East – otherwise it would risk losing essential partners for these efforts. At the end of the day, the EU, and particularly its southern member states, appears to prefer stable, authoritarian and Western-oriented regimes to the potential instability and Islamist electoral victories that genuine democratization processes in this region are likely, in some cases, to produce.[39]

Finally, domestic conditions in most neighbouring countries stand in the way of effective political conditionality. Most of the 'European neighbourhood' from Belarus via the Caucasus to Northern Africa is governed by autocratic states for which complying with the EU's political conditions would be tantamount to regime change. Even in the democratizing countries of the Western Balkans, Eastern Europe, and Turkey, legacies of ethnic conflict, extreme political polarization, and severe weaknesses in governance capacity block the road to further EU integration.[40] In sum, this special issue starts from the assumption that the EU's most studied and, arguably, most successful strategy of democracy promotion is losing its prominence and effectiveness, and that alternative models are potentially becoming more relevant. These other models have been less well theorized and less systematically researched than EU political conditionality.

As for linkage, there is statistical evidence that geographic proximity to the EU is systematically correlated with democracy.[41] This, however, is only a proxy for a mixed bag of transnational exchanges, contacts, and similarities (and probably other unspecified influences related to distance). We do not yet know which kinds of linkages are relevant for democracy promotion and what the specific EU contribution is. In addition, the literature is generally sceptical as far as EU democracy support from below is concerned. Studies on EU support in the southern neighbourhood point out, for instance, that EU assistance has remained extremely modest, focused on a narrow sector of civil society (such as secular organizations that are approved by, and often connected to, Middle Eastern and Northern African partner governments)[42] and privileged non-political community services. An important reason for the modest and timid support is the fact that the most governments of the neighbourhood region regard direct linkage as illegitimate interference in their internal affairs and that the EU has an overriding strategic or economic interest in securing intergovernmental cooperation.[43] Finally, the domestic conditions for bottom-up support appear unfavourable in most neighbourhood countries because democratic civil society is weak and lacks autonomy.

Since linkage is thus unlikely to be an effective alternative to leverage, we turn to the governance model in this special issue. This model has been much less explored in the literature than linkage. At the same time, it appears to suit the conditions for democracy promotion in the EU's neighbourhood better than either leverage or linkage. First, it is in line with the main thrust of the EU's external action and the ENP: the creation of policy networks and the transfer of EU policy rules (see Note 31). Second, it is less overtly political. Because democratic governance rules come as an attachment to material policies, do not target change in basic structures of political authority, and focus on the administration rather than societal actors, they are less likely to arouse suspicion and opposition by third country governments.

Contributions

The contributions to this special issue deal with the problems and limits of the leverage model as well as the potential of the governance model of democracy promotion in the EU neighbourhood. Some contributions analyse the problems of leverage, whereas others explore the potential of democratic governance promotion. For the reasons mentioned above, the linkage model is not the main focus of the issue.

Paul Kubicek analyses the effects of EU leverage (conditionality) in Turkey between 2000 and 2009 and draws comparisons to the effects of linkage (cultivation of civil society). Whereas the first half of the decade was characterized by significant democratic reforms, they stalled in the second half. In Kubicek's analysis, the change in democratization had mainly do with a variation in the conditions of conditionality. Reforms between 2000 and 2005 were triggered by the EU's recent commitment to Turkish membership and received further momentum in 2002 when the reform-oriented Justice and Development Party AKP removed the Kemalist parties from power. A large and credible incentive was thus matched by lower political costs of reform. The credibility of the EU's commitment appeared high and was confirmed by the EU's decision, in 2005, to open accession negotiations. These conditions worsened after 2005. Popular disapproval across the EU and the principled opposition of major EU member state governments cast doubt on the EU's commitment; further reforms and the implementation of promises made became more costly for the government; and the envisaged duration of accession negotiations moved any reward for these reforms far into the future. By contrast, the cultivation of civil society was less relevant in the first phase, and could not compensate for the worsened conditions of leverage in the second. As Kubicek points out, Turkey is a hard case of democracy promotion compared to the Central European countries. In comparison to the other target countries studied in this special issue, however, it is the one with the most favourable conditions of leverage.

Raffaella Del Sarto and Tobias Schumacher start from the observation that the EU has moved from negative to positive conditionality in its relations with the Mediterranean countries. Whereas the association agreements threatened the partner countries with the termination or suspension of cooperation when basic standards were violated, the ENP envisaged rewarding democratic progress with intensified cooperation. In either case, however, the effective use of leverage requires clear conceptual underpinnings; its credibility hinges on well-defined democratic conditions. In a comparison of the EU's ENP Action Plans with Jordan and Tunisia, however, Del Sarto and Schumacher show that the benchmarks are vague, arbitrary, inconsistent, incomplete, and thus useless for credible conditionality. Whereas the inconsistency is partly due to the principle of 'co-ownership', which allows partner countries to co-define the Action Plans according to their own priorities, it also shows a lack of determination on the part of the EU. At a conceptual level, Del Sarto and Schumacher thus confirm the widespread assessment that the EU's democracy promotion is inconsistent. This finding applies to the ENP in general – and is not invalidated by the fact that in countries with a relatively strong domestic democratization and EU integration agenda such as Ukraine we may observe clear and determinate benchmarks in the Action Plan.[44]

Tom Casier analyses EU democracy promotion in Ukraine, arguably the Eastern ENP country that has made most progress in democratization. Casier distinguishes two tracks of intergovernmental cooperation on democracy outlined in the ENP Action Plan: one focusing on formal democracy, i.e. the constitutional and institutional framework of democracy, the other on substantive democracy, i.e. the governmental practices within these institutions. He observes an asymmetric outcome for both tracks. Whereas Ukraine has made significant progress with regard to formal democracy, substantive democracy clearly lags behind. To a large extent, the discrepancy can be explained by the fact that formal institutional change can be achieved faster than the change of practices. The continuation of old practices also allows vested interests to reduce the costs of democratic institutional change. According to Casier's study, however, the discrepancy is reinforced by the EU's focus on formal institutions and the weaker visibility of substantive practices. On the one hand, the case of Ukraine thus shows that, in the absence of a credible membership incentive, EU democracy promotion can work via 'self-imposed conditionality': if the elites of the target state are strongly committed to European integration and regard democratic reforms as a way to demonstrate their commitment and induce the EU to perceive their country as a viable candidate. On the other hand, however, self-imposed conditionality is likely to remain at the level of formal institutional reform and does not appear to improve substantive democracy.

Democratic governance and the governance model of democracy promotion are the focus of the three remaining contributions. Anne Wetzel asks whether the transgovernmental promotion of democratic governance might be less affected by inconsistency than intergovernmental leverage. In a comparison of three policies – the regulation of genetically modified organisms (GMO), water governance and fisheries – she shows that this is not the case. When economic interests are threatened by stakeholder participation, as they were in the GMO and fisheries cases, democratic governance promotion is likely to be downgraded. Regarding the 'input'side of democracy promotion, that is, the EU's consistency and determination, 'governance' therefore does not seem to have an advantage over leverage.

By contrast, the joint contribution by Tina Freyburg, Sandra Lavenex, Frank Schimmelfennig, Tatiana Skripka, and Anne Wetzel analyses the 'output' side of the governance model and the conditions of effective democratic governance promotion. In a comparison of three policies (competition, environment, and migration policy) and four countries, two from the Eastern neighbourhood (Moldova and Ukraine) and two from the Southern neighbourhood (Jordan and Morocco), the study shows that country-level political variables (membership aspirations and the degree of political liberalization) do not explain the variation in outcomes. This finding demonstrates that the governance model is indeed an independent model and that the promotion of democratic governance operates differently from leverage. The authors argue that the transfer of democratic governance norms follows a sectoral dynamic and match the conditions stipulated by the governance model. Accordingly, the adoption of democratic governance provisions by the target states is the more successful, the more strongly these provisions are codified in the sectoral *acquis*, the more institutionalized the cooperation between the EU and ENP states is, the more interdependent the parties are, and, finally, the lower adoption costs are for national governments and sectoral authorities. However, the analysis also reveals that legislative adoption is generally not followed by rule application. As in the two-track case presented by Tom Casier, changes mainly remain formal. Because the contribution by Freyburg et al. is based on the most-likely ENP countries for effective democratic governance promotion, the lack of application can be generalized to the entire neighbourhood.

In the final contribution, Tina Freyburg shifts the focus from macro-level of domestic legislation to the micro-level. She asks whether participation in transgovernmental policy networks influences the attitudes of state officials regarding democratic governance. In a comparative analysis of two EU twinning projects in Morocco, she finds conditional support for the effectiveness of democratic governance promotion. Whereas in the issue area of environmental policy, the participants in the twinning project exhibited a significantly higher support for democratic governance than the non-participants, this was not the case for the twinning project on competition policy. The difference cannot be accounted for by properties of the state officials such as their linkage experiences but is best explained by the difference in politicization (the intensity of the political actors' interests at stake) between the two sectors. The finding that non-politicized sectors are more conducive to democratic governance promotion matches the results of the previous contribution.[45]

Conclusions

Studies on EU democracy promotion largely concur that EU leverage has been an effective model of democracy promotion in the (potential) candidate countries for membership. But what happens if the EU does not offer membership in return for democratic consolidation, or if its membership promise lacks credibility? Does leverage still work, or are alternative strategies more promising? The contributions to this special issue study different models of EU democracy promotion in the European neighbourhood, which does not have a membership perspective, and in Turkey whose accession process appears to have slowed down or even stalled. What can we learn from these cases?

Leverage is reaching its limits. The ineffectiveness of leverage even appears over-determined in the neighbourhood countries. The EU's lack of consistency, determinacy, and credibility combines with high political costs on the part of the partner governments. This is not the end of democratic reforms as recent developments in Turkey show.[46] Self-imposed, anticipatory conditionality in Ukraine is another partial substitute for strong external incentives, and partner governments may use the EU as an external anchor for reforms in the face of domestic resistance (see Note 44). But both examples also show the limits of 'conditionality-lite'.[47] Reforms often remain constrained by domestic constellations of power and interests or remain superficial, and self-imposed conditionality is unlikely to go far in the absence of EU responsiveness.

Linkage however is not an alternative. The contributions to this special issue have not systematically assessed the linkage model but the patchy evidence assembled here confirms the expectation of low impact. In the case of Turkey, the cultivation of civil society could not compensate for lack of credibility and external incentives (see Note 46), and in the case of Moroccan state officials, the variation in transnational experiences and exchanges did not account for the variation in socialization effects.[48]

What about the governance model of democracy promotion then? Sector-specific cooperation in transgovernmental networks seems capable, indeed, of influencing the legislation as well as the attitudes of state officials in favour of democratic governance.[49] Democratic governance promotion, however, proves to be as vulnerable to contrary economic and strategic interests and costs,[50] and as susceptible to superficial implementation (see Note 45), as leverage. In addition, it needs to be emphasized again that sector-specific participation, transparency, and accountability cannot compensate for the absence of democratic elections, representation, and the rule of law at the highest political level, nor does it replace an active civil society and socio-economic preconditions at the most basic level of democratization. Clearly, the governance model is no panacea and no substitute for EU leverage. But it provides a track of democracy promotion that is worth exploring further. At any rate, while the contributions to this special issue differentiate analytically between the three models of external democracy promotion, their empirical results document very much the interplay and mutual interdependence between external incentives for political institutions, the development of civil society, and democratization at the level of sectoral governance.

Postscript

When this special issue was finalized and ready to go to press, the successful revolts in Tunisia and Egypt, the popular unrest spreading across Northern Africa and the Middle East, and the uncertain prospects of democratization in the region demonstrated once again the need and timeliness to reflect on the EU's democracy promotion agenda in its neighbourhood countries. While the EU's long-standing focus on stabilizing the southern Mediterranean region with the help of autocratic regimes is discredited, the EU is struggling with defining its strategy to assist democratization processes under the new circumstances. As the transition countries will not be considered for membership even in the longer term, leverage is unlikely to be viable. In this respect there is nothing to be added to the conclusions of this special issue. By contrast, the anti-regime movements have in some countries opened up new opportunities for the impact of linkage that we considered highly unlikely when we planned this issue. Yet, given the weakness of civil society in the region and of the EU's ties to the anti-regime movements, direct linkage will be difficult to implement; and indirect linkage is by definition a long-term project.

For these reasons, the promotion of democratic governance may yet turn out to be the EU's best chance in the short term. Many regimes in the region are likely to survive the wave of unrest; in these cases, there is hardly an alternative to the governance model. Those countries that experience regime change will continue to cooperate with the EU across a wide range of policy issues and to seek its assistance. The established transgovernmental policy networks with the EU are likely to persist. In addition, however, these countries will be more open towards transparent, accountable, and participatory policy-making and policy implementation than their predecessors.

Acknowledgements

This contribution summarizes the theoretical framework of a project on 'Promoting Democracy in the EU's Neighbourhood' led by Sandra Lavenex and Frank Schimmelfennig within the Swiss National Centre for Competence in Research 'Challenges to Democracy in the 21st Century'. Financial support by the Swiss National Science Foundation is gratefully acknowledged. The authors would like to thank the two external reviewers and the editors of the Journal for helpful comments on earlier versions of the contribution.

Notes

1. For the juxtaposition of 'leverage' and 'linkage' as main models of external democracy promotion, see Levitsky and Way, 'International Linkage'.
2. See, e.g. Smith, 'European Union Foreign Policy', 122–29.
3. The ENP applies to Algeria, Armenia, Azerbaijan, Egypt, Georgia, Israel, Jordan, Lebanon, Moldova, Morocco, Palestine, Tunisia, and Ukraine. Belarus, Libya, and Syria qualify for participation but have hitherto not concluded the corresponding agreements.
4. See Horng, 'Human Rights Clause'.
5. Vachudova, *Europe Undivided*; Schimmelfennig, Engert, and Knobel, *International Socialization*.
6. Schimmelfennig, 'Europeanization beyond Europe'.
7. European Commission, 'European Neighbourhood Policy'.
8. European Commission, 'Governance in the European Consensus', 6; Freyburg et al., 'EU Promotion of Democratic Governance in the Neighbourhood'.
9. Allen and Smith, 'Western Europe's Presence'; Hill, 'Capability-Expectations Gap'.
10. Duchêne, 'Europe's Role'.
11. Manners, 'Normative Power Europe'.
12. Kubicek, *The European Union and Democratization*; Kelley, *Ethnic Politics*.
13. Going back to Lipset, 'Some Social Requisites'.
14. Lipset, *Political Man*, 31.
15. Boix, *Democracy and Redistribution*; Acemoglu and Robinson, *Economic Origins of Dictatorship*.
16. Inglehart and Welzel, *Modernization*.
17. Schimmelfennig and Sedelmeier, *The Europeanization of Central and Eastern Europe*, 12–16.
18. Ibid.
19. For the following, see Schimmelfennig, 'The EU: Promoting Liberal Norms'.
20. Kelley, *Ethnic Politics*; Schimmelfennig, Engert, Knobel, *International Socialization*.
21. Schimmelfennig, Engert, and Knobel, *International Socialization*; Vachudova, *Europe Undivided*.
22. Schimmelfennig and Scholtz, 'EU Democracy Promotion'.
23. Schimmelfennig and Sedelmeier, *The Europeanization of Central and Eastern Europe*.
24. Hughes and Sasse, 'Monitoring the Monitors'; Schimmelfennig and Schwellnus, 'Politiktransfer'.
25. Schimmelfennig, 'Strategic Calculation'; Schimmelfennig and Scholtz, 'EU Democracy Promotion'.
26. Schimmelfennig, Engert, and Knobel, *International Socialization*.
27. Beetham, 'Democracy and Human Rights', 4–5; see also Freyburg et al., 'Democracy between the Lines?'.
28. Cf. the concept of 'stakeholder democracy', Matten and Crane, 'What Is Stakeholder Democracy'. In this sense, democratic governance is similar to, but goes beyond, good governance (see, e.g. Kaufmann, Kraay, and Mastruzzi, 'Governance Matters'). Good governance refers mainly to the effectiveness of governance and need not be democratic.

29. Lavenex, 'EU External Governance'.
30. The EU *acquis* mainly comprises the entire body of EU primary (treaty) and secondary law in force. In addition, it includes politically binding declarations (as in the EU's foreign and security policy).
31. Lavenex, 'A Governance Perspective'.
32. For concrete examples, see Freyburg et al., 'Democracy Promotion'.
33. Lavenex and Schimmelfennig, 'EU Rules'.
34. Slaughter, *A New World Order*; Lavenex, 'A Governance Perspective'.
35. See, e.g. Kelley, *Ethnic Politics*; Pridham, *Designing Democracy*; Vachudova, *Europe Undivided*; Schimmelfennig, Engert, Knobel, *International Socialization*.
36. Mayer and Schimmelfennig, 'Shared Values', 40–42.
37. Bosse, 'Values in the EU's Neighbourhood Policy'; Baracani, 'The European Neighbourhood Policy'. See also the contributions in Pace, Seeberg, and Cavatorta, 'The EU's Democratization Agenda'.
38. Warkotsch, 'The European Union and Democracy Promotion'.
39. Gillespie and Whitehead, 'European Democracy Promotion', 196; Gillespie and Youngs, *The European Union and Democracy Promotion*, 12–13; Youngs, *The European Union and Democracy Promotion*, 42; Jünemann, 'Security-Building', 7; Pace, Seeberg, and Cavatorta, 'The EU's Democratization Agenda'.
40. On Croatia, see Freyburg and Richter, 'National Identity Matters'.
41. Kopstein and Reilly, 'Geographic Diffusion'; Schimmelfennig and Scholtz, 'EU Democracy Promotion'.
42. Gillespie and Whitehead, 'European Democracy Promotion', 197; Haddadi, 'Two Cheers'; Haddadi, 'The EMP and Morocco; Jünemann, 'From the Bottom to the Top'; Schlumberger, 'Dancing with Wolfes', 45; Youngs, *The European Union and Democracy Promotion*, 55–57; Youngs, *The European Union and the Promotion of Democracy.*
43. We thank one of the reviewers for alerting us to this point.
44. Casier, 'The EU's Two-Track Approach'.
45. Freyburg et al., 'Democracy Promotion through Functional Cooperation?'.
46. Kubicek, 'Political Conditionality'.
47. Sasse, 'The European Neighbourhood Policy'.
48. Freyburg, 'Transgovernmental Networks'; Freyburg, 'Demokratisierung durch Zusammenarbeit?'.
49. Freyburg, 'Transgovernmental Networks'; Freyburg et al., 'Democracy Promotion through Functional Cooperation?'.
50. Wetzel, 'The Promotion of Participatory Governance'.

Notes on contributors

Sandra Lavenex is Professor of International Politics at the University of Lucerne, Switzerland.

Frank Schimmelfennig is Professor of European Politics at the ETH Zurich, Switzerland.

Bibliography

Acemoglu, Daron, and James A. Robinson. *Economic Origins of Dictatorship and Democracy.* Cambridge: Cambridge University Press, 2006.
Allen, David, and Michael Smith. 'Western Europe's Presence in the Contemporary International Arena'. *Review of International Studies* 16, no. 1 (1990): 19–39.

Baracani, Elena. 'The European Neighbourhood Policy and Political Conditionality: Double Standards in EU Democracy Promotion?' In *The External Dimension of EU Justice and Home Affairs. Governance, Neighbours, Security*, ed. Thierry Balzacq, 133–53. Basingstoke, Palgrave Macmillan, 2009.

Beetham, David. *Democracy and Human Rights.* Cambridge: Polity Press, 1999.

Boix, Carles. *Democracy and Redistribution* Cambridge: Cambridge University Press, 2003.

Bosse, Giselle. 'Values in the EU's Neighbourhood Policy: Political Rhetoric of Reflection of a Coherent Policy?' *European Political Economy Review* no. 7 (2007): 38–62.

Casier, Tom. 'The EU's Two-Track Approach to Democracy Promotion. The Case of Ukraine' *Democratization* 18, no. 4 (2011): 956–977.

Duchêne, François. 'Europe's Role in World Peace'. In *Europe Tomorrow: Sixteen Europeans Look Ahead*, ed. Richard Mayne, 32–47. London: Fontana Collins, 1972.

European Commission. 'Governance in the European Consensus on Development. Towards a Harmonised Approach within the European Union'. Commission Communication, COM(2006) 421 final, Brussels: 30 August 2006.

European Commission. 'European Neighbourhood Policy: Strategy Paper'. Communication from the Commission, COM(2004) 373 final, Brussels: 12 May 2004.

Freyburg, Tina. 'Demokratisierung durch Zusammenarbeit? Funktionale Kooperation mit autoritären Regimen und Sozialisation in demokratischem Regieren'. *Zeitschrift für Internationale Beziehungen* 18, no. 1 (2011): 5–46.

Freyburg, Tina. 'Transgovernmental Networks as Catalysts for Democratic Change? EU Functional Cooperation and Socialization into Democratic Governance'. *Democratization* 18, no. 4 (2011): 1001–1025.

Freyburg, Tina, Sandra Lavenex, Frank Schimmelfennig, Tatiana Skripka, and Anne Wetzel. 'Democracy Promotion through Functional Cooperation? The Case of the European Neighbourhood Policy'. *Democratization* 18, no. 4 (2011): 1026–1054.

Freyburg, Tina, Sandra Lavenex, Frank Schimmelfennig, Tatiana Skripka, and Anne Wetzel. 'EU Promotion of Democratic Governance in the Neighbourhood'. *Journal of European Public Policy* 16, no. 6 (2009): 916–34.

Freyburg, Tina, and Solveig Richter. 'National Identity Matters: The Limited Impact of EU Political Conditionality in the Western Balkans'. *Journal of European Public Policy* 17, no. 2 (2010): 262–80.

Freyburg, Tina, Tatiana Skripka, and Anne Wetzel. 'Democracy between the Lines? EU Promotion of Democratic Governance via Sector-Specific Co-Operation'. (NCCR Democracy Working Paper 5, 2007). http://www.nccr-democracy.uzh.ch/publications/ workingpaper/pdf/WP5.pdf (last accessed June 5, 2011).

Gillespie, Richard, and Laurence Whitehead. 'European Democracy Promotion in North Africa: Limits and Prospects'. In *The European Union and Democracy Promotion: The Case of North Africa,* ed. Richard Gillespie and Richard Youngs, 192–206. London: Cass, 2002.

Gillespie, Richard, and Richard Youngs, eds. *The European Union and Democracy Promotion: The Case of North Africa.* London: Cass, 2002.

Haddadi, Said. 'The EMP and Morocco: Diverging Political Agendas?' *Mediterranean Politics* 8, no. 2 (2003): 73–89.

Haddadi, Said. 'Two Cheers for Whom? The EU and Democratization in Morocco'. *Democratization* 9, no. 1 (2002): 149–69.

Hill, Christopher. 'The Capability-Expectations Gap, or Conceptualising Europe's International Role'. *Journal of Common Market Studies* 31, no. 1 (1993): 305–28.

Horng, Der-Chin. 'The Human Rights Clause in the European Union's External Trade and Development Agreements'. *European Law Journal* 9, no. 5 (2003): 677–701.

Hughes, James, and Gwendolyn Sasse. 'Monitoring the Monitors: EU Enlargement Conditionality and Minority Protection in the CEECs'. *Journal on Ethnopolitics and Minority Issues in Europe* 1, no. 1, 2003: 1–37.

Inglehart, Roland, and Christian Welzel. *Modernization, Cultural Change and Democracy. The Human Sequence.* Cambridge: Cambridge University Press, 2005.

Jünemann, Annette. 'From the Bottom to the Top: Civil Society and Transnational Non-Governmental Organizations in the Euro-Mediterranean Partnership'. *Democratization* 9, no. 1 (2002): 87–105.

Jünemann, Anette. 'Security-Building in the Mediterranean After September 11'. *Mediterranean Politics* 8, no. 2 (2003): 1–20.

Kaufmann, Daniel, Aart Kraay, and Massimo Mastruzzi. 'Governance Matters Vi: Governance Indicators for 1996–2007' (The World Bank Policy Research Working Paper 4954, 2007). http://econ.worldbank.org/external/default/main?entityID= 000016406_20070710125923&menuPK=64166093&pagePK=64165259&piPK= 64165421&theSitePK=469372 (last accessed June 5, 2011).

Kelley, Judith. 'New Wine in Old Wineskins: Promoting Political Reforms through the New European Neighborhood Policy'. *Journal of Common Market Studies* 44, no. 1 (2006): 29–55.

Kelley, Judith G. *Ethnic Politics in Europe. The Power of Norms and Incentives.* Princeton: Princeton University Press, 2004.

Kopstein, Jeffrey, and David Reilly. 'Geographic Diffusion and the Transformation of the Postcommunist World'. *World Politics* 53, no. 1 (2000): 1–37.

Kubicek, Paul J. 'Political Conditionality and the European Union's Cultivation of Democracy in Turkey'. *Democratization* 18, no. 4 (2011): 910–31.

Kubicek, Paul J., ed. *The European Union and Democratization.* London: Routledge, 2003.

Lavenex, Sandra. 'A Governance Perspective on the European Neighbourhood Policy: Integration beyond Conditionality?'. *Journal of European Public Policy* 15, no. 6 (2008): 938–55.

Lavenex, Sandra. 'EU External Governance in "Wider Europe"'. *Journal of European Public Policy* 11, no. 4 (2004): 688–708.

Lavenex, Sandra, and Frank Schimmelfennig. 'EU Rules beyond EU Borders: Theorizing External Governance in European Politics'. *Journal of European Public Policy* 16, no. 6 (2009): 791–812.

Levitsky, Stephen, and Lucan A. Way. 'International Linkage and Democratization'. *Journal of Democracy* 16, no. 3 (2006): 20–34.

Lipset, Seymour M. *Political Man. The Social Bases of Politics.* New York: Doubleday, 1960.

Lipset, Seymour Martin. 'Some Social Requisites of Democracy: Economic Development and Political Legitimacy'. *The American Political Science Review* 53, no. 1. (1959): 69–105.

Manners, Ian. 'Normative Power Europe: A Contradiction in Terms?'. *Journal of Common Market Studies* 40, no. 2 (2002): 235–58.

Matten, Dirk, and Andrew Crane. 'What Is Stakeholder Democracy? Perspectives and Issues'. *Business Ethics* 14, no. 1 (2005): 107–22.

Mayer, Silvia, and Frank Schimmelfennig. 'Shared Values: Democracy and Human Rights'. In *Governing Europe's Neighbourhood. Partners or Periphery?*, ed. Katja Weber, Smith Michael, and Michael Baun, 39–57. Manchester: Manchester University Press, 2007.

Pace, Michelle, Peter Seeberg, and Francesco Cavatorta. (ed.) 'The EU's Democratization Agenda in the Mediterranean: A Critical Inside-Out Approach'. *Democratization* 16, no. 1 (2009): 3–19.

Pridham, Geoffrey. *Designing Democracy. EU Enlargement and Regime Change in Post-Communist Europe*. London: Palgrave, 2005.

Sasse, Gwendolyn. 'The European Neighbourhood Policy: Conditionality Revisited for the EU's Eastern Neighbours'. *Europe-Asia-Studies* 60, no. 2 (2008): 295–316.

Schimmelfennig, Frank. 'Europeanization beyond Europe'. *Living Reviews in European Governance* 4, no. 3 (2009). http://www.livingreviews.org/lreg-2009-3.

Schimmelfennig, Frank. 'Strategic Calculation and International Socialization: Membership Incentives, Party Constellations, and Sustained Compliance in Central and Eastern Europe'. *International Organization* 59, no. 4 (2005): 827–60.

Schimmelfennig, Frank. 'The EU: Promoting Liberal Democracy through Membership Conditionality'. In *Socializing Democratic Norms. The Role of International Organizations for the Construction of Europe*, ed. Trine Flockhart, 106–26. Basingstoke: Palgrave Macmillan, 2005.

Schimmelfennig, Frank, Stefan Engert, and Heiko Knobel. *International Socialization in Europe: European Organizations, Political Conditionality, and Democratic Change* Basingstoke: Palgrave Macmillan, 2006.

Schimmelfennig, Frank, and Guido Schwellnus. 'Politiktransfer durch politische Konditionalität. Der Einfluss der EU auf die Nichtdiskriminierungs- und Minderheitenschutzgesetzgebung in Mittel- und Osteuropa'. In *Transfer, Diffusion und Konvergenz von Politiken (PVS-Sonderheft 38)*, ed. Katharina Holzinger et al., 271–96. Wiesbaden: VS-Verlag, 2007.

Schimmelfennig, Frank, and Hanno Scholtz. 'EU Democracy Promotion in the European Neighbourhood – Political Conditionality, Economic Development and Transnational Exchange'. *European Union Politics* 9, no. 2 (2008): 187–215.

Schimmelfennig, Frank, and Ulrich Sedelmeier, eds. *The Europeanization of Central and Eastern Europe*. Ithaca: Cornell University Press, 2005.

Schlumberger, Oliver. 'Dancing with Wolves: Dilemmas of Democracy Promotion in Authoritarian Contexts'. In *Democratization and Development. New Political Strategies for the Middle East*, ed. Dieter Jung, 33–60. Basingstoke: Palgrave Macmillan, 2006.

Slaughter, Anne-Marie. *A New World Order*. Princeton: Princeton University Press, 2004.

Smith, Karen. *European Union Foreign Policy*. London: Polity Press, 2008.

Vachudova, Milada Anna. *Europe Undivided. Democracy, Leverage, and Integration Since 1989*. Oxford: Oxford University Press, 2005.

Warkotsch, Alexander. 'The European Union and Democracy Promotion in Bad Neighbourhoods. The Case of Central Asia'. *European Foreign Affairs Review* 11, no. 4 (2006): 509–25.

Wetzel, Anne. 'The Promotion of Participatory Governance in the EU's External Policies: Compromised by Sectoral Economic Interests?'. *Democratization* 18, no. 4 (2011): 978–1000.

Youngs, Richard. *The European Union and the Promotion of Democracy: Europe's Mediterranean and Asian Policies* Oxford: Oxford University Press, 2001.

Youngs, Richard. 'The European Union and Democracy Promotion in the Mediterranean: A New or Disingenuous Strategy'. *Democratization* 9, no. 1 (2002): 40–62.

Political conditionality and European Union's cultivation of democracy in Turkey

Paul Kubicek

Department of Political Science, Oakland University, Rochester, MI, USA

This contribution assesses the effectiveness of the European Union's (EU's) efforts to promote democracy in Turkey through strategies of political conditionality (leverage) and via the cultivation of Turkish civil society (linkage). Testing various hypotheses about leverage and linkage, it finds that the EU's efforts, particularly those emphasizing conditionality, were far more effective from 2000 to 2005, prior to the beginning of accession talks with Turkey. Since that period, ambiguities about conditionality and whether Turkey will be able to gain admission, as well as internal political developments in Turkey, have slowed political reform in Turkey. Examination of the Turkish case, therefore, shows both the possibilities and constraints of EU democracy promotion via linkage and leverage.

Introduction

The possible accession of Turkey to the European Union (EU) challenges the EU in a number of ways. With Turkey being a large, relatively poor country, its member-ship will likely put a strain on the EU's budget, affect the EU's decision-making, and test the EU's commitment to free movement of EU citizens. Turkish accession would push the boundaries of the EU further to the east, adding foreign policy and security questions. Most obviously, perhaps, as a Muslim-majority state, Turkey will change the cultural fabric of the EU, a fact that has made many in Europe uneasy. These issues, however, will come to pass only if Turkey does, in fact, gain entry into the EU. Whereas accession negotiations with Turkey began in 2005, its membership remains in doubt for a number of reasons, including opposi-tion to Turkish membership by governments and public in several EU states, Turkey's disputes with Cyprus, and concerns about the strength of Turkey's democracy, particularly given the efforts made in 2008 to ban Turkey's governing party, the AKP [*Adalet ve Kalkinma Partisi*, Justice and Development Party], and revelations in 2009–2010 of coup plots against the AKP government by its opponents in the military, media, and state bureaucracy.[1] Thus, at present, one of the primary challenges that the EU faces with respect to Turkey is ensuring that the democratic political reforms undertaken in Turkey in the 2000s – reforms that were made with explicit EU encouragement – are preserved.

Seen in this context, Turkey thus constitutes an important case for those interested in EU democracy promotion. Whereas the EU employed both leverage (conditionality) and pursued various policies of linkage (e.g. cultivation of civil society and transnational ties) in East Central Europe in the 1990s, one could make a strong case that the democratic outcomes in those states had been over-determined and that, in many cases, the EU played more the role of a guardrail than an initiator in the democratization processes of these countries.[2] In Turkey, the EU has employed leverage and linkage in the 2000s and played a key role in the reform process, but the EU's efforts have encountered more opposition and obstacles in Turkey than in East Central Europe. Turkey thus illustrates both the possibilities and limits of the EU's efforts to promote democracy, and the results in Turkey to date with respect to both leverage and linkage confirm many of the hypotheses advanced by Lavenex and Schimmelfennig in the introductory piece of this volume.[3]

This contribution aims to explain the EU's achievements and difficulties in Turkey, analysing the reasons behind the apparent success of EU approaches in the early 2000s and problems encountered in the later half of the decade. In doing so, it will revisit some of the claims made about political conditionality, illustrating how the Turkish domestic political environment, as well as the application of conditionality by the EU, over time became more problematic in Turkey than in Central and Eastern Europe (CEE). As for linkage, EU's possibilities for the development of civil society were also more constrained than in CEE countries. In short, whereas most of the factors – internal and external – lined up propitiously in CEE, various factors in Turkey have short-circuited a process whereby EU encouragement for reforms produces those very reforms which then lead to accession. Instead, after some progress, reforms in Turkey slowed, while at the same time, a 'grand coalition' in both Europe and Turkey has emerged in favour of something less than full membership for Turkey. This unfortunate development, in turn, may foster a 'vicious circle' that may stop or even reverse democratization in Turkey.[4]

The logic of conditionality and cultivation

The EU has been a vocal and often successful advocate for democratization. Through pressure, blandishments, and technical assistance, it has attempted to foster political liberalization and greater respect for human rights in a number of states. As noted by Lavenex and Schimmelfennig, EU policies work on various levels and through different causal mechanisms.[3] The present analysis will focus on the application of conditionality (leverage) and the cultivation of civil society (a key aspect of linkage).

Conditionality has been a cornerstone of the EU democratization strategy and is especially relevant in the case of membership candidate countries. Pared down to its core principle, the logic is clear: do X to get Y. In this case, the requirement is to democratize sufficiently to meet the conditions necessary for EU membership.

While the basic logic of conditionality is relatively simple and an analysis of the EU's democracy promotion experience in CEE countries might lead one to believe that the conditionality's effectiveness is 'self-evident',[5] several factors affect its likelihood of succeeding. As noted by Lavenex and Schimmelfennig, there is a consensus in the literature about when conditionality is most likely to work.[3] Most obviously, given that conditionality works on a cost–benefit analysis, the benefit must be greater than the cost of democratizing. Past studies have demonstrated that the benefits have to be tangible and large, with the carrot of EU membership being the most effective incentive for promoting democratization.[2,6] This approach, however, may not be enough. While a simple model of conditionality might suggest that domestic elites roll over to the demands of the EU, they may be reluctant to do so, particularly if reforms such as democratization carry, in Schimmelfennig's terms, high 'adaptation costs' that could jeopardize their hold on power, their conception of identity, or the integrity of the state.[6] Furthermore, if elites or the wider public question the intentions of the EU's agenda, or if a country has other political, economic, and security options besides the EU (e.g. in Turkey's case, this might include ties to the Middle East and Central Asia), a cost–benefit calculation may work against the adoption of democratic reforms as required by the EU.[7] Thus, when looking at the costs and benefits, it is important to look at a state's options, assess how reforms may affect domestic politics, and examine the standing of the EU within the target country. On this score, one should investigate to see if the calculus in Turkey is different from what it was for most states in CEE.

A second consideration is that the rewards offered by conditionality must be credible. If the ostensible reward is very costly for the EU itself, if it is promised to be delivered far in the future, or if EU members disagree over whether the EU should ever bestow the reward, the expected utility of democratization for elites in the targeted state declines. Why assume the costs if benefits are uncertain? These considerations all have relevance in the case of Turkey, as membership is at best a medium-term proposition and many EU states have reservations about Turkish accession, even if Turkey meets the Copenhagen Criteria.

A third consideration is the strength and determinacy of conditionality, referring to the consistency of conditionality and the clarity and formality of rules. If conditionality is inconsistently applied or is otherwise weak, targeted states might doubt that policy change has bearing on EU policy and may thus try to obtain rewards without fulfilling EU conditions. If the rules are unclear, targeted states may try to take advantage of ambiguity and reform only partially or, particularly if they perceive that the EU is arbitrarily changing the rules, they may question the sincerity of the EU and lose confidence that they can ever meet EU conditions. In either case, the reform push is weakened. While the EU would be reluctant to acknowledge that conditionality is unclear or arbitrary, the Copenhagen Criteria can become 'highly debatable and slippery concepts' that can lead to a 'highly politicized process'.[8] For example, it is hard to say with any precision how much 'democracy' or 'rule of law' will be enough in a particular case. Moreover, studies have shown that the EU has not always rigorously or consistently applied conditionality, particularly if it fears that its pressure could lead to counterproductive results.[9]

In contrast to the top-down vision of democratization suggested by conditionality, the EU has a number of programmes in place to cultivate democracy 'from below'. Many of these are designed to strengthen the demand side of the democratic equation: domestic actors such as political parties, civil society organizations, and the media, which will form a constituency and lobby group for democratization and civic education. The logic here is that such non-governmental organizations (NGOs) can play a crucial role in preventing the state from dominating society by both challenging undemocratic practices and providing information to elites so that democratic shortcomings can be corrected.[10] Beyond cultivating the quantitative growth of non-governmental actors in civil society, part of EU's tasks in these endeavours is political socialization through implanting and fostering democratic norms.

The EU democratization programmes attempt to improve the scope, depth, coordination, and democratic orientation of civil society, usually through funding and partnerships with associations in the targeted country. As noted by Lavenex and Schimmelfennig, the success of these strategies – part of what they identify as linkage – is conditioned by a number of factors.[3] An obvious one is that the intensity of EU support – through funding or contacts between the EU and the target society – matters. The more money or the more involvement there is, the better. Some EU support, as noted by Lavenex and Schimmelfennig, may be more indirect and long term, such as fostering economic development or education.[11] As with conditionality, however, one could further hypothesize that the effectiveness of EU aid or socialization efforts will depend upon how the EU is viewed in the targeted society as well as conditions within it. For example, if the EU's activities are viewed as legitimate and the EU norms have some resonance with those present in the given state – what might be dubbed a 'cultural match'[12] – EU's efforts to bolster civil society and transnational networks are likely to be easier. The legal environment is also an important concern. If civil society organizations are freer to organize and express themselves, EU's job in fostering democracy 'from below' becomes simplified. Finally, one might suggest that the unity and orientation of the organizations in civil society matter. If they are divided along ideological, sectarian, or ethnic lines, or if many civic groups are disinclined to support political liberalization, it may be more difficult to forge a broad-based, unified movement 'from below' that can push for democracy.

Bearing these considerations about conditionality and cultivation in mind, we shall now turn to the Turkish case, focusing, in particular, on why strategies that seemed to have much promise in the early 2000s later ran into serious roadblocks, so that by 2010 both Turkish accession to the EU and the stability of Turkish democracy remain in doubt.

2000–2005: the 'golden age' of reforms

Whereas Turkey undertook some political and economic reforms in the mid-1990s in order to fulfil requirements for the 1995 Customs Union with the EU, both the ability of the EU to push for reforms and the commitment of Turkish elites for ambitious changes were limited due to the absence of a membership perspective.[13] Calculations changed in late 1999, when the EU, reversing a decision from 1997, decided that it would consider a Turkish membership bid. This put before Turkey the same conditions demanded from applicant countries in East Central Europe, while at the same time, the EU increased aid programmes to Turkey, including funding for programmes designed to cultivate civil society and broader social support for democratization. In other words, the EU became much more serious about using leverage and linkage to push democratization in Turkey.

Conditionality and top-down reforms

EU's 1999 decision to consider the possibility of Turkish membership produced a 'political avalanche of democratization' in Turkey in the early 2000s.[14] One content analysis of Turkish parliamentary debates noted that a consensus in favour of sweeping democratization emerged as the EU opened its door to Turkey, with the then Prime Minister Bülent Ecevit even stating that 'the Copenhagen Criteria are not imposed on us by foreigners but they offer a life standard that we ourselves deserve'.[15] As quickly as July 2000, the government-created Supreme Board of Coordination for Human Rights issued a report on political reforms to comply with the Copenhagen Criteria, and the government adopted its recommendations as objectives.[16] In the following year, the Turkish government passed the National Programme for the Adoption of the EU *Acquis* and pushed through 34 constitutional amendments that were in line with the EU's recommendations. In 2002, the government built upon these moves by advancing various reform packages through the Turkish National Assembly. These actions included changes on a variety of fronts: abolition of the death penalty, expansion of freedom of expression, curtailment of the power of the military, release of political prisoners, and more freedom for the use and study of Kurdish, which previously had been prohibited. In November 2002, the AKP, which had a pronounced Islamic orientation, won parliamentary elections and its leader, Recep T. Erdoğan, became Prime Minister. The AKP, however, was not the same as previous Islamist parties in several respects, including the fact that it was fundamentally pro-Europe and in favour of political liberalization. The AKP government established an EU Harmonization Commission and adopted the UN Covenants on Civil and Political Rights and on Economic,

Social, and Cultural Rights. In a period of 2 years, it passed six reform packages through parliament, arguably the most ambitious liberalization programme in the history of the Turkish Republic.

The reforms of 2000–2004 fundamentally changed the political environment in Turkey by liquidating 'a very large part of the semi-authoritarian legacy' of the military government of the early 1980s.[17] The 1982 Turkish Constitution, which had been drafted by the military, and a host of supporting laws had limited civic and political rights in various ways, including limiting freedom of expression and assembly, restricting the formation and orientations of political parties, and legitimizing a political and judicial role for the military. Many of these provisions were eliminated or altered. For example, Article 13 of the Constitution was amended to make it harder to restrict fundamental rights and liberties, and rights to privacy and personal liberty were strengthened by amending Articles 19–23. Article 34 was amended by deleting text which gave reason for limiting freedom of assembly. The preamble of the Constitution was changed so that only 'activity' and not, as before, 'thought and opinions' contrary to state interests can be prohibited. Freedom of expression was also expanded by the third reform package, passed in 2002, which removed barriers to broadcasting and education in Kurdish. Furthermore, Articles 68 and 69 were altered to make bans on political parties more difficult. Constitutional changes and new laws changed the composition of the National Security Council (NSC) as well to strengthen the civilian presence in that body and limited many of the privileges and prerogatives (e.g. ability to try civilians in military courts, special State Security Courts) granted to the military by the Constitution.[18]

In some cases, threats of EU sanctions prevented backsliding.[19] For example, during debates over revisions to the Turkish Penal Code in September 2004, Erdoğan pushed a proposal to criminalize adultery. This made many in Europe question AKP's agenda. Eventually, this proposal was scrapped. The lines of cause and effect were rather clear and are underscored by the fact that debates on revisions of the Penal Code were put on the agenda and rushed through parliament in order to have these reforms in place before a critical European Commission report on whether to recommend the launch of accession talks.

Overall, reforms in the early 2000s were far more extensive than those in the 1990s and were largely in line with EU concerns, which centred on freedom of expression and association (including for Kurds), elimination of torture, curtailing rights of the military, and abolition of the death penalty.[20] As Turkish law fell in line with the Copenhagen Criteria, the EU, in turn, responded favourably. For example, Guenther Verheugen, then EU's Commissioner for Enlargement, acknowledged in 2003 that the 'passage of reforms through [the Turkish] parliament shows the strong determination of the Turkish government to get in shape for EU membership'.[21] By the end of 2004, the European Council noted that Turkey had sufficiently fulfilled the Copenhagen Criteria in order to open membership negotiations.[22]

Cultivation of civil society

Together with the top-down political reforms, there were also growth and increased activity in Turkish civil society, which according to most accounts suffered historically from underdevelopment and/or government suppression.[23] Civil society organizations had their initial flowering in the 1990s, and they were further bolstered by their heroic activity (and the government's failures) during the 1999 earthquakes.[24] Some organizations – notably the Turkish Industrialists' and Businessmen's Association (*Turk Sanayicileri ve Isadamlari Dernegi* – TUSIAD) and the Human Rights Association (*Insan Haklari Dernegi* – IHD) – became particularly outspoken and visible on issues of political reform. The EU thus did not have to create a domestic reform constituency from scratch.

That said, there is little doubt that the EU's efforts since 2000 have bolstered Turkish civil society.[25] The non-governmental sector in Turkey in the early 2000s worked closely with European groups and agencies through exchanges, seminars, conferences, and partnerships. EU's Civil Society Development Programme was active in Turkey and was charged to 'develop capacity for citizen's initiatives and dialogue, domestically and abroad, and to help establish a more balanced relationship between citizens and the state, thereby contributing to the maturing of democratic practice'.[26] In 2003–2004, for example, it spent €8 million in five defined areas: local civic initiatives, Greek–Turkish dialogue, trade unions, business chambers, and police professionalism, all of which emphasized transnational ties with international partners. Some initiatives were apolitical (e.g. bird watching organizations), but others were clearly more political, such as support for Kurdish and women's organizations. One success was the campaign of over 125 women's organizations to promote changes of the definition of 'family' in the Civil Code, to integrate a gender equality approach in the Penal Code, and to ensure women's sexual, bodily, and reproductive rights.[27] Other EU programmes stressed human rights development and education, and in June 2003, the European Initiative for Democracy and Human Rights launched a competition for funding for micro-projects on issues of torture, anti-discrimination, and good governance. Such assistance was vital to groups that did not enjoy powerful patrons within Turkey, and cooperation with European and other international actors bolstered the standing and legitimacy of NGOs in the eyes of Turkish political elites. Lastly, one should emphasize that some of the political reforms touched on earlier in this contribution (e.g. liberalizing the Law on Associations), which were encouraged by the EU, have created a better legal environment for civil society organizations in Turkey. In 2004, the EU even launched a project to improve NGO–public sector cooperation, which supported a department within the Turkish Ministry of Interior that engages in outreach to civic associations.[26]

Turkish civic organizations, with an eye towards the EU, have also taken the initiative to organize themselves.[28] In 2002, 175 Turkish NGOs formed the European Movement (*Avrupa Haraketi*), which advocated political and social reforms to bolster Turkey's EU bid. In 2004, the Turkish Economic Development

Foundation took the lead in bringing together 269 organizations in the Turkey Platform, a group that lobbied both Brussels and Ankara in favour of Turkish membership. The common desire to join the EU, at least in the early 2000s, often brought disparate groups (e.g. secular, liberal, Kurdish, and Islamic) in Turkish civil society together, whereas in the past, their ideological diversity had weakened their effectiveness as a counter-weight to the state.[24,29] Turkish civic organizations also played an important role in providing information to the EU and then putting a Turkish face on EU initiatives, which otherwise risked being perceived as patronizing or ignorant of Turkish reality. Some Turkish civic organizations, most notably TUSIAD, have also opened offices in Brussels and are major advocates for Turkey within the EU.

Accounting for success

Although it is hard to demonstrate 100% conclusively, there is much evidence to suggest that since joining the EU became a 'national obsession'[30] in the early 2000s, EU policy has been decisive in sparking reforms in Turkey. Earlier political liberalization in the 1990s remained limited and did not address fundamental issues such as the powers of the NSC and rights of the Kurds. Pointedly, leading figures in the Turkish government prior to 1999 denied that there was even a 'Kurdish' problem and asserted that reforms that 'go against the fiber of our country are not matters upon to discussion'.[31] According to Öniş, if previously one witnessed a 'vicious circle of delayed reforms and slow progress toward full membership', EU pressure helped foster a 'virtuous circle' conducive to wide-ranging reforms.[4] The reforms of 2000–2004 were, in his view, 'inconceivable in the absence of powerful incentives and pressures from the EU' (see Note 4). Indeed, given the fact that most of the government's reforms addressed issues identified in various EU 'progress reports' on Turkey (e.g. role of the NSC, death penalty, and freedom of expression), one can be fairly confident in identifying the EU's actions as a causal factor.

What accounts for the apparent success of EU's democracy promotion policy? Drawing from the above discussion, one may conclude that the various factors conducive to the effective application of conditionality lined up positively in the early 2000s in Turkey. First, as noted, the benefit – EU membership – was much larger than what had been offered previously. It is true that there were costs to reform and some opposition to the EU's use of conditionality, most notably from the Nationalist Action Party, which was in the coalition government until 2002. However, the desire for EU membership was so strong, both in terms of public opinion[32] and in terms of the country's long-term Europeanization agenda that harkens back to the days of Atatürk, that the benefits were widely viewed to be worth the costs.[33] It also bears noting that the AKP, which assumed power in 2002, was explicitly pro-EU, viewing the EU reform agenda as a potential ally in its own domestic political battles with the secular, Kemalist establishment that in the past had been willing to ban Islamic-oriented parties.[34] For the AKP then, the costs of reform were relatively low, and it did not, as earlier Islamic parties had, think that Turkey had geopolitical options (e.g. in the Middle East or Central Asia) outside of joining the EU.[35] As for the credibility and consistency of conditionality, these were not salient concerns. It is true that Turks, no doubt, realized that East Central European states were likely to join the EU before they would, but the EU appeared enthusiastic about the expansion project, and its 1999 decision to open the door to Turkey had overcome previously expressed opposition to Turkish membership. Conditionality in this period seemed straightforward enough and was not subject to problems (e.g. the situation regarding Cyprus) that appeared later. In other words, Turkish elites believed that if they implemented reforms, they could join the EU.[36]

The cultivation of civil society was also relatively problem free, although one can debate the centrality of civil society and various transnational linkages in the reform process.[37] In the early 2000s, the EU increased funding for democratization efforts in Turkey, particularly those involving civil society. This gave the EU more of a role than it had had in the past. Two Turkish civil society activists concede that prior to 1999, the work of civil society groups failed to produce concrete results. It was, in their view, the political discipline provided by the EU prospect and greater involvement by the EU in assisting Turkish civic organizations that changed the environment to the benefit of reformers in Turkey.[38] Moreover, as noted, there was a strong consensus in Turkish society about the desirability of EU membership, thus giving EU's activities legitimacy. Changes in the legal environment augured well for a stronger role for civil society, and civic groups themselves demonstrated a strong degree of unity and purpose in embracing the democratization agenda, uniting behind the EU project in contrast to internecine conflict that emerged after the glow of their 1999 post-earthquake accomplishments had begun to dissipate.[24]

2005–2009: the EU project stalls

The opening of accession talks in October 2005 marked a highpoint in Turkish–EU relations. Since then, political liberalization in Turkey has markedly slowed, while EU–Turkish relations have run into various difficulties. These phenomena allow one to look at changes over time within the single case study of EU policies towards Turkey, thereby facilitating the effort to assess what causal factors changed and may have broken the 'virtuous circle' that earlier promoted Turkish democratization.

The slowdown in top-down reforms

Whereas the EU and other outside observers were often effusive in their praise for the reforms of 2001–2005, since then the tone has increasingly been one of scepticism and doubt. Part of the issue was that the focus turned from adoption of reforms to their actual implementation. For example, the 2005 and 2006 EU Progress Reports noted problems on elimination of torture and illegal detentions, access to Kurdish language courses, and continued limits on freedom of expression, all of which were supposedly remedied by various reform packages.[39] Some accused the 'deep state' (the military, the courts, and the bureaucracy) of foot-dragging and of taking actions that undermined Turkey's EU bid.[40] One of the most notorious examples was the trial in late 2005, brought by a Turkish prosecutor not affiliated with the AKP government, against Nobel prize-winning author Orhan Pamuk, who was charged under Article 301 of the Criminal Code for insulting Turkishness by discussing the killings of Armenians during World War I with a Swiss newspaper. The EU sent a delegation to observe the trial, and charges against Pamuk were dropped on a technicality, but other writers were convicted under this statute. One, Hrant Dink, a Turkish citizen of Armenian origin, was jailed in 2006 for referring to 'genocide' against the Armenians and, after his release, was killed in January 2007 by a gunman with ties to nationalist groups in the military and bureaucracy.

By 2008 and 2009, the European Commission progress reports became harsher in their assessments.[41] Among other items, the 2009 report noted several areas where Turkish laws and practices did not meet the EU standards, including rules on political parties, promotion of minority languages, trade union rights, alle-gations of torture, corruption, non-discrimination on basis of sexual orientation, bans on Internet sites, use of the Anti-Terror law against Kurdish groups, the lack of a gender equality body, and the continued political influence of the military. It noted that 'overall limited concrete progress was made [in 2008–09] on political reforms' and that 'little progress can be reported on effective implementation of [previous] political and constitutional reforms'.[42] The European Commission was also troubled by court cases brought by state prosecutors to close the ruling AKP (ultimately unsuccessful) and the primarily Kurdish Democratic Society Party (DTP), the closure of which in December 2009 drew EU's criticism. Specifi-cally, the EU Presidency noted that the Venice Commission of the Council of Europe concluded that Articles 68 and 69 of the Turkish constitution used to ban political parties violated the European Convention of Human Rights and called for Turkey to make appropriate changes to its constitution.[43]

The European Commission also noted its general disappointment with the AKP government. While it acknowledged the government's commitment to the accession process, it reported in 2008 that 'the government did not put forward a consistent and comprehensive Programme of political reforms'.[44] For example, the government's proposal to engage with civil society organizations in an ambitious project to adopt a new constitution better aligned with international standards on political and civil rights – an idea welcomed by the EU – was aban-doned in 2007 in favour of pushing forward amendments to lift the headscarf ban on university students. It was this effort that prompted the lawsuit against the AKP, in which AKP narrowly avoided being shut down.

Most troubling of all, perhaps, were revelations about the actions of AKP's opponents, which, as uncovered by investigations in Turkey, suggested that fac-tions within the military and bureaucracy were planning a coup against the AKP as early as 2003 and that they had turned against Turkey's alignment with the West.[45] While AKP's efforts to prosecute the alleged coup plotters was looked upon largely favourably by the EU, this action had created new frictions with the military and thrown the future of the democratization project into some doubt.

What role for civil society?

If momentum for reform 'from above' stalled after the first half of the 2000s, what can be said of civil society and 'movement from below'? First, it is evident that Turkish civil society remains vibrant. Nearly 100,000 civic associations exist in Turkey, and at times, civic groups have been able to mobilize sizeable segments of the population. For example, in early 2007, a mass protest against the killing of Dink brought up to a million people out on the streets of Istanbul chanting the slogan 'We are all Armenians.' Later that year, amid tensions between the government and the military, nationalist and pro-secular groups spearheaded massive demonstrations against the nomination of Abdullah Gül of AKP to become the president of Turkey because of his alleged Islamic orientation. The latter gathering implicitly backed threats of a military coup and the closure of AKP and included harsh criticism of the EU, suggesting that the growth or mobilization of civil society *per se* may not portend positive development for liberalization or Turkish–EU relations.

Secondly, one should note that the EU has stepped up efforts to promote Turkish civil society. Since 2005, the EU has funded the EU–Turkey Civil Society Dialogue, which is designed to foster ties between Turkish groups and associations in EU countries. According to an EU representative in Turkey, one of the programme's main goals is to 'overcome mutual misperceptions', 'give Turkish citizens the chance to learn more about the EU', and improve knowledge of Turkey within the EU.[46] From 2005 to 2007, this programme spent €4.3 million on 70 different projects. Among its self-proclaimed success stories, the EU trumpets the 'Bridges of Knowledge' programme, which created 27 partnerships between Turkish and European civic associations and led to numerous seminars, workshops, and publications. This project had a broad focus (e.g. energy, environment, and human rights) and was the first project to emphasize training and development from a civil society perspective.[47] In 2006, the Turkish government and the EU devoted €29.5 million towards additional civil society development, including a grant programme, which is envisioned to support over 100 civic organizations in various areas. In 2008, the EU sponsored a Turkey–EU Democracy Forum, which brought policy-makers and civic activists together to discuss political reforms and how to engage better with civil society. On-going EU involvement includes €10 million for an NGO Grant Facility and €3 million in 2007–2010 for the European Instrument for Democracy and Human Rights, which funded projects that include rehabilitation of torture victims, a dialogue on secularism, women's and minority rights, media freedom, and efforts to promote human rights through textbooks. In 2009, the EU announced a new project, 'Access-TR', designed to involve non-governmental actors more directly in the accession process.

However, the impact of these activities is hard to discern. The aforementioned 2008 Progress Report highlighted the fact that contact between the government and various NGOs lacks a legal framework and is often limited. For example, the Turkish government's Human Rights Advisory Board has not met since 2004. Consultations that do occur 'do not result in tangible policy outputs'.[48] Areas that were highlighted by criticism were the failure of the government to work with NGOs on women's issues and the lack of progress to pass legislation to ensure trade union rights. In 2009, these areas were again singled out as deficient.[49] Moreover, the EU reports found that groups that receive foreign funding (including EU funds) and those working on Kurdish issues have been subjected to harassment by state authorities. The findings expressed in these reports echo the results of academic research among civil society organizations, in which they noted in response to surveys that their groups are organizationally weak, have a low impact on public policy, and operate in a legal environment that is often unsupportive. In addition, representatives from civil society organizations are overall neutral with respect to whether civil society functions in a manner that contributes to democratization within Turkey, due in part to lack of commitment among civil society groups to democratic principles and divisions among groups within Turkish civil society.[10]

What went wrong?

How can one account for these outcomes, which stand in such contrast to those in the early 2000s? Several of the previously advanced hypotheses help provide answers, as they point to how changes within the Turkish domestic environment as well as application of EU policy affect the receptiveness and responsiveness to the EU's agenda.

While it is true that the reward – accession – remained the same, the credibility of the reward as well as the general perception of the EU changed markedly after 2005. In short, Turks found it less and less likely that, regardless of what they did, they would gain entry into the EU. 'Enlargement fatigue' in Europe from the 2004 and 2007 expansions is clearly working against Turkey, but there are specific factors in the Turkish case that have led many Turks to doubt that they would be approved for EU membership. For example, in December 2006, the EU suspended negotiations on several chapters of the accession talks, because Turkey refused to allow (Greek) Cypriot ships and planes into Turkish facilities. Given Turkish and Turkish Cypriot support for and Greek Cypriot rejection in 2004 of the UN-sponsored Annan Plan to reunify the island, many Turks felt that this decision was unwarranted and evidence of the EU's 'unbalanced' approach to this question.[50] Expressions of anti-Turkish sentiment from European leaders also contributed to the problem. These took various forms. One was a proposal, broached even before accession talks commenced, to permanently limit Turkish labour mobility within the EU, creating, in effect, a secondary type of 'European' status for Turks. This was widely denounced in Turkey.[51] Some European leaders, including Germany's Angela Merkel and France's Nicholas Sarkozy, have spoken out forcefully against Turkish membership in principle, with Sarkozy in 2007 even rejecting the long-standing notion that Turkey was a 'European' country.[52] A public opinion survey in 2008 found only 31% of the citizens in the EU favoured membership for Turkey, with 55% opposing, the largest opposition for any prospective EU member. Majorities in France, Germany, Austria, and Greece opposed Turkish membership even if Turkey complied with all the conditions required by the EU.[53]

Given this change, many Turks began to sour both on the EU and on Turkey's accession prospects. The Turkish Secretary General for EU Affairs suggested that 'EU leaders' habit of using Turkey's population, geography and culture as arguments for a "privileged partnership" instead of full membership weakens the Turkish public's trust in the EU'.[54] In 2009, for example, a survey from the German Marshall Fund showed that positive views of EU membership were only 48% (compared with 73% in 2004) and that only 28% of Turks thought that they would someday become an EU member compared with 65% who thought it unlikely.[55] Turks also accuse the EU of double standards and hypocrisy. Demands beyond the Copenhagen Criteria (e.g. recognition of the Armenian genocide) have been placed on Turkey, while the idea of stopping accession talks in favour of a 'privileged partnership' was not broached with other states, for example. Proposals to hold referendums to approve further EU expansion – suggested in both Austria and France – are clearly directed against Turkey. Examination of the EU reports also shows, according to one study, that conditionality was much more rigorously and consistently applied to other countries (e.g. Romania) than to Turkey.[9] This concern also touches upon the clarity of and determinacy of EU criteria. Indeed, reading the EU Progress Reports through the 2000s, one can get the impression that each year, the EU adds more and more to the Turks' to-do list, with the final goal – how strong must 'democracy' and the 'rule of law' and other criteria be in order to gain membership – being decidedly unclear. The contrast with accession negotiations on more technical or economic issues highlights how the question of democratization can be contested or easily become politicized. Examination of Turkish public opinion affirms this notion, with a majority (59%) saying as early as 2002 in a survey by the Turkish Economic and Social Studies Foundation that they thought the EU was insincere and hypocritical toward Turkey.[56]

The key point from this discussion is that as both the credibility of the prize of EU membership has declined and more Turks question the sincerity of the EU and the desirability of the EU membership itself, there is less incentive for Turkey to comply with the EU's democratization agenda. It is true that the reform process has not ended entirely – the referendum on constitutional changes in the judicial system scheduled to be held in September 2010 is designed to bring Turkey more in line with the European norms and practices[57] – but it has perceptively slowed, and opposition to various reforms, particularly those that limit the power of the military or give more room for religious expression in public life, has hardened with Turkey. While some might be willing to cut the AKP government some slack – given the shrinking domestic constituency in favour of the EU and its battles with its secularist and nationalist opponents – there is clearly a sense of disappointment in the EU. Ria Oomen-Ruijten, the European Parliament's Rapporteur on Turkey, noted that the Turkish government has been side-tracked from reform and that by 2008 the credibility of the reform process was at stake. Given the fact, as she observed, that the 2008 report was the third one to note the slowdown in reform, many might wonder if the 'virtuous circle' of the 'golden age' of reforms can be re-created.[58]

Another factor that has gained currency among those who noted the slowdown of reforms in Turkey is that the Turkish government may feel that it has other options besides the EU. Several scholars have suggested how ideas of 'neo-Otto-manism' and the desire for greater engagement with the Muslim world have animated Turkish foreign policy under the AKP government.[59] Part of the motivation is economic, as Turkish economic interaction with its non-EU neighbours grew markedly in the second half of the 2000s. With the Turkish economy growing by over 10% in 2010 while European economies remained stagnant, some began to question how much Turkey really needs Europe.[60] Older strategic alliances are also being re-considered. For example, in 2009–2010, Turkey stepped up criticism of Israel and made friendly overtures to Iran. In the wake of the Israelis' seizure of Turkish vessels that tried to deliver supplies to Gaza and the resulting anti-Israel (and anti-Western) demonstrations in Turkey, some suggested that Turkey, rebuffed by Europe, was turning East. While this new emphasis in Turkish foreign policy seems to have boosted Erdoğan's standing both at home – where anti-European and anti-American attitudes are gaining strength[61] – and in the wider Middle East, his actions, which include feting the leaders of Sudan and Iran in Ankara, have raised questions in Europe and the USA about Turkey's long-standing Western orientation.[62]

As for linkage and civil society, its role is increasingly constrained. As the EU reports cited above noted, the government is not engaging it as a player in the policy-making process. It is true that the EU has been supporting many groups in Turkish civil society, particularly those lobbying for women's and minority rights, but it is hard at present to draw clear lines of causation between the actions of NGOs and policy change, particularly given the Turkish government's inclination not to engage with many of these groups. The EU officials concede that it is hard to judge their efforts to cultivate civil society, with one official noting that 'it will take time to see these micro results [of supporting civil society] spreading to the larger public'.[63] At minimum, as noted above, one could say that both questions about the EU's credibility and image as well as some incongruence with respect to a 'cultural match' (e.g. views on what secular-ism requires) hampers the EU's efforts to forge a more united civil society to push forward the EU's agenda for political liberalization. In this respect, one must acknowledge that civil society in Turkey reflects Turkish society itself and the divisions over EU membership. Whereas there was consensus on joining both the EU and the political reform process in the early 2000s, this consensus broke down in the later half of the 2000s.

A key consideration here is that the perceived costs of reforms – their 'adaptative costs' – have grown in Turkey, while the level of social consensus on what the end-point should be is far more contested. In East Central Europe, the critical issues were democratization and marketization, and there was a fairly high level of consensus on the vision of a liberal democracy and market-oriented economy. Hence, in these states, both parties of the right and the left could advance the reform agenda. The situation in Turkey is different. Whereas there was a consensus on the need for reform in 1999, over time this broke down as some actors, implicitly or explicitly, began to question the wisdom or applicability of a liberal democratic model in Turkey. Two issues stand out. One is minority relations, as many Turks fear that the granting of cultural rights to certain groups (e.g. the Kurds) will fatally undermine the Turkish state.[64] The other is secularism. Although some EU states (e.g. France) adopt a version of secularism (more accurately, *laïcité*) similar to Turkey's, the thrust of the reforms required by the EU would open up more space for Islamic-oriented groups and curtail the powers of the military, the actor that traditionally has seen itself as the guardian of order and secularism. Even though the EU is formally neutral on the hotly contested headscarf issue, its statements against efforts to ban the AKP must be disconcerting for those who believe that the AKP is committed to 'dismantling the republic as it has existed'.[65] For some in Turkey, the choice between satisfying an EU that *might* grant Turkey membership and protecting the Turkish state from elements hostile to basic tenets of Kemalism is obvious. Many groups that were pro-EU in the early 2000s, particularly those with pro-Western, secular leanings, are increasingly concerned that the EU's democratization agenda is being used by the AKP to further an Islamic agenda. For example, the main opposition party, the Republican Peoples' Party (CHP), was staunchly pro-EU in the 1990s, but throughout the 2000s, it became more and more 'Euro-pessimist' as it embraced secularism and Turkish nationalism while growing sceptical of the value of EU-inspired reforms.[66] Thus, the domestic constellation of forces in Turkey, mixed between pro-reform and reform-sceptical forces, create, as Schimmel-fennig observed in East Central Europe, 'stop and go' reforms.[6]

It is also worth noting that pro-Western attitudes in Turkey always contained a bit of ambivalence, linked in large part to suspicions about Western motives. One set of Turkish scholars noted that the Turkish nationalistic tradition 'tends to per-ceive Western powers as a source of conspiracy that threatens the national indepen-dence of Turkey'.[67] At times, this could be hidden, as Kemalist principles were believed to be congruent with Westernization. Now, however, with the EU making demands that might radically overhaul the Turkish polity, there has been a backlash, with some opponents to the EU and the AKP also embracing elements of 'neo-Ottomanism' by suggesting that Turkey turn to Middle Eastern states, Central Asia, or Russia as an alternative to joining the EU. While some might dismiss this as fanciful, the fact that foreign policy thinking in Turkey – notably both within the AKP government and within the opposition[68] – is increasingly interested in pursuing options in 'the East' might diminish the attractive power and leverage of the EU to produce political reform within Turkey.

Conclusion

While the final outcome of Turkey's bid to join the EU is still unknown, examination of Turkish democratization and Turkish–EU relations in the 1990s and 2000s shows that the Turkish case, while far more contested than those in East Central Europe, sheds much light on the possibilities and limits of the EU's democratization agenda. Most of the hypotheses suggested by Lavenex and Schimmelfennig as well as those posited at the beginning of this contribution are supported by looking at the ups and downs of Turkish democratization over the past decade.

On the one hand, it is clear that leverage through the prospect of membership – a sizeable and valued incentive – did spur political liberalization in Turkey. The line of cause and effect in the early 2000s is fairly clear in this respect. The EU made membership conditional on political reforms, and Turkish governments adopted a number of sweeping reforms that in the 1990s were politically impossible to adopt and were largely in line with EU's recommendations. EU's efforts to bolster civil society – linkage – were also important in this regard, building a domestic constituency for political change. For a time, it looked as if the EU's efforts might be enough to encourage an erstwhile 'reluctant democratizer' to liberalize to European standards.

By 2005, however, the democratization agenda in Turkey had clearly stalled, as the EU reports became more and more critical about the lack of follow-through in implementation and continued restrictions on political and civil liberties. Whereas this slowdown was caused in part by domestic political factors, it is also apparent that the impact of the EU was not as substantial as it had been earlier in the decade. Hypotheses about the limits of conditionality and linkage are relevant here. As Turks became less convinced that the EU would deliver on the promise of membership, as the public soured on the EU, and as some leaders began to believe that Turkey had other options besides the EU, the incentive to comply with EU demands declined. At the same time, the consensus in favour of reforms broke down as some – particularly in the political opposition – began to note that there were potentially high costs in adopting the EU's recommendations. By the end of the decade, one saw the emergence of a 'grand coalition' of actors within Turkey and the EU in favour of something less than full membership for Turkey.[4] Such an arrangement, provided that it holds, would mean that political liberalization would be more limited and that membership-driven conditionality would be off the table. As for Turkish civil society, while it now operates in a better legal environment and has become more active, it is subject to many of the same cleavages that divide Turkish political parties, and it was never fully engaged as a partner by the government. By itself, it cannot drive the reform process.

This is not to suggest that the EU has abandoned Turkey or vice versa. Membership is still, technically at least, on the table, and EU aid to Turkey in 2010 was twice that of 2005. EU officials continue to lobby for reforms and the EU has funded a civil society dialogue between itself and Turkish organizations. Turkish elites still affirm the goal of EU membership, and in February 2010, the government convened, for the first time since 2003, its Reform Monitoring Group, which has met on numerous occasions to bolster the reform process and involve a variety of groups in the accession process. In May 2010, the main opposition party, the CHP, elected a new leader Kemal Kiliçdaroğlu, who has given full support to Turkey's EU bid. In September 2010, Turkish voters approved a referendum of several constitutional reforms – the most significant of which pertain to the judiciary – that address long-standing concerns of the EU. The EU November 2010 progress report on Turkey, while critical of the lack of implementation of some reforms, the closure of the DTP, and continuing concerns on freedom of expression (including prosecutions under Article 301) and the state's treatment of journalists and the media, was more upbeat than reports in the previous two years. It acknowledged progress on a variety of issues, ranging from gender equality to cultural rights for Kurds to civilian oversight of the security forces to constitutional reforms.[69] Looking further ahead, the AKP government has declared that passing an entirely new constitution, free of the constraints in the military-drafted constitution of 1982, will be one of its top priorities should it be re-elected in 2011.

While these developments have yet to re-establish completely the optimism of 2005 when accession talks began, they do constitute progress, giving hope that the previous 'virtuous circle' of political reform leading to accession can be re-animated. However, the preceding analysis should make it clear that the dynamic between Turkey and the EU is not as straightforward as the one between the EU and Hungary or Slovenia. Serious doubts about Turkey's future as an EU member remain, the credibility of the EU within Turkey has declined, Turkish foreign policy is less beholden to Europe than in years past, and the domestic political situation in Turkey remains unsettled. It suffices to say that the EU's application of leverage and linkage to foster democracy in Turkey will remain contested and problematic.

Notes

1. Tocci, 'Unblocking'.
2. Kubicek, *The European Union*. See also Vachudova, *Europe Undivided*.
3. Lavenex and Schimmelfennig, 'Models'. This article does not consider governance, an approach suggested by Lavenex and Schimmelfenning. Certainly, given negotiations of accession chapters (half of which are suspended as of late 2010), this is occurring in Turkey. However, the thrust of the EU democratization programme in Turkey, particularly in the 2000s, worked through leverage and linkage. Governance may be of more relevance in those cases (e.g., the Middle East, Central Asia, and Ukraine) where more direct forms of EU democracy promotion fail or are minimally attempted. See Freyburg et al., 'Democracy Promotion', in this volume.

4. Öniş, 'Turkey–EU Relations'.
5. Grabbe, 'European Union Conditionality', 249.
6. Kubicek, *The European Union*; Vachudova, *Europe Undivided*; and Schimmelfennig, 'Strategic Calculation'.
7. In addition to Lavenex and Schimmelfennig, 'Models', hypotheses in this section are also developed in Kubicek, *The European Union*.
8. Grabbe, 'European Union Conditionality', 251–52. The 1993 Copenhagen Criteria state 'Membership requires that candidate country has achieved stability of institutions guaranteeing democracy, the rule of law, human rights, respect for and protection of minorities, the existence of a functioning market economy as well as the capacity to cope with competitive pressure and market forces within the Union. Membership pre-supposes the candidate's ability to take on the obligations of membership including adherence to the aims of political, economic and monetary union.'
9. Saatcioğlu, *Political Membership Conditionality.*
10. Toros, 'Understanding the Role'.
11. While these could play an important role, attributing specific outcomes to EU policies promoting economic development and education is not easy. Moreover, whether one should expect significant outcomes over a single decade – the time frame for this analysis – is debatable. The long-term impact of the EU is thus downplayed in the present analysis.
12. Checkel, 'Norms'.
13. Mehmet Uğur refers to this as an 'anchor-credibility dilemma'. See Uğur, *The European Union and Turkey.*
14. Avcı, 'Turkey's EU Politics', 141. See also Carkoğlu and Rubin, *Turkey and the European Union*; and Özbudun, 'Democratization Reforms'.
15. Taniyici, 'Europeanization', 186.
16. European Commission, *Turkey 2000*, 11.
17. Özbudun, 'Democratization Reforms', 195.
18. A good source for these reforms is Özbudun, 'Democratization Reforms'.
19. Kubicek, 'Turkish Accession'.
20. For example, see European Commission, *Turkey 2000.*
21. *The Turkey Update*, 'Reforming'.
22. Council of the European Union, 'Presidency Conclusions', p. 6.
23. Grigoriadis, *Trials of Europeanization.*
24. Kubicek, 'The Earthquake'.
25. This section relies heavily upon Kubicek, 'Grassroots Democratization'; Göksel and Güneş, 'Role of NGOs'; Arabaci, 'Explaining Transformation'; and Grigoriadis, *Trials of Europeanization.*
26. European Union, *EU-Funded Programmes*
27. Özdemir, 'Empowering Civil Society', 12.
28. See Kubicek, 'Grassroots Democratization'.
29. Kubicek, 'The Earthquake'; and Şimsek, 'The Transformation of Civil Society'.
30. Smith, 'The Politics of Conditionality', 127.
31. Kubicek, 'The Earthquake', 774.
32. In 2002 and 2004 Eurobarometers, 65% and 71% of Turkish respondents, respect-ively, thought that EU membership would be good for Turkey. Over 50% of the respondents had a positive view of the EU compared with 24% (in 2002) and 12% (in 2004) who had a negative image. See Kubicek, 'Political Cleavages', and detailed analysis of a 2001 survey in Turkey in Carkoğlu, 'Who Wants?'.
33. For more on Turkish public opinion in this period, see Carkoğlu, 'Who Wants?'.
34. The most prominent case was the ban on the *Refah* (Welfare) Party in 1998.

35. The biggest cost, as became apparent in the later half of the 2000s, was in engendering opposition from the military and bureaucracy within Turkey, but in the early 2000s, these groups seemed solidly behind the goal of joining the EU. For more on the AKP, see Cizre, *Secular and Islamic*.

36. Tocci, 'Europeanization in Turkey', notes that this perception that EU membership was a credible prospect changed elite calculations.

37. Şimsek, 'The Transformation of Civil Society', 46, concluded that the impact of civil society on political life had been 'trivial'. It is far easier to draw a line between application of EU conditionality and top-down reforms in Turkey than to point to a comprehensive role for Turkish civil society, although, as noted earlier, on some issues (e.g. women's rights), groups were particularly active. This article's main focus is not attributing primacy to one agent or strategy over another, but for a perspective that argues that change in Turkey was more an endogenous process than one driven by the EU, see Tocci, 'Europeanization in Turkey'.

38. Göksel and Güneş, 'The Role of NGOs'.

39. European Commission, *Turkey 2005* and European Commission, *Turkey 2006*.

40. Among other sources, see Note 4 and Kaya, 'The Rise and Decline'.

41. European Commission, *Turkey 2008*, and European Commission, *Turkey 2009*.

42. European Commission, *Turkey 2009*, 8–10.

43. 'EU criticizes'.

44. European Commission, *Turkey 2008*, 7.

45. See, for example, Kaya, 'The Rise and Decline'.

46. Vogele, 'Civil Society Dialogue'.

47. The best source for these projects is the EU and Civil Society pages on the website of the European Commission Delegation to Turkey at http://www.avrupa.info.tr/EUCSD.html.

48. European Commission, *Turkey 2008*, 18.

49. For example, the 2009 report noted that there is a lack of 'effective dialogue with the civil society organizations with the government on gender-related issues'. European Commission, *Turkey 2009*, 27.

50. Despite rejecting the UN effort to re-unify the island, the Greek Cypriots still obtained EU membership, while the EU has maintained an economic embargo on Northern (Turkish) Cyprus. See Öniş, 'Turkey–EU Relations', 42.

51. Keyman and Aydin, 'The Principle of Fairness'.

52. See Sarkozy's interview with The National Interest, April 17, 2007, when he states 'I do not think Turkey has a right to join the European Union because it is not European'. Available online at http://nationalinterest.org/commentary/making-france-a-power-for-the-future-part-i-1536 (accessed February 13, 2011).

53. European Commission, 'Standard Eurobarometer 69'.

54. 'Turks increasingly "distrustful"'.

55. German Marshall Fund, 'Transatlantic Trends', 24–25. For more on Turkish public views on Europe, see Kubicek, 'Political Cleavages'.

56. Yilmaz, 'Indicators'.

57. This referendum is not without controversy, as some in Turkey see it as an effort by the AKP to decrease the power of the one branch of government that it does not control and that has in the past acted to limit imposition of more 'Islamic' elements of its platform. For more, see Turan, 'Checking the Opposition'.

58. Rita Oomen-Ruijten, reports on ABHaber.com, February 8, 2008, and March 12, 2009, www.ABhaber.com (accessed September 10, 2010).

59. See Öniş and Yilmaz, 'Between Europeanization', and Walker, 'Reclaiming Turkey's Imperial Past'.

60. See Linden, 'Battles', and Kirişci, 'The Transformation'. See also Thomas, 'Turkey Prospers by Turning East'.
61. German Marshall Fund, 'Transatlantic Trends', 24–25.
62. For examples, see Friedman, 'Letter from Istanbul' and *The Economist*, 'Is Turkey turning?'.
63. Vogele, 'Civil Society Dialogue', 8.
64. This is sometimes referred to as the 'Sevres syndrome', in reference to the 1920 Treaty imposed upon Ottoman Turkey that envisioned a separate Kurdish state. Turkey's disputes with Denmark over Danish refusal to close Roj TV, a pro-Kurdish satellite station, are but one example of this.
65. Rubin, 'Where is Turkey Going?'
66. Gülmez, 'The EU Policy'.
67. Ayata and Ayata, 'The Center-Left Parties', 224.
68. Walker, 'Reclaiming Turkey's Imperial Past'.
69. European Commission, *Turkey 2010*. See also 'Publish and be damned'.

Notes on contributor

Paul Kubicek is Professor of Political Science at Oakland University in Rochester, Michigan. He has previously taught at Koç University and Boğaziçi University in Turkey. His publications on Turkish politics have appeared in *Political Studies*, *World Affairs*, *Turkish Studies*, and *Mediterranean Politics*, and he is the editor of *The European Union and Democratization* (Routledge).

Bibliography

Arabaci, Ahmet. 'Explaining Transformation of Turkish Civil Society in the EU Accession Process', *Insight Turkey* 10, no. 4 (2008): 77–94.
Avcı, Gamze. 'Turkey's EU Politics: What Justifies Reform?', in *Enlargement in Perspective*, ed. Helene Sjursen, 129–49. Oslo, Norway: ARENA, 2005.
Ayata, Sencer, and Ayşe-Güneş Ayata. 'The Center-Left Parties in Turkey'. *Turkish Studies* 8, no. 2 (2007): 211–32.
Carkoğlu, Ali. 'Who Wants Full Membership? Characteristics of Turkish Public Support for EU Membership'. *Turkish Studies* 4, no. 1 (2003): 171–94.
Carkoğlu, Ali, and Barry Rubin, eds., *Turkey and the European Union*. London: Frank Cass, 2003.
Checkel, Jeffrey. 'Norms, Institutions, and National Identity in Contemporary Europe'. *International Studies Quarterly* 43, no. 1 (1999): 83–114.
Cizre, Ümit. *Secular and Islamic Politics in Turkey: The Making of the Justice and Development Party* London: Routledge, 2008.
Council of the European Union. *Brussels European Council, 16/17 December 2004 Presidency Conclusions*. Brussels, Belgium: Council of the European Union, February 2005.
The Economist. 'Is Turkey turning?', June 12, 2010.
The Economist. 'Publish and be Damned', November 13, 2010.
'EU criticizes Turkey's court ban of Kurdish party'. *Euractiv.com*, December 15, 2009, http://www.euractiv.com (accessed November 10, 2010).
European Commission. *Turkey 2000: 2000 Regular Report from the Commission on Turkey's Progress Toward Accession*. Brussels, Belgium: European Commission, 2000.
European Commission. *Turkey 2005 Progress Report*. Brussels, Belgium: European Commission, 2005.

European Commission. *Turkey 2006 Progress Report*. Brussels, Belgium: European Commission, 2006.
European Commission. *Turkey 2008 Progress Report*. Brussels, Belgium: European Commission, 2008.
European Commission. 'Standard Eurobarometer 69', Spring 2008, http://ec.europa.eu/public_opinion/archives/eb/eb69/eb69_annexes.pdf (accessed June 6, 2011).
European Commission. *Turkey 2009 Progress Report*. Brussels, Belgium: European Commission, 2009.
European Commission. *Turkey 2010 Progress Report*. Brussels, Belgium: European Commission, 2010.
European Union. *European EU-Funded Programmes in Turkey 2003–2004*. Ankara, Turkey: European Commission Representation to Turkey, 2003.
Friedman, Thomas. 'Letter from Istanbul', *New York Times*, June 15, 2010.
Freyburg, Tina et al. 'Democracy Promotion Through Functional Cooperation: The Case of the European Neighbourhood Policy'. *Democratization*18, no. 4 (2011): XXX.
German Marshall Fund. 'Transatlantic Trends: Key Findings 2009'. http://www.gmfus.org/trends/2009/docs/2009_English_Key.pdf (accessed September 10, 2010).
Göksel, Diba Nigar, and Rana Birden Güneş. 'The Role of NGOs in the European Integration Process – the Turkish Experience'. *South European Society and Politics* 10, no. 1 (2005): 57–72.
Grabbe, Heather. 'European Union Conditionality and the *Acquis Communautaire*'. *International Political Science Review* 23, no. 3 (2002): 249–68.
Grigoiadis, Ioannis N. *Trials of Europeanization: Turkish Political Culture and the European Union*. New York: Palgrave, 2009.
Gülmez, Seckin Baris. 'The EU Policy of the Republican People's Party: An Inquiry on the Opposition Party and Euro-Skepticism in Turkey'. *Turkish Studies* 9, no. 3 (2008): 423–36.
Kaya, Serdar. 'The Rise and Decline of the Turkish "Deep State": The Ergenekon Case'. *Insight Turkey* 11, no. 4 (2009): 99–113.
Keyman, E. Fuat, and Senem Aydin. 'The Principle of Fairness in Turkey-EU Relations'. *Turkish Policy Quarterly* 3, no. 3 (2004): 83–93.
Kirişci, Kemal. 'The Transformation of Turkish Foreign Policy: The Rise of the Trading State'. *New Perspectives on Turkey*, no. 40 (2009): 29–57.
Kubicek, Paul. 'The Earthquake, The European Union, and Political Reform in Turkey'. *Mediterranean Politics* 7, no. 1 (2002): 1–18.
Kubicek, Paul, ed. *The European Union and Democratization*. London: Routledge, 2003.
Kubicek, Paul. 'Turkish Accession to the European Union: Challenges and Opportunities'. *World Affairs* 168, no. 2 (2005): 67–78.
Kubicek, Paul. 'The European Union and Grassroots Democratization in Turkey'. *Turkish Studies* 6, no. 3 (2005): 361–77.
Kubicek, Paul. 'The European Union and Political Cleavages in Turkey'. *Insight Turkey* 11, no. 3 (2009): 109–26.
Lavenex, Sandra, and Frank Schimmelfennig. 'Models of EU Democracy Promotion: Leverage, Linkage, and Governance'. *Democratization* 18, no. 4 (2011): XXX.
Linden, Ronald. 'Battles, Barrels, and Belonging: Turkey and Its Black Sea Neighbors'. in *Turkey and Its Neighbors: Foreign Relations in Transition*, ed. Ronald H. Linden, Ahmet Evin, Kemal Kirişci, Thomas Straubhaar, Nathalie Tocci, Juliette Tolay, and Joshua W. Walker. Boulder CO: Lynne Reinner, 2011.
Öniş, Ziya. 'Turkey–EU Relations: Beyond the Current Stalemate'. *Insight Turkey* 10, no. 4 (2008): 35–50.
Öniş, Ziya, and Şuhnaz Yilmaz. 'Between Europeanization and Euro-Asianism: Foreign Policy Activism in Turkey During the AKP Era'. *Turkish Studies* 10, no. 1 (2009): 7–24.

Özbudun, Ergun. 'Democratization Reforms in Turkey, 1993–2004'. *Turkish Studies* 8, no. 2 (2007): 179–96.

Özdemir, Nalan. 'Empowering Civil Society in Turkey'. *EU Turkey Review*, no. 9 (2007): 10–12.

Rubin, Barry. 'Where is Turkey Going and Why: A Panel Discussion'. *Middle East Review of International Affairs* 13, no. 1 (2009), http://www.gloria-center.org/meria/2009/03/discussion.html (accessed November 9, 2010).

Saatcioğlu, Beken. *The European Union's Political Membership Conditionality: Myth or Reality?* PhD diss., Department of Politics, University of Virginia, 2009.

Schimmelfennig, Frank. 'Strategic Calculation and International Socialization: Membership Incentives, Party Constellations, and Sustained Compliance in Central and Eastern Europe'. *International Organization* 59, no. 4 (2005): 827–60.

Şimsek, Sefa. 'The Transformation of Civil Society in Turkey: From Quantity to Quality'. *Turkish Studies* 5, no. 3 (2004): 46–74.

Smith, Thomas W. 'The Politics of Conditionality: The European Union and Human Rights Reform in Turkey'. in *The European Union and Democratization*, ed. Paul Kubicek, 111–31. London: Routledge, 2003.

Taniyici, Şaban. 'Europeanization of Political Elite Discourses in Turkey: A Content Analysis of Parliamentary Debates 1994–2002'. *Turkish Studies* 11, no. 2 (2010): 181–96.

The Turkey Update. 'Reforming for Europe'. August 4, 2003, http://csis.org/files/media/csis/pubs/tu030804.pdf (accessed September 10, 2010).

Thomas, Landon, Jr. 'Turkey Prospers by Turning East'. *The New York Times*, July 6, 2010.

Tocci, Nathalie. 'Europeanization in Turkey: Trigger or Anchor for Reform?'. *South European Society and Politics* 10, no. 1 (2005): 71–81.

Tocci, Nathalie. 'Unblocking Turkey's EU Accession'. *Insight Turkey* 12, no. 3 (2010): 27–31.

Toros, Emre. 'Understanding the Role of Civil Society as an Agent for Democratic Consolidation: The Turkish Case'. *Turkish Studies* 8, no. 3 (2007): 395–416.

Turan, İlter. 'Checking the Opposition, Balancing the Judiciary: Constitutional Reform Debates in Turkey'. *On Turkey*, March 31, 2010, http://www.gmfus.org//doc/Turan%20_OnTurkey_0410_Final2.pdf (accessed September 10, 2010).

'Turks increasingly "distrustful" of EU membership process', *Euractiv*, November 1, 2007, http://www.euractiv.com (accessed November 10, 2010).

Uğur, Mehmet, *The European Union and Turkey: An Anchor/Credibility Dilemma*. Aldershot, UK: Ashgate, 1999.

Vachudova, Milada A. *Europe Undivided: Democracy, Leverage, and Integration after Communism*. Oxford: Oxford University Press, 2005.

Vogele, Michel. 'Civil Society Dialogue in Turkey'. *EU Turkey Review*, no. 9 (2007): 8–9.

Walker, Joshua. 'Reclaiming Turkey's Imperial Past'. in *Turkey and Its Neighbors: Foreign Relations in Transition*, ed. Ronald H. Linden, Ahmet Evin, Kemal Kirişci, Thomas Straubhaar, Nathalie Tocci, Juliette Tolay, and Joshua W. Walker. Boulder, CO: Lynne Reinner, 2011.

Yilmaz, Hakan. 'Indicators of EuroSupportiveness and EuroScepticism in the Turkish Public Opinion'. *Observatory of European Foreign Policy*, no. 12 (2003), http://www.iuee.eu/pdf-dossier/12/5Bsly6VPIfP0dJjdGXNH.PDF (accessed June 6, 2011).

From Brussels with love: leverage, benchmarking, and the action plans with Jordan and Tunisia in the EU's democratization policy

Raffaella A. Del Sarto[a] and Tobias Schumacher[b]

[a]The Oxford Centre for Hebrew and Jewish Studies/Middle East Centre, St Antony's College, University of Oxford, Oxford, UK; [b]Centre for Research and Studies in Sociology (CIES), Lisbon University Institute (ISCTE-IUL), Lisbon, Portugal

With the adoption of the European neighbourhood policy (ENP) in 2003, the European Union (EU) for the first time introduced benchmarking procedures in the realm of democracy promotion, while also establishing the principles of 'positive conditionality' and differentiation. In order to exploit its full potential, however, this strategy must be able to define how political development can effectively be measured and monitored, along with the benchmarks chosen for this purpose. Applying insights of democratic and transition theories to the Action Plans concluded with Jordan and Tunisia, the contribution shows that the ENP suffers from the absence of analytical depth as far as concepts and processes of democratization are concerned, along with an arbitrary and largely useless selection of pseudo-benchmarks. While undermining the effectiveness of the leverage model of democratization policies, the EU's lack of clarity and determination seriously contradicts the declared objectives of its democracy promotion policy.

Introduction

With the adoption of the Euro-Mediterranean partnership (EMP) in November 1995, the promotion of political reform, broadly speaking, became a declared objective within the policies of the European Union (EU) vis-à-vis its 'neighbourhood' in North Africa and the Middle East. In contrast to previous approaches towards the region which focused purely on trade and economic cooperation, the EMP – or Barcelona process – committed the governing elites of all southern partner countries to develop democracy and the rule of law in their political systems and to act in respect of the UN Charter and the Universal Declaration of Human Rights. Considered a major innovation in Euro-Mediterranean relations at the time,[1] political, economic and cultural cooperation did, however, not generate processes of political reform, at the end of which democratic rule and good governance would supersede authoritarianism – the predominant governance pattern in North Africa and the Middle East. Undoubtedly, the reluctance of Arab regimes to embark on such processes in conjunction with the EU's unwillingness to make use of the principle of 'negative conditionality' that is incorporated in the respective Euro-Mediterranean Association Agreements is the primary reason for the bleak balance sheet of the Union's democracy promotion efforts in the framework of the Barcelona process.[2]

Developed in 2002–2003 as an alternative to EU enlargement, the European neighbourhood policy (ENP) envisaged the creation of a 'ring of friends'[3] east and south of the EU. More importantly, the new policy set out to address the issue of political reform beyond the EU's borders from a different and ideally more effective tri-dimensional angle. The cornerstone of this approach was meant to be the combination of 'positive conditionality', that is economic or political rewards in exchange of reform, differentiation, and benchmarking.[4] Whereas the Barcelona Declaration stipulated that the 'strengthening of democracy and the respect for human rights' were central for the overall objective of turning the Mediterranean 'into an area of dialogue, exchange and cooperation guaranteeing peace, stability and prosperity',[5] the ENP is more explicit as it speaks of a 'commitment to shared values', including human dignity, liberty, democracy, equality, the rule of law, and the respect for human rights.[6] The eventual inclusion of the countries covered by the ENP into the much-quoted 'ring of friends' shall depend on the degree to which they respect these values and the extent to which processes of political reform are being undertaken by their governments. In other words, this 'everything-but-institutions' (see Note 3) approach, as former European Commission President Prodi coined it, promises reform-minded countries a substantial stake in the EU's Internal market, and finally the integration into its four freedoms,[7] in return for compliance with the commitment to shared values and progress in sector- and area-specific reform areas.[8] The Action Plans that the EU has hitherto concluded with seven Mediterranean partners in the framework of the ENP were meant to reflect this new approach.

The de facto replacement of the so-called Bulgaria clause[9] that underpins the notion of negative conditionality with the ENP's principle of positive conditionality was somewhat a logical step given that Brussels never applied the former, not even in the event of blatant human rights violations. A prime example of the non-use of the clause was the EU's inaction in the case of Sa'ad Eddin Ibrahim, who was imprisoned by the Egyptian authorities in 2000 on the grounds of alleged embezzlement of EU funds (which the EU denied) and besmirching Egypt's name internationally. Thus, theoretically, the new approach opened a window of opportunity for the EU to be more successful in its efforts to promote democracy in its southern neighbourhood, as the policy offers tailor-made incentives and realistic rewards to the states in the south. Hence, relying on political conditionality as main instrument, the ENP espouses a leverage model of democracy promotion following the classification of Lavenex and Schimmelfennig.[10] Rooted in a top-down approach, this model envisages a gradual introduction of democratic change in the partner state institutions which would eventually impact positively upon the behaviour of political agents. The ENP's conditionality instrument that is typical for the leverage model is, however, modified so as to offer incentives instead of 'punishment' (or a mix of both). Given that the ENP is not offering EU membership, the policy's incentives are also weaker than, for instance, those in the EU's enlargement policy, but, at least theoretically, they are sound and credible. Indeed, at least for some countries in the Middle East and North Africa – most of which are not interested in EU membership at any rate – the prospect of gradually participating in the Union's Internal Market and of being part of EU programmes and projects may exceed the domestic material and non-material costs associated with political reforms. Yet, considering the 'soft' conditionality approach and the choice given to the partner countries on the extent of cooperation with the EU, the ENP also contains aspects of the governance model of democracy promotion. In his vein, weak compliance or non-compliance in the field of democratization and human rights of the partner states may not necessarily prevent cooperation in other fields, as Lavenex and Schimmelfennig point out.[11] This outcome, however, may also be a problem of inconsistent conceptualization and implementation of the ENP, which may undermine the leverage logic of the ENP.

Indeed, the EU's declared objective of defining clear benchmarks against which the partner countries' political reform process can be measured and to which rewards are coupled promised an effective leverage strategy – at least in theory. Practically, however, the process of translating a seemingly proactive strategy into a sustainable and effective reform-inducing instrument turned out to be far more difficult than what policy-makers in Brussels may have envisaged. With more than seven years into the ENP, both the Maghreb and the Mashreq have proven to remain, broadly speaking, immune to wide-ranging and sustainable political reforms[12] and thus to the policy's incentives. This also applies to a large extent to those countries that have been actively participating in the ENP and which were extensively rewarded by Brussels, such as Morocco and, more disturbingly, Tunisia – the latter having been characterized by a continuous curtailment of political liberties under Ben-Ali's regime.[13] Even the EU itself seems to have put the issue of political reform in North Africa and the Middle East increasingly on the backburner. Indeed, these issues do not feature in the rather apolitical and project-based Union for the Mediterranean (UfM) – the latest incarnation of the Barcelona process.[14] Whether the UfM's sectoral cooperation approach could serve as a useful example of alternative models of democracy promotion[15] remains to be seen.

This study is interested in the constraints and limits of the leverage model in the EU's democratization policy by specifically analysing how the principles of positive conditionality and benchmarking are conceptualized and implemented in the ENP. It argues that there is a dysfunctional relationship between the conceptual and structural underpinnings of the ENP on the one hand, and the desired policy outcomes on the other. Applying insights of democratic theory and transition theories to the ENP 'Action Plans' concluded with Jordan and Tunisia, the contribution will show that the ENP suffers from an outspoken superficiality in its alleged benchmarking efforts, along with a clear lack of determination, both of which can be expected to negatively impact on the effectiveness of the leverage model of democratization.[16] Indeed, without providing any definitions or clear criteria, the terms 'democracy', 'the rule of law' and 'good governance' are used interchangeably in the Action Plans, while the Action Plans are also based on an arbitrary and largely useless selection of pseudo-benchmarks. These factors not only question the scope and effectiveness of the EU's alleged benchmarking efforts in the realm of democratization, but also raise serious doubts about the EU's commitment to promote democracy in its neighbourhood in the first place. Hence, this contribution links up to the broader argument of this special issue on the waning effectiveness of what used to be the EU's most successful strategy of democracy promotion in the context of EU enlargement. Vis-à-vis the EU's southern periphery, it may, thus, indeed be worthwhile to explore alternative models of democracy promotion[17] or, alternatively, to reflect on the adjustment of existing ones. Analysing the underlying reasons for the fading clout of the leverage model in EU democracy promotion – which is not only a matter of EU membership not being on offer – is a crucial starting point of such an endeavour. Conceptualizing adequate models of democracy promotion and assistance is all the more important in view of the popular uprisings that, at the time of writing, are sweeping through North Africa and the Middle East and which may lead to regime changes in the EU's southern periphery.

The contribution is structured as follows. Based on a brief analysis of the notion of benchmarking, the first section reflects on a number of key concepts and their main criteria in the realm of human rights and democratization, along with the potential of developing useful indicators, or benchmarks, for a democratization strategy. The second section shifts the focus of attention to the ENP Action Plans concluded with Tunisia and Jordan by analysing whether these documents can be considered useful examples of an exercise of benchmarking democratic development in practice. The two countries have been chosen as they differ in terms of geographical location and the degree of authoritarianism, with Jordan being partly free and Tunisia being unfree, according to the two most influential international indices.[18] The different-case-comparison can be further justified with the relative importance of the EU in the two countries' foreign policy agenda and, thus, with the different types of interdependence with the EU. While in both political and economic terms the EU is certainly Tunisia's most important partner, Jordan has a somewhat more diversified foreign policy.[19] Indeed, in spite of the EU being its major trade partner, Jordan attributes particular importance to close political and trade relations with the USA as well as with its regional neighbourhood. While reflecting on the reasons why the EU has not shown more commitment to supporting democratic reforms in its southern periphery, the study will conclude by arguing for the need to introduce analytical depth, conceptual clarity, and determination into the EU's Mediterranean democracy promotion agenda if its leverage approach is to be effective.

A benchmarking approach to democratization?

With Brussels stressing that the introduction of benchmarks would be a novelty in its democracy promotion policy within the ENP, a closer look at what benchmarks are and how benchmarking ideally works is imperative for our discussion.[20] In a nutshell, any benchmarking effort presupposes clear and pre-defined indicators or benchmarks, which provide quantitative and/or qualitative measurement criteria.[21] As benchmarking is meant to evaluate progress over time, it also necessitates detailed and transparent timetables. Furthermore, effective benchmarking must be based on *ex-ante* decisions with respect to the measurement and data collection methods as well as the commitment of all actors involved. The existence and strict application of this complex set of criteria determines whether the process corresponds to what is widely called 'intelligent benchmarking' or degenerates into 'naïve benchmarking', mainly characterized by intuition and superficial comparison.[22]

Benchmarking was added in the mid-1990s to the EU's tool box as the European Commission sought to evaluate and compare the efficiency of national labour markets.[23] Yet, seeking to benchmark processes of democratization is a particularly complex task. One of the difficulties is that, in spite of the important theoretical insights on democratization and regime types,[24] there still is much disagreement among both academics and practitioners on concepts and processes of democratization.[25] Yet, a number of sound indicators characterizing democratic regimes and reforms have been identified in the literature.[26] These could serve as a basis for developing more concrete benchmarks in the EU's democratization strategy towards North Africa and the Middle East. As will be discussed below, however, even the most basic criteria are either absent from the ENP Action Plans or used in a completely arbitrary and inconsistent manner.

The challenge of benchmarking democracy, good governance, and the rule of law

With many myths on the emergence of democracy persisting,[27] the objective of applying a benchmarking approach to democratization processes faces the challenge that there is no universal agreement in the literature on the key features of democracy. It has been defined in terms of mass participation and contested elections with universal adult suffrage in open and fair elections, while the accountability of elected officials, resulting from the norms of political pluralism and open competition, has also been stressed.[28] The respect for core human rights counts as another central feature of democratic governance, along with the occurrence of political change without violence.[29] Certainly, the aim of defining democratic governance remains challenging as the term refers to an ideal type that hardly exists in the real world, and there are variegated types and models of democratic systems. Democracies may also vary in their quality.[30] More importantly, democracy is generally associated with liberalism. Yet, while historically both ideas developed independently from each other – with many liberal thinkers of the eighteenth and nineteenth century actually opposing democracy[31] – liberal democracies consist of two different ingredients: first, democratic procedures in selecting governments, and second, constitutional liberalism aimed at protecting individual rights. A neglect of the latter leads to what Zakaria has termed 'illiberal democracies'.[32]

Thus, broadly speaking, a (liberal) democracy can be defined as a *political system characterized by mass participation and contestation through open and fair elections, genuine competition for executive office, accountability, institutional checks on power, and the respect for core human rights* Although these features are complex in themselves, they provide a list of criteria that may be translated into benchmarks in the framework of democratization strategies.

Alternative – and somewhat fashionable – concepts used by practitioners and scholars, such as 'good governance' and the 'rule of law', are similarly vague and intricate, but may nonetheless offer a number of reasonable benchmarking criteria. 'Good governance', for instance, came to include public sector management, the transparency of decision-making, and the rule of law from an economic perspective.[33] In the late 1990s, the UN Development Programme broadened the concept so that it now also entails the legitimacy, accountability, and competence of governments, along with the protection of human rights.[34] More recently, the efficacy of legislation and oversight, the accountability of political leadership, and the independence of the judiciary have been added.[35]

As for the concept of the 'rule of law', in its *minimalist* sense it is theoretically compatible with (enlightened) authoritarianism, as it omits any reference to the *quality* of the legal and political system.[36] Yet, in its *maximalist* sense, the concept entails that the law must be fairly, consistently, and equally applied to all citizens by an independent judiciary and that the laws themselves must be clear, publicly known, stable, universal, and non-retroactive. Moreover, the legal system must defend the political and civil rights of citizens as well as the procedures of democracy (if in place); and it must reinforce the authority of agencies that ensure horizontal accountability, along with the legality and appropriateness of official actions.[37] As several studies have indicated, the degree to which the rule of law is implemented in a democratic state may well reflect on the *quality* of that democracy.[38] However, it is also true that a certain extent of liberalism under the rule of law may exist without democratic governance, as was historically the case in Western Europe (see Note 31). Thus, while promoting the rule of law cannot be the final or sole objective of democratization, it remains a crucial ingredient. At the same time, the concept embodies potentially useful benchmarks as far as the respect for civil and political rights, the implementation of the law, and the independence of the judiciary are concerned.

The challenge of benchmarking human rights

Human rights are central to all the concepts discussed so far. Indeed, the respect for human rights is a key ingredient of liberal democracies; human rights are part of the otherwise rather hybrid concept of 'good governance'; and they are also a key component of the rule of law in its maximalist sense. As potential benchmarks, human rights have a number of advantages: first, the international community has recognized them as being universal (as is most visible in the UN Universal Declaration of Human Rights); their importance is generally not contested. Second, a state's commitment to international human rights agreements is documented by the respective body (such as the UN or the European Convention on Human Rights), and various organizations regularly monitor both *de jure* and *de facto* protection of human rights. Hence, a large amount of data is available here. Third, human rights have been codified in international law as well as in national legal frameworks. Thus, developing human rights indicators that can be applied to different states is a relatively manageable task, also because a growing number of organizations started adopting the standardized system for indicators and methodologies of the Human Rights Documentation Systems, a global network of human rights organizations.

Of course, some debate persists on *which* human rights deserve priority, with the literature generally arguing in favour of the precedence of civil and political rights over economic and social rights.[39] While the realization of the latter category is certainly a key concern for *developing* countries, as recognized by the UN's Millennium Development Goals,[40] the priority conceded to political and civil rights may also be justified by the fact that these rights are by now recognized as being central to economic development as well.[41] Hence, in the framework of a democratization strategy based on leverage and benchmarks, the respect for political and civil rights should serve as the most important benchmark – and starting point.[42]

Transitology or a focus on process

As both benchmarking and democratization are processes, benchmarking is theoretically well-suited to monitor processes of regime transformation. Yet, basing a leverage approach to democratization on benchmarks is, perhaps unsurprisingly, analytically not a particularly easy task. Indeed, democratization may proceed at different paces and along different trajectories while involving different phases, dimensions, and conditions.[43] Moreover, the terminology has remained problematic, as the terms 'liberalization', 'transition', 'democratization', or 'reforms' are often used interchangeably. Yet, they may mean very different things. For instance, autocratic regimes may engage in processes of political reforms (or liberalization) involving a greater degree of political freedom without truly transforming the polity into a democracy.

Yet, for an effective application of benchmarking procedures, the conceptualization of democratization as consisting of *different phases* may be an extremely helpful analytical tool. Following Schneider and Schmitter, one possibility is to subdivide democratization processes between first, a phase of *political liberalization of autocratic regimes*, second, a phase of *democratic transition*, and third, a phase of *democratic consolidation*.[44] As each phase is characterized by different features, such as guaranteeing human rights in the first phase, contested elections with mass participation for the second, and the acceptance of the election results by the governing elite and the electorate for the third phase,[45] benchmarks can be set according to these criteria. Of course, reality is, however, rather reluctant to follow clearly distinctive phases and automatic sequencing. As illustrated by the case of Morocco and, albeit less accentuated, Jordan, autocratic regimes may sustain a phase of liberalization over extensive periods of time without transforming themselves into democracies. Liberalization processes may also be reversed, as the case of Egypt shows.[46]

Thus, if benchmarking is indeed the EU's preferred method of promoting democracy in the Middle East and North Africa within an approach based on 'positive conditionality' and leverage, it is imperative to first think through the key concepts and main criteria of democracies and democratization processes. Setting clear benchmarks and time tables – preferably in relation to different analytical stages of democratization – is also indispensable. As the discussion has shown, the respect for civil and political rights is an easily applicable and factually crucial benchmark, while more specific indicators could be developed regarding the independence of the judiciary – the efficacy of legislation and oversight, the accountability of governments and policies, the transparency of decision-making, and, subsequently, open and fair elections with mass participation. To be fair, such an endeavour is certainly not without difficulties. But neither is impossible. As the following discussion of the ENP Action Plans concluded with Jordan and Tunisia shows, however, it is doubtful whether the EU made any respective attempt at all.

The ENP action plans with Jordan and Tunisia: a case of leverage and benchmarking?

With a view to assess the ENP's declared objective of introducing benchmarking to democratization and human rights in its bilateral relations with Jordan and Tunisia, this section analyses the democracy- and human rights-related provisions of the two ENP Action Plans that both countries agreed upon at the end of 2004.[47] The ENP Country Reports that were prepared by the European Commission ahead of the Action Plans as a blueprint of sorts are the only documents that could serve as terms of reference for discussing the contents of the Action Plans.[48] This is, however, not unproblematic, as all country reports are characterized by a relatively uncritical approach and, both in tone and substance, remain behind relevant reports of international human rights organizations.[49] While this already hints at the general outlook of the Action Plans and may be detrimental to a sound benchmarking exercise, a second potentially problematic feature is equally noteworthy: like the Barcelona Declaration, the Action Plans are not legally binding. They are merely supposed to (re-)define the priorities of the EU's bilateral relations with each signatory. At the same time, bilateral ties are also based on the Association Agreements, which were signed by Jordan and Tunisia on 24 November 1997 and 17 July 1995, respectively. Unlike the Action Plans, these documents are legally binding and, thus, subject to international law. From a legal point of view, it can be argued that the association agreements are superior; yet, such a view may underestimate the *political* weight of the Action Plans, not least due to the EU's refusal to apply the principle of negative conditionality enshrined in the association agreements.[50] With the simultaneous adoption of two very different conditionality approaches, and the omission of any explicit reference as to when and under which circumstances positive or negative conditionality applies, the ENP contains an in-built problem to the extent that this dual existence contributes to structural vagueness with respect to the benchmarking process as such. Although such vagueness can be said to be a natural outcome of intense bilateral political bargaining – the Action Plans were indeed negotiated with the respective partner government – it does eventually undermine the EU's own leverage in its efforts to induce democratic change in Jordan and Tunisia.

Which indicators and benchmarks do the Action Plans stipulate with regard to democracy and human rights? Whereas the Action Plan concluded with Jordan by and large reflects the 'Jordan First' reform programme, initiated by King Abdullah II in late 2002, the Tunisian Action Plan is not based on any domestically generated document of good intentions. Hence, the section on 'Democracy and the Rule of Law' in the Jordanian Action Plan at first glance promises to be somewhat more wide-ranging as it focuses on 'stability and effectiveness of institutions strengthening democracy and the rule of law including good governance and transparency'.[51] The Tunisia Action Plan, in comparison, is more superficial by stating the 'strengthening [of] institutions and the judiciary'[52] as its objective. Both Action Plans contain a section entitled 'Human Rights and Fundamental Freedoms', while Tunisia's Action Plan also includes a separate section on 'Fundamental Social Rights and Core Labour Standards'.[53] The structure of the Action Plans thus already points to a notoriously superficial use of the concepts of democracy, the rule of law, good governance, fundamental freedoms, and reforms. These concepts are also highly inconsistently employed across the two Action Plans, as well as across all other Action Plans, including those that were concluded with transition countries in Eastern Europe. Perhaps unsurprisingly, no definitions of any of these notions are provided in the documents (or any other ENP document, for that matter), nor is there any reference to the key criteria associated with these concepts.

Democracy and the rule of law

The first issue area addressed by Jordan's Action Plan is the promotion of 'the stability and effectiveness of institutions strengthening democracy and the rule of law'.[54] The document omits any detailed specification of how this admittedly broad objective should be implemented. Instead, it lists five target areas, including the establishment of a dialogue between the Jordanian and the European Parliament, the support of 'ongoing efforts to improve good governance and transparency', the promotion of a 'national dialogue on democracy, political life and relevant issues', the reform of political parties and the electoral law, and the implementation of a government plan for public sector reform.[55] All of these 'targets' are supposed to function as sub-objectives, but, as a matter of fact, they are equally vague. For instance, it is not clear why an inter-parliamentary dialogue with the EU in general, and the European Parliament in particular, is supposed to contribute to the increase the stability and effectiveness of institutions that strengthen democracy and the rule of law. Probably with the exception of the fifth target which is somewhat more explicit than the others by addressing the respect of human rights and fundamental freedoms in line with Jordan's international commitments, the entire section is characterized by analytical imprecision, an arbitrary choice of vague indicators such as 'stability' and 'effectiveness', and an absence of any criteria-specific time-tables. Indeed, it is incomprehensible why other relevant reform areas, such as relations between the executive and the legislative, their prerogatives in the decision-making process, the Royal Court's dominant position, or the (limited) extent to which civil society can exert political influence, to name but a few, were omitted from this list. Moreover, as the Action Plan speaks of institutions that are meant to be '*strengthening* democracy and the rule of law',[56] the misleading impression is being generated as if Jordan already was a functioning democracy.

In contrast, Tunisia's Action Plan stipulates the strengthening of institutions, but only with a view to *guarantee* democracy and the rule of law.[57] While one may be tempted to assume that such a wording was chosen deliberately in order to refrain from labelling the (authoritarian) Tunisian polity, the Action Plan's reference to party politics does seem to consider Tunisia's political developments as geared towards a democratic end. Indeed, it states that the Tunisian regime should 'continue' to support political parties 'so as to further strengthen their involvement in the democratic process',[58] thereby ignoring bluntly the massive interpenetration between the state apparatus and the ruling Constitutional Democratic Rally, Tunisia's hegemonic party, as well as the regime's highly repressive practices. According to the Action Plan, this issue, together with administrative reform and greater transparency, shall be addressed by a subcommittee on human rights and democracy to be set up under Article 5 of the Association Agreement, and ideally, these topics shall also be dealt with in the context of 'exchanges of experiences between Tunisian and European members of parliament'.[59] In the meantime, the subcommittee was established, and so were the subcommittees with the other ENP partner countries; yet the actual impact of these bilaterally structured bodies – comprised of representatives of both the EU and the 'southern' partners – as regards the benchmarking of progress, stagnation or even retrogression has been extremely limited.[60]

Apart from the fact that the democracy-related clauses resemble those of the Jordan Action Plan in that they keep silent about the nature of the political system, they are noteworthy to the extent that they do not even address any of the most relevant issues. These include, for instance, the strong executive powers of the president, the weakness of parliament, the absence of political pluralism and thus the very opaque rules regarding the setting up of a political party. The Action Plan remains thus behind the Country Report, which, albeit rather regime-friendly, bothers to point out at least some of these shortcomings. This gap can be explained by the fact that the Action Plans were negotiated bilaterally with the Tunisian and the Jordanian governments, respectively. While diplomacy often thrives on ambiguity, processes of political bargaining tend to generate diluted and imprecise results.[61] In addition, at the time of the negotiations of the Action Plans, the European Commission was not in a position to impose neither on the Tunisian nor the Jordanian regime too strong a chapter on democracy-related issues. A stronger EU position on these chapters may have put the participation of Jordan and Tunisia in the ENP at risk and thus jeopardized the entire process. In fact, already during the first Association Council meeting in 1998 Tunisia threatened to discontinue the talks if the domestic human rights situation was to be discussed. In a way, this attitude has constantly been characterizing Tunisia's position under Ben Ali, irrespective of whether talks were held in the Association Council or the ENP subcommittee. Clearly, negotiating over potential democratization objectives and benchmarks puts into question the feasibility and seriousness of the entire process, with significant implications not only for Jordan and Tunisia, but also for the EU. Given the vagueness of the documents, all parties may thus find it easier to renege on what was agreed upon than to fully comply, or to defend their own interpretation of the provisions.

It is in this light that the Action Plan clauses regarding the rule of law in both countries have to be read. Both limit the issue to reform of the judiciary without specifying what type of reform is envisaged. Both documents are also marked by a minimalist notion of the concept of the rule of law which, as mentioned above, may be compatible with authoritarianism, and both leave the timetables during which reforms should take place undefined.

In the case of Jordan, two objectives under the rule of law provisions are being defined: first, the Jordanian government commits itself 'to implement its Judicial Upgrading Strategy 2004–2006, to simplify judicial procedures, and to improve the speed and efficiency of decisions'.[62] The second objective is 'to strengthen the capacity and efficiency of the justice administration, including adequate training of judges'.[63] Interestingly, under the heading of 'impartiality and independence of the judiciary', the latter's efficiency and modernisation are being pointed out, but impartiality and independence of judges – arguably two issues that are of much greater relevance to the rule of law – are not even mentioned.[64] In contrast, Tunisia's Action Plan does indeed refer to the independence of the judiciary. Yet, it speaks of its 'consolidation', rather than of its reform, and thus seems to have adopted the official jargon of the regime.[65] While it is undoubtedly the case that Tunisia can be considered as a regional frontrunner in what regards the judiciary's handling of economic issues and property rights cases, judges, who are constitutionally considered as independent, are exposed to potentially considerable political pressure, as they are appointed by the Superior Council of the Judiciary, which is in turn was headed by former President Ben Ali.

Tunisia's Action Plan lists two more objectives: like the Jordan Action Plan, it addresses the issue of efficiency of the judiciary, but is slightly more comprehensive as it also addresses prison conditions and envisages relevant improvements.[66] The stipulated measures meant to lead to greater efficiency of the judiciary are, however, formulated in a vague fashion, as they speak only of the strengthening of judicial procedures, the right of defence, and the reform of the penal code. Thus, Brussels leaves the Tunisian regime a considerable room for interpretation. It allows Tunis to undertake just cosmetic reforms while, formally speaking, still being in compliance with the Action Plan. The same applies to the provisions related to improvements of prison conditions. By speaking of improving prisoners' rights, the training of prison staff, the development of alternatives to incarcerations, the setting up of reintegration schemes, and prisoners' access to justice, the Action Plan has a rather limited focus and does not explain the difference between means and ends either.[67]

In the case of the Jordan Action Plan the issue of prisoners' rights is not explicitly mentioned. The document only refers to the effective application of 'existing legislation against ill treatment',[68] which assumedly refers to prisoners, but features in the section on human rights and fundamental freedoms. These structural shortcomings, all of which can be considered incomplete benchmarks, in conjunction with the absence of explicit time tables, cast serious doubts on the EU's understanding of benchmarking the rule of law and bereft the stipulations of their actual value. They also highlight an insufficient reflection on the concept of the rule of law *per se* and its relationship to democratization processes.

Human rights and fundamental freedoms

At least in terms of the structure of the human rights provisions, there is a certain consistency. Indeed, both the Jordan and the Tunisia Action Plan contain provisions on the two countries' compliance with international human rights conventions, specifically mentioning freedom of association, freedom of expression, media pluralism, and gender equality. The Jordan Action Plan is somewhat more wide-ranging, as it also contains clauses related to social rights and labour standards.

As regards the two countries' international commitments to human rights and fundamental freedoms, the Jordan Action Plan contains some rather vague references. They include, first, the implementation of international human rights conventions to which Jordan is party, second, the 'strengthening [of] the capacity and effectiveness of the National Commission for Human Rights',[69] and third, the establishment of a dialogue for human rights and democratization with the EU. While the relevant section in Tunisia's Action Plan is similar, the paragraphs that touch upon the envisaged human rights dialogue only mention the objective to 'pursue and extend dialogue on human rights issues'.[70] Hence, it does neither contain any clarification of the actors and the scope of such a dialogue nor does it make any explicit reference to the above-mentioned EU–Tunisia subcommittee that, as a matter of fact, is supposed to specifically deal with this matter and that, as noted above, is suffering from Tunisia's rather confrontational attitude with respect to any meaningful human rights dialogue.

Although, as discussed above, human rights could theoretically serve as useful benchmarks, the contents and structure of the human rights-related sections of both Action Plans are consistently formulated in a nebulous fashion, marked by selectivity and the omission of clearly specified short- or medium-term objectives. Regarding the adoption of optional protocols to international human rights conventions, Tunisia's Action Plan vaguely states that Tunis should 'examine the possibility of accession'.[71] Unsurprisingly, it is not specified which optional protocols are meant and neither is the formulation particularly committing. All it says subsequently is that Tunisia's national legislation should comply with international standards.

After a rather disconnected reference to the objective of providing support training measures of law enforcement officers on human rights – an objective that is not substantiated neither by a contextualization nor a precise definition of the type of training that is being referred to – Tunisia's Action Plan subsequently deals, in the same fashion, with a number of political and civil rights. Here, the document mentions the right to associate and to assemble, the freedom of expression and opinion, the role of NGOs, data protection, media liberalization, and the right to have internet access [sic!].[72] EU–Tunisian cooperation of 'voluntary sectors' and bilateral cooperation in the realm of civil society and human rights are also listed. What is striking here is that all of these provisions are blatantly superficial and by far lag behind those specified in the Commission's Country Report.[73] In fact, this proves once more that the southern partners were in a favourable negotiation position vis-à-vis the Commission, as they could always rely on the EU's unwillingness to endanger the entire ENP for the sake of 'saving' some stipulations of the original Country Reports. At the same time, however, it points to the order of priorities in the foreign policy interests of both the EU and the states of North Africa and the Middle East of recent years, with stability, security cooperation, and the upholding of mutually beneficial trade relations clearly on the top of the agenda.

The Country Reports explicitly refer to specific violations of the freedom of association and expression, the harassment of human rights activists and journalists, the government's denial of granting recognition to associations, the difficulties of Tunisian NGO's in receiving foreign funding, the widespread censorship of the media, and the authorities' control over the private media.[74] While these provisions potentially offer measurable benchmarks of sorts, the Action Plan refrains from making use of them. Remaining vague and not being underpinned by any time table, these provisions are in fact a blow to the efforts of the very few remaining reform actors in Tunisia who already operate with a very-restricted room for manoeuvre. In this regard, a case in point is the arrest of Tunisian journalist Muhammad Abou, who was condemned to a three-year prison term in early 2005 after publishing an article on a banned website comparing President Ben Ali to then Israeli Prime Minister Ariel Sharon. The most recent violation of fundamental freedoms is the entering-into-force on 1 July 2010 of an amendment to the Tunisian penal code that allows the regime to 'criminalize' and, thus, prosecute any person who has international links, regardless of whether these contacts are with international NGOs, international organizations, or even with foreign govern-ments.[75] Obviously, these developments, which are indicative of the Tunisian regime's general approach to the upholding of fundamental freedoms, occurred in spite of the existence of the Action Plans and did not provoke any noteworthy reaction on the part of the EU.

The same assessment applies to the relevant clauses in the Jordan Action Plan, which also remain behind the Commission's Country Report. The latter referred to *de facto* and *de jure* restrictions on the right of association and the harassment of human rights activists. It is rather specific on Jordan's treatment of prisoners, ill-treatment of political detainees, including arbitrary arrests and *incommunicado* detention, while pointing out that the death penalty continues to be applied.[76] The Action Plan, however, speaks only of the freedom of association, the reform of the legislation on associations – this being the only item that is defined as a medium-term objective – and the 'development of civil society' (see Note 62). It does not in any way refer to torture, arbitrary detention, and the death penalty, and neither does it state that effective protection of the existing civil society shall be a priority.[77] Consequently, neither the death of two Jordanian men one week after they were beaten by Jordanian police officers in November 2009, nor the adop-tion of yet another temporary election law in May 2010 by the Jordanian cabinet reinforcing the long-standing violation of electoral rights and discrimination of urban voters, affected EU–Jordan relations in any way or even triggered the slight-est debate within Europe over the potential application of conditionality.[78] In view of the general trend of securitization of policies, visible in Jordan since 11 Septem-ber 2001, and the adoption of new anti-terrorism laws that curb civil liberties, this is highly problematic. It also contradicts the EU's self-proclaimed objective of being a transformative power that tries to export its Copenhagen criteria beyond the EU–European space and undermines seriously the credibility of the ENP and hence its conditionality approach.

This impression is substantiated even further by an analysis of the provisions on gender equality and women's rights. Unlike the Country Reports, the two Action Plans are unspecific and incomprehensive as they do not even address per-taining issues such as divorce, inheritance, pension, social benefits, or other persisting legal discriminations against women. Domestic violence, *de jure* punish-able in Tunisia and to some extent also in Jordan (although article 301 of the con-stitution leaves ample space for different interpretations), is being ignored too, thus allowing male members of families to continue dealing with this issue outside of the juridical space. The provision in the Action Plan that Jordan shall transpose 'international Conventions to which Jordan is party concerning women's rights' (see Note 68) into national legislation is simply insufficient in this regard,[79] par-ticularly since the Action Plan explicitly mentions that such a transposition shall only lead to implementing 'measures strengthening [the] punishment of crimes'.[80] The second and third action areas in the field of gender equality are drafted in the same fashion, i.e. in the medium term female participation in econ-omic and political life shall be achieved through the adoption of a 'plan', while all developments in that regard shall be subject to an exchange of information and the development of reliable statistics (see Note 68). Adopting plans and compiling statistics, however, are everything but a bullet-proof recipe for implementing gender equality and curbing violence against women, let alone for monitoring progress in this regard.

Conclusions

In view of our analysis, the EU's commitment to the promotion of democracy and human rights in the Middle East and North Africa must seriously be questioned. Without providing any definition of the basic and indispensable features of democracy, the rule of law, and good governance, along with the relationship between these notions, the ENP Action Plans are characterized by a striking superficiality that hides behind an extremely nebulous language. While using the terms of democracy, rule of law, and reforms interchangeably, the Action Plans concluded with Jordan and Tunisia also refer to the *guaranteeing* or *strengthening* of democracy, thus giving the impression as if democratic procedures were already in place in these two countries. It is also evident that the ENP Action Plans cannot be considered examples of 'intelligent' benchmarking, as they do not comply with any of the prerequisites that such a process requires. In addition to not addressing the basic elements of a (liberal) democracy, both Action Plans lack clear-cut benchmarks and omit precise time tables. In conjunction with the fact that the underlying data collection methods have not even been tackled, one cannot but conclude that the EU's ENP is not even close to 'naïve benchmarking' of sorts.

While the ENP clearly signals the EU's abandonment of the principle of negative conditionality in favour of a lofty idea of positive conditionality based on incentives and benchmarking, it is problematic that in line with the leverage model on EU democracy promotion civil society organizations were largely excluded from the negotiations on the Action Plans. While local NGOs would probably have put forward a well-informed and comprehensive reform agenda, the prerogative of defining the priorities in the realm of political reforms and human rights was given to southern governments instead. Indeed, under the buzzword of 'co-ownership' – another much-touted novelty of the ENP – the Action Plans were negotiated with the governments of the ENP partner countries in North Africa and the Middle East in the bilaterally structured Association Councils. While the principle of 'co-ownership' and hence the negotiated character of the Action Plans sits uneasily with a leverage approach to democratization – even if the latter is solely based on 'positive conditionality' and incentives – Brussels in fact adopted the strategy of letting the fox guarding the chickens.

These sobering conclusions are reinforced by the lack of commitment that both the EU and Jordan and Tunisia have displayed since the entering into force of their respective Action Plans in the area of democracy and human rights. The establishment of the EU–Tunisia subcommittee supposed to deal with human rights and political issues related to the Action Plan is indicative of the EU's visible attitude of benign neglect. Not only did it take until November 2007 for the first meeting to take place, but the nature of the political system and the regime's measures to uphold authoritarianism were never discussed. In fact, the Commission's progress report of 2008 on Tunisia is rather telling in this regard, as it states, albeit in a diplomatic and highly inoffensive fashion, that five years into the ENP both parties continue to disagree on the involvement of civil society in the societal debate on democracy in Tunisia.[81] Similarly, the impact of Jordanian anti-terrorism laws on political and civil liberties never entered the bilateral agenda. The EU's ignorance towards *de facto* political developments in both countries is also reflected in the European Commission's Progress Reports of 2006, which avoid any criticism of the two regimes. In this vein, the Progress Report on Jordan praises the country as it 'remains strongly committed to a number of political and economic reforms',[82] which is as meaningless as are, in fact, the ambiguous provisions of the Action Plans themselves. Tone and substance of subsequent progress reports have slightly changed to the extent that some shortcomings are nowadays pointed out. Yet, embellished statements such as 'the holding of [the second meeting of the EU–Tunisia subcommittee on human rights and democracy] have yet not been followed by concrete results as regards the respect of human rights in [Tunisia]'[83] exemplify that the Commission and, thus, the EU are still shying away from voicing frank criticism and from using the progress reports as a means to raise public awareness for the democratic deficits. Finally, the EU's granting of 'advanced status' to Morocco,[84] and, more recently, Jordan, indicates that even the EU's already meagre implementation of positive conditionality is about to vanish in the future. The predominantly project-based character of the UfM further substantiates this prospect. Indeed, the states in North Africa and the Middle East that have been rewarded with an advanced type of relations by Brussels and that are likely to achieve this status in the near future, such as Tunisia, have not fulfilled the vague commitments specified in their respective Action Plans, let alone achieved a reasonable status of democratic governance and human rights protection.

Yet, the EU could well exert more pressure on some countries in the region to move towards democratic reforms and hence use its leverage, particularly in view of the fact that interdependence between the EU and Jordan and between the EU and Tunisia respectively is asymmetrically favouring the EU – this being one of the criteria for the leverage model of EU democracy promotion to be most effective. This is most notably the case for Tunisia, which is trade dependent on the EU, receives a high percentage of MEDA funds, is of limited strategic importance and is not (or not yet) characterized by a noticeable 'threat' of a potential Islamic opposition[85] – a consideration that often serves as a justification for not insisting on even a minimum level of human rights protection. However, until the Jasmine revolution of January 2011 – the impact of which is too early to tell – developments in Tunisia did certainly not show any sign of democratization. The country was economically liberalizing, stable, and persistently autocratic, while the formerly ruling Trabelsi family was preparing the succession of the aging President Ben Ali (see Note 13).

The EU's modalities of promoting democracy and human rights in its southern periphery are thus not only seriously flawed but also counterproductive, as they signal to autocratic governments that they can get away with repressive policies and the infinite postponement of democratic reforms. As the discussion has shown, any serious attempt of benchmarking democratization requires a clear definition of concepts, objectives, processes, strategies, and incentives, as well as the political will of the parties engaged in the benchmarking exercise to take seriously their mutually agreed commitments. Particularly the protection of human rights is a reasonable minimum requirement for any significant democratization process, which could be benchmarked and monitored with a relative ease. The EU's failure to do so demonstrates that it is not particularly concerned, determined, or clear regarding the question of what it actually wants to promote in the Middle East and North Africa, particularly since any EU membership perspective is categorically ruled out for these countries. Thus, the EU's conspicuous lack of seriousness, determination, and commitment, clearly undermines any leverage Brussels may have with regard to the support of democratization in North Africa and the Middle East. However, these flaws and omissions reflect the real foreign policy agenda of the EU, its member states, and the Mediterranean partners, indicating that Brussels indeed prefers some sort of indistinct reform for the sake of stability in its southern periphery. While connecting the European core with its southern 'borderlands' in areas of trade, energy, and infrastructure, Brussels seems far more interested in *co-opting* the governments in North Africa and the Middle East in specific EU governance patterns (while excluding them from EU decision-making) than in the spread of democracy.[86] Thus, in spite of lofty rhetoric vis-à-vis its southern periphery, EU policies seem to rather *strengthen* (semi-)authoritarianism than to reform it.

Acknowledgements

The authors would like to thank Sandra Lavenex, Frank Schimmelfennig, two anonymous reviewers, along with the participants of the authors' workshop on EU Democracy Promotion which took place at the ETH Zurich on 4 June 2009, for their insightful comments on a previous version of this contribution. The usual disclaimers apply.

Notes

1. See, for example, Barbé, 'The Barcelona Conference', 37.
2. See Aliboni, 'EMP Approaches'; Youngs, *The EU and the Promotion of Democracy*.
3. Prodi, 'A Wider Europe'.
4. See Commission of the European Communities (henceforth 'Commission'), *European Neighbourhood Policy: Strategy Paper*.
5. Barcelona Declaration.

6. Commission, *Wider Europe – Neighbourhood*.
7. The 'four freedoms' defining the EU's internal market include the free movement of goods, people, service, and capital, as stipulated in the European Single Act of 1986. Aiming at establishing the internal market, the European Single Act was the first major revision of the 1957 Treaty of Rome that established the European Communities.
8. Del Sarto and Schumacher, 'From EMP to ENP'.
9. The term Bulgaria clause is derived from the fact that it was incorporated for the first time and in identical form in the Europe association agreements with Bulgaria and Romania and used as standard clause in association agreements ever since. The Bulgaria clause replaces the so-called Baltic clause, which was still used in the association agreements with the Baltic countries and Albania as explicit suspension clause. The Bulgaria clause leaves the contracting parties somewhat more room for manoeuvre, as it stipulates that 'The parties reserve the right to suspend this Agreement in whole or in part with immediate effect if a serious breach of its essential provisions occur'.
10. See Lavenex and Schimmelfennig, forthcoming.
11. Ibid.
12. Schumacher, 'Middle East and North Africa'.
13. Sadiki, 'Democracy and EU Association'.
14. See Kausch and Youngs, 'The End of the Euro-Mediterranean Vision'; Schumacher, 'A Fading Mediterranean Dream'.
15. See Lavenex and Schimmelfennig, forthcoming; Freyburg et al., forthcoming.
16. Ibid.
17. Ibid.
18. See http://www.bertelsmann-transformation-index.de/16.0.html?&L=1 and http://www.freedomhouse.org.
19. Hillal Dessouki and Abul Kheir, 'Foreign Policy'; Ryan, *Inter-Arab Alliances.*
20. For an extensive analysis of the evident conceptual confusion and ambiguity within the EU's democratization strategy vis-à-vis the Middle East and North Africa, see the first section of a EuroMeSCo report prepared by the authors, Del Sarto et al., *Benchmarking Human Rights.*
21. Bogan and English, *Benchmarking for Best Practices.*
22. Ibid.
23. Commission, *Benchmarking the Competitiveness of European Industry.*
24. Sandschneider, *Stabilität und Transformation;* Merkel, *Systemtransformation;* Morlino, *Hybrid Regimes.*
25. Munck, 'The Regime Question'.
26. See, for example, Landman and Häusermann, *Map-Making and Analysis.*
27. Halperin, 'Power to the People'.
28. Dahl, *Polyarchy;* Collier, *Paths toward Democracy;* Sartori, *Democratic Theory;* Sartori, *Democrazia.*
29. Diamond, *Developing Democracy;* Dahrendorf, 'The Challenge of Democracy', 103.
30. Morlino, *Democrazie e democratizzazioni*, 225–55; Morlino, 'What is a "Good" Democracy?'
31. Hobson, 'Beyond the End of History'.
32. Zakaria, 'The Rise of Illiberal Democracies'.
33. The concept originally entailed the transparent and accountable management of a country's resources; see World Bank, *Development and Good Governance.*
34. UNDP, *Governance for Sustainable Human Development.*
35. UNDP, *Arab Human Development Report 2004*, 63.
36. The Rule of Law in its minimalist sense implies that 'whatever law exists is written down and publicly promulgated by an appropriate authority before the events

meant to be regulated by it'. The law must also be 'fairly applied by relevant state institutions including the judiciary'. O'Donnell, 'Why the Rule of Law Matters', 33.

37. Ibid.

38. Ibid.; Diamond and Morlino, 'The Quality of Democracy'; Linz and Stepan, *Problems of Democratic Transition.*

39. Political and civil human rights, or the first generation of human rights, are codified in the 1966 UN Covenant on Civil and Political Rights; economic and social rights, or second generation of human rights, are specified in the UN Covenant on Economic, Social, and Cultural Rights, also of 1966. Both are also codified in the 1948 United Nations Universal Declaration of Human Rights. The recognition of the more recently developed third generation of human rights, which include self-determination, the right to peace and development, the right to a healthy environment, and the right to intergenerational equity, is controversial.

40. Aiming at 'sustainable development', the UN's Millennium Development Goals (UN, 2000) incorporate the right to a universal primary education, a decent standard of living and freedom from hunger, and the right to a safe working environment. See United Nations General Assembly, *United Nations Millennium Declaration.*

41. See UNDP, *Integrating Human Rights.* It should be noted that the preference granted to social an economic rights of autocratic elites often serves as a cover for the continuous violation of political and civil rights. See, for example, Howard and Donnelly, 'Human Rights in World Politics', 26–27.

42. There is a broad agreement in the literature that the core of civil and political rights include the freedom from torture and other cruel or inhumane treatment by authorities; humane treatment of prisoners; non-discrimination on the basis of race, sex, religion, ethnicity, etc.; freedom of thought, opinion, and speech; freedom of conscience and religious conviction; freedom of movement; freedom of assembly and association; the sanctity of the private home and correspondence; *habeas corpus* ensuring freedom from arbitrary and unlawful arrest or detention; and a number of legal standards, such as the right to a fair hearing before an impartial tribunal, equality before the law, the presumption of innocence until proven guilty, a prompt and fair trial, the right to counsel, and the right to review by a higher court.

43. Linz and Stepan, *Problems of Democratic Transition*; Collier, *Paths toward Democracy*; Morlino, *Democracy between Consolidation and Crisis*; Morlino, *Democrazie e democratizzazioni*; O'Donnell and Schmitter, *Transitions from Authoritarian Rule*; Croissant and Merkel, 'Consolidated or Defective Democracy?'

44. Schneider and Schmitter, 'Liberalization, Transition and Consolidation'; see also Merkel, *Systemtransformation.*

45. Schneider and Schmitter, 'Liberalization, Transition and Consolidation'.

46. On Morocco, see for example Wegner and Pellicer, 'Prospects for a PJD-USFP Alliance'; on Jordan see Lust-Okar, 'Elections under Authoritarianism'; on Egypt see, for example, Kienle, *A Grand Delusion.*

47. See Commission, *EU/Jordan Action Plan*; and Commission, *EU/Tunisia Action Plan*, respectively. It should be noted that of all ENP partner countries, Jordan was the first to adopt the ENP Action Plan, already on 11 January 2005 (even six weeks before it was adopted by the EU). In contrast, it took the Tunisian government until 4 July 2005 to adopt its Action Plan.

48. See Commission, *European Neighbourhood Policy: Country Report Tunisia*; and Commission, *European Neighbourhood Policy: Country Report Jordan.*

49. See for example http://www.amnesty.com and http://www.hrw.org.

50. It could be argued that the Action Plans represent soft forms of legalisation and therefore provide the EU with potentially alternative ways to infringe on the sovereignty of the Mediterranean partners. Such an interpretation would, however, ignore that soft

forms of legalisation tend to be based on reduced precision, less stringent obligations, stipulations that allow for weak delegation, and rather high discretion. See Abbott, et al., 'The Concept of Legalization'; Abbott and Snidal, 'Hard and Soft Law'.

51. Commission, *EU/Jordan Action Plan*, 3. The original document does not contain page numbers; in this and the following references the page numbers refer to those given by the Adobe software in the downloaded pdf version.

52. Commission, *EU/Tunisia Action Plan*, 4. The original document does not contain page numbers; the references refer here to the page numbers given by the Adobe software in the downloaded pdf version.

53. See Commission, *EU/Jordan Action Plan*, 4–5, and Commission, *EU/Tunisia Action Plan*, 5, respectively.

54. Commission, *EU/Jordan Action Plan*, 3.

55. Ibid., 4.

56. Ibid., 3.

57. See Commission, *EU/Tunisia Action Plan*, 4.

58. Ibid.

59. Ibid.

60. Interview with Official, DG External Relations, European Commission, 8 October 2010.

61. On the vague wording of the ENP Action Plan concluded with Israel, resulting from intense negotiations that eventually permitted both sides to claim success in defending their principles, see Del Sarto, 'Wording and Meaning(s)'.

62. Commission, *EU/Jordan Action Plan*, 4.

63. Ibid.

64. Ibid.

65. Ibid.

66. Ibid.

67. Ibid.

68. Commission, *EU/Jordan Action Plan*, 5.

69. Ibid.

70. Commission, *EU/Tunisia Action Plan*, 5.

71. Ibid.

72. Ibid.

73. See Commission, *European Neighbourhood Policy: Country Report Tunisia*, 7–10.

74. Ibid, 7–8.

75. See Human Rights Watch, 'The Price of Independence'; Kausch, 'EU incentives'.

76. Commission, *European Neighbourhood Policy: Country Report Jordan*, 7–10.

77. Commission, *EU/Jordan Action Plan*, 4–5.

78. Democracy Reporting International, *Jordan's New Election Law.*

79. Although not explicitly mentioned, reference is here to the The Convention on the Elimination of All Forms of Discrimination against Women (CEDAW), adopted in 1979 by the UN General Assembly, which Jordan has signed, but not incorporated into national law.

80. Commission, *EU/Jordan Action Plan*, 5. For a discussion of women's rights in Jordan, here particularly the rights of women migrant workers, see Amnesty International, 'Isolated and Abused'.

81. Commission, *Rapport de Suivie Tunisie*, 2008.

82. Commission, *ENP Progress Report Jordan* (2006), 2.

83. Commission, *Rapport de Suivie Tunisie*, 2009, 4; authors' translation.

84. Martín, 'EU-Morocco Relations'; Schumacher, 'Morocco's Advanced Status'.

85. Durac and Cavatorta, 'Strengthening Authoritarian Rule'.

86. Del Sarto, 'Borderlands'.

Notes on contributors

Raffaella A. Del Sarto is the Pears Fellow in Israel and Mediterranean Studies, Oxford Centre for Hebrew and Jewish Studies and Middle East Centre, St Antony's College, University of Oxford, Oxford, UK, and Adjunct Professor of Middle East Studies and International Relations, The Paul H. Nitze School of Advanced International Studies, Johns Hopkins University, Bologna Center, Italy.

Tobias Schumacher is Senior Researcher in Political Science, Centre for Research and Studies in Sociology (CIES), Lisbon University Institute (ISCTE-IUL), Portugal.

Bibliography

Abbot, Kenneth, and Duncan Snidal. 'Hard and Soft Law in International Governance'. In *Legalization and World Politics*, ed. Judith Goldstein, Miles Kahler, Robert Keohane, and Anne-Marie Slaughter, 37–72. Cambridge, MA: MIT Press, 2001.

Abbott, Kenneth, Robert Keohane, Andrew Moravcsik, Anne-Marie Slaughter, and Duncan Snidal. 'The Concept of Legalization'. In *Legalization and World Politics*, ed. Judith Goldstein, Miles Kahler, Robert Keohane, and Anne-Marie Slaughter, 17–36. Cambridge, MA: MIT Press, 2001.

Aliboni, Roberto. 'EMP Approaches to Human Rights and Democracy'. In *The Euro-Mediterranean Partnership: Assessing the First Decade*, ed. Haizam Amirah Fernández and Richard Youngs, 47–58. Madrid: Real Instituto Elcano and FRIDE, 2005.

Amnesty International. 'Isolated and Abused: Women Migrant Domestic Workers in Jordan Denied their Rights'. October 2008.

Barbé, Esther. 'The Barcelona Conference: Launching Pad of a Process'. *Mediterranean Politics* 1, no. 1 (1996): 25–42.

Bogan, Christopher E., and Michael J. English. *Benchmarking for Best Practices: Winning through Innovative Adaptation* Columbus: McGraw-Hill, 1994.

Collier, Ruth Berins. *Paths toward Democracy: Working Class and Elites in Western Europe and South America* New York: Cambridge University Press, 1999.

Commission of the European Communities (henceforth 'Commission'). *Benchmarking the Competitiveness of European Industry*. COM(1996) 463, 9 October 1996.

Commission. *ENP Progress Report Jordan*. SEC(2006) 1508/2, 4 December 2006.

Commission. *EU/Jordan Action Plan*. Published 9 December 2004. http://ec.europa.eu/world/enp/pdf/action_plans/jordan_enp_ap_final_en.pdf (accessed 1 March 2011).

Commission. *EU/Tunisia Action Plan*. Published 9 December 2004. http://ec.europa.eu/world/enp/pdf/action_plans/tunisia_enp_ap_final_en.pdf (accessed 1 March 2011).

Commission. *European Neighbourhood Policy: Country Report Jordan*. SEC(2004) 564, 12 May 2004.

Commission. *European Neighbourhood Policy: Country Report Tunisia*. SEC(2004) 570, 12 May 2004.

Commission. *European Neighbourhood Policy: Strategy Paper*, Communication from the Commission, Brussels. COM(2004) 373 final, 12 May 2004.

Commission. *Rapport de Suivi Tunisie*. SEC(2009) 401, 3 April 2008.

Commission. *Rapport de Suivi Tunisie*. SEC(2009) 521/2, 23 April 2009.

Commission. *Wider Europe – Neighbourhood: A New Framework for Relations with our Eastern and Southern Neighbours* COM(2003) 104 final, 11 March 2003.

Croissant, Aurel, and Wolfgang Merkel, eds. 'Consolidated or Defective Democracy? Problems of Regime Change'. Special issue of *Democratization* 11, no. 5 (2004).

Dahl, Robert A. *Polyarchy: Participation and Opposition*. New Haven, CT: Yale University Press, 1970.

Dahrendorf, Ralf. 'The Challenge of Democracy'. *Journal of Democracy* 14, no. 4 (2003): 101–14.

Del Sarto, Raffaella A. 'Borderlands: The Middle East and North Africa as the EU's Southern Buffer Zone'. In *Mediterranean Frontiers: Borders, Conflicts and Memory in a Transnational World*, ed. Dimitar Bechev and Kalypso Nicolaidis, 149–67. London: I.B. Tauris, 2010.

Del Sarto, Raffaella A. 'Wording and Meaning(s): EU-Israeli Political Cooperation according to the ENP Action Plan'. *Mediterranean Politics* 11, no. 1 (2007): 59–74.

Del Sarto, Raffaella, and Tobias Schumacher. 'From EMP to ENP: What's at Stake with the European Neighbourhood Policy towards the Southern Mediterranean?'. *European Foreign Affairs Review* 10, no. 1 (2005): 17–38.

Del Sarto, Raffaella A., with Tobias Schumacher, Erwan Lannon, and Ahmed Driss. *Benchmarking Human Rights and Democratic Development in the Euro-Mediterranean Context: Conceptualising Ends, Means, and Strategies*. EuroMeSCo Annual Report. Lisbon: IEEI/EuroMeSCo Secretariat, 2006.

Democracy Reporting International. *Jordan's New Election Law: Much Ado about Little*. Briefing Paper 06. Berlin: DRI Press, 2010.

Diamond, Larry. *Developing Democracy: Toward Consolidation*. Baltimore: Johns Hopkins University Press, 1999.

Diamond, Larry, and Leonardo Morlino. 'The Quality of Democracy: An Overview'. *Journal of Democracy* 15, no. 4 (2004): 20–31.

Durac, Vincent, and Francesco Cavatorta. 'Strengthening Authoritarian Rule through Democracy Promotion? Examining the Paradox of the US and EU Security Strategies: The Case of Bin Ali's Tunisia'. *British Journal of Middle Eastern Studies* 36, no. 1 (2009): 3–19.

Freyburg, Tina, Sandra Lavenex, Frank Schimmelfennig, Tatiana Skripka, and Anne Wetzel. 'Democracy Promotion Through Functional Cooperation: The Case of the European Neighbourhood Policy'. *Democratization* 18, no. 4 (2011): 1026–54.

Halperin, Sandra. 'Power to the People: Nationally Embedded Development and Mass Armies in the Making of Democracy'. *Millennium: Journal of International Studies* 37, no. 3 (2009): 605–30.

Hillal Dessouki, Ali E., and Karen Abul Kheir. 'Foreign Policy as a Strategic National Asset: The Case of Jordan'. In *The Foreign Policy of Arab States: The Challenge of Globalization*, ed. Bahgat Korany and Ali E. Hillal Dessouki, 253–82. Cairo, NY: AUC Press, 2008.

Hobson, Christopher. 'Beyond the End of History: The Need for a "Radical Historicisation" of Democracy in International Relations'. *Millennium: Journal of International Studies* 37, no. 3 (2009): 631–57.

Howard, Rhoda E., and Jack Donnelly. 'Human Rights in World Politics'. In *International Handbook of Human Rights*, ed. Rhoda E. Howard and Jack Donnelly, 1–27. New York: Greenwood Press, 1987.

Human Rights Watch. 'The Price of Independence'. 21 October 2010.

Kausch, Kristina. 'Tunisia: EU Incentives Contributing to New Repression'. *IPRIS Maghreb Review* 4 (2010): 1–2.

Kausch, Kristina, and Richard Youngs. 'The End of the Euro-Mediterranean Vision'. *International Affairs* 85, no. 5 (2009): 963–75.

Kienle, Eberhard. *A Grand Delusion: Democracy and Economic Reform in Egypt*. London: I.B. Tauris, 2001.

Landman, Todd, and Julia Häusermann. *Map-Making and Analysis of the Main International Initiatives on Developing Indicators on Democracy and Good Governance*. Essex: University of Essex, Human Rights Centre, 2003. http://www.oecd.org/dataoecd/0/28/20755719.pdf. (accessed 2 September 2010)

Lavenex, Sandra, and Frank Schimmelfennig. 'Models of EU Democracy Promotion: Leverage, Linkage, and Governance', *Democratization* 18, no. 4 (2011): 885–909.

Linz, Juan J., and Alfred Stepan. *Problems of Democratic Transition and Consolidation: Southern Europe, South America and Post-Communist Europe.* Baltimore: Johns Hopkins University Press, 1996.

Lust-Okar, Ellen. 'Elections under Authoritarianism: Preliminary Lessons from Jordan'. *Democratization* 13, no. 3 (2006): 456–471.

Martín, Ivan. 'EU-Morocco Relations: How Advanced Is the "Advanced Status"?'. *Mediterranean Politics* 14, no. 2 (2009): 239–45.

Merkel, Wolfgang. *Systemtransformation: Eine Einführung in die Theorie und Empirie der Transformationsforschung.* Opladen, Germany: Leske+Budrich, 1999.

Morlino, Leonardo. *Democracy between Consolidation and Crisis: Parties, Groups, and Citizens in Southern Europe.* New York: Oxford University Press, 1998.

Morlino, Leonardo. *Democrazie e democratizzazioni.* Bologna, Italy: Il Mulino, 2003.

Morlino, Leonardo. *Hybrid Regimes or Regimes in Transition?.* Madrid: FRIDE Working Paper 70, 2008.

Morlino, Leonardo. 'What is a "Good" Democracy?'. *Democratization* 11, no. 5 (2004): 10–32.

Munck, Gerardo L. 'The Regime Question: Theory Building in Democracy Studies'. *World Politics* 54 (2001): 119–44.

O'Donnell, Guillermo. 'Why the Rule of Law Matters'. *Journal of Democracy* 15, no. 4 (2004): 32–46.

O'Donnell, Guillermo, and Philippe C. Schmitter. *Transitions from Authoritarian Rule: Tentative Conclusions about Uncertain Democracies.* Baltimore: Johns Hopkins University Press, 1986.

Prodi, Romano. 'A Wider Europe – A Proximity Policy as The Key to Stability', speech delivered at the Sixth ECSA-World Conference, Jean Monnet Project, Brussels, 5–6 December 2002, Speech/02/619. http://europa.eu/rapid/pressReleasesAction.do?reference=SPEECH/02/619&format=HTML&aged=0&language=EN&guiLanguage=en (accessed 1 March 2011).

Ryan, Curtis. *Inter-Arab Alliances: Regime Security and Jordanian Foreign Policy.* Miami: University Press of Florida, 2009.

Sadiki, Larbi. 'Democracy and EU Association in Bin Ali's Tunisia: Where to?'. *IPRIS Maghreb Review* 3 (2010): 2–3.

Sandschneider, Eberhard. *Stabilität und Transformation politischer Systeme: Politikwissenschaftliche Aspekte einer Theorie der Systemtransformation.* Opladen, Germany: Leske+Budrich, 1995.

Sartori, Giovanni. *Democratic Theory.* 2nd ed. Westport, CT: Greenwood Press, 1973.

Sartori, Giovanni. *Democrazia: cosa è.* Milano, Italy: Rizzoli, 1993.

Schneider, Carsten Q., and Phillipe C. Schmitter. 'Liberalization, Transition and Consolidation: Measuring the Components of Democratization'. *Democratization* 11, no. 5 (2004): 59–90.

Schumacher, Tobias. 'A Fading Mediterranean Dream'. *European Voice*, 16 July 2009.

Schumacher, Tobias. 'Middle East and North Africa'. In *Bertelsmann Transformation Index 2008: Political Management in International Comparison*, ed. Bertelsmann Stiftung, 126–245. Gütersloh: Verlag Bertelsmann Stiftung, 2008.

Schumacher, Tobias. 'Morocco's Advanced Status or "The Spirits that I called..."'. *IPRIS Maghreb Review* 1, no. 2 (2010): 3–4.

UNDP (United Nations Development Programme). *Arab Human Development Report 2004: Towards Freedom in the Arab World.* Amman, Jordan: National Press, 2005.

UNDP. *Governance for Sustainable Human Development: A UNDP Policy Document* United Nations Development Programme, January 1997.

UNDP. *Integrating Human Rights with Sustainable Human Development: A UNDP Policy Document*. New York and Washington: UNDP, 1998.

United Nations General Assembly. *United Nations Millennium Declaration*. A/RES/55/2. 18 September 2000.

Wegner, Eva, and Michel Pellicer. 'Prospects for a PJD-USFP Alliance in Morocco'. *IPRIS Maghreb Review* 1, no. 5 (2010): 1–2.

World Bank. *Development and Good Governance*. Washington, DC: World Bank, 1992.

Youngs, Richard. *The EU and the Promotion of Democracy*. Oxford: Oxford University Press, 2001.

Zakaria, Fareed. 'The Rise of Illiberal Democracies'. *Foreign Affairs* 76, no. 6 (1997): 22–43.

The EU's two-track approach to democracy promotion: the case of Ukraine

Tom Casier

*Brussels School of International Studies, University of Kent, Boulevard de la Plaine 5,
1050 Brussels, Belgium*

This contribution argues that the European Union (EU) promotes two forms of democracy in its policy towards Ukraine: formal democracy (institutions and procedures at polity level guaranteeing a free and fair electoral process) and substantive democracy (principles and mechanisms that allow for an ongoing societal control over policy processes). While the first form of democracy is mainly promoted through intergovernmental channels, the latter is promoted both at a transgovernmental and more weakly at an intergovernmental level. The question raised is why more progress has been made in formal democratic reforms in Ukraine (between 2006 and 2009), than in the field of substantive democracy. Two explanations are put forward: the higher visibility of formal democratic reforms in the framework of Ukraine's legitimacy seeking with the EU and the strategic behaviour of domestic actors. It is argued that institutional democratic reforms are regarded as the litmus test for Ukraine's feasibility for future EU membership and act to a degree as a sort of 'self-imposed' conditionality. This, however, is counterbalanced by strategic behaviour of domestic actors, resisting deeper democratic change to compensate for the power they lose as a result of a more democratic electoral process. The EU's one-sided emphasis on the promotion of formal democracy over substantive democracy facilitates this.

Introduction

In order fully to understand the role the European Union (EU) can play in democracy promotion, we must distinguish between two different tracks that seem to be underlying the EU's approach to democratization beyond its borders. The first track is aimed at the export of a democratic institutional framework, in which free and fair elections determine the formation of a government and the separation of powers provides checks and balances. The second track is formed by the promotion of less tangible elements of democracy, most notably transparency, accountability and active citizen participation outside the formal election process. Following Pridham's distinction, we refer to the first form of democracy as 'formal or procedural democracy', to the second form as 'substantive democracy'.[1]

This contribution focuses on the EU's promotion of democracy in Ukraine. It is in the first place reflecting on the models of leverage and governance, presented in the introduction of this special issue, two areas in which the EU has been most visible as democracy promoter.[2] As mentioned in the introduction to this issue, the models of leverage, governance and linkage are ideal types. Democracy promotion is considered to vary independently across the four main dimensions (target level, outcome, channel and instruments). This contribution explores how the EU promotes both formal and substantive democracy along different channels: intergovernmental channels, characteristic of the leverage model, and transgovernmental channels, characteristic of the governance model.

The contribution does not focus on the modes of democracy promotion, but rather on the outcomes and factors determining their effectiveness. It aims to assess why in Ukraine some progress has been made in the field of formal democratization (the establishment of democratic institutions at polity level), but little progress has been made in the field of substantive democratization (the creation of transparency, accountability and participation in policy processes). In other words, this contribution seeks to answer the question why democratic reforms promoted by the EU have progressed more on the polity level than on the governance front. It is hypothesized that diverging results have to do with the way they interfere with domestic structures and European integration strategies in Ukraine. This is neither to claim that limited progress in the field of substantive democracy is due to the EU, nor to claim that the EU solely should be credited for progress in formal democratization. Clearly, the impact of democracy promotion by one actor is likely to interfere with democratization efforts of other actors (such as the Council of Europe, USA or individual EU member states) as well as with independent domestic developments.

In the first part of this contribution, we introduce the conceptual distinction between formal and substantive democracy, as well as their policy relevance. Next, we present the factors which explain the transfer of EU rule to its Eastern neighbours in general. This sets the context for a study of the EU's two-track democracy promotion in Ukraine. The next part compares the democratization envisaged by the EU with its effective outcomes in Ukraine. Finally, we explain the diverging results in both democratization tracks on the basis of the instrumental purposes they serve among Ukrainian elites.

Two types of democracy

The major part of the literature on democracy focuses on 'major institution and laws of government about participation in elections'.[3] A regime can only be labelled as democratic when the necessary mechanisms are in place to give citizens the opportunity to participate in the electoral process and to guarantee free and fair competition – directly or indirectly – for major public posts. The focus is then on free and fair elections, and the conditions they imply, namely a multi-party system, and on a number of basic institutional requirements such as the separation of powers and the rule of law. This, however, is only a minimal definition of democracy. Pridham distinguishes between 'formal' (or procedural) democracy and 'substantive democracy' 'Formal or procedural democracy involves establishing rules, procedures and institutions for the purpose of what Schumpeter called, in his definition of democracy, "arriving at political decisions in which individuals acquire the power to decide by means of a competitive struggle for the people's vote"'.[4] Formal democracy is an incomplete form of democracy. If the ultimate criterion for democracy is 'popular control over collective decision-making',[5] then more is needed than a set of rules for free electoral competition. Pridham defines substantive democracy as 'a way of regulating power relations so as to maximize the opportunities for individuals to influence debates about the key decisions that affect society' (see Note 4). Crucially 'substantive democracy relates to deeper dimensions of political life'.[6] Citizens get the chance to participate, to debate, to impact on the agenda and to have access to information. Pridham emphasizes 'the presence of an active civil society, including independent associations, that may serve to check abuses of state power' (see Note 6).

Norberto Bobbio's concepts of 'political democracy' and 'societal democracy' express a similar distinction, but he gives civil society participation in different spheres of policy-making an even greater role. Bobbio speaks of political democracy when the control of the ruled over the rulers is mainly guaranteed by the electoral process, in which parties compete for the support of the electorate.[7] It reduces a democracy to a pure delegation of power. According to Bobbio, it needs to be supplemented by other forms of ongoing control by society. Societal democracy[8] refers precisely to 'ascending power ... spreading to various spheres of civil society'.[9] Societal democracy is crucial to balance the power of the elected leaders by creating forms of societal control over different policy processes. A developed and well-functioning civil society counterbalances a strong state, controls the legitimacy of its acts and exerts pressure on that state. The political sphere gets 'included in a much larger sphere, that of society as a whole; political decisions are conditioned, even determined, by what happens in the social sphere'.[10] In other words, the higher the level of participation and the wider number of contexts in which participation takes place, the better the quality of the democracy.[11] Obstacles which may withhold a political democracy from developing into a societal democracy may include a lack of transparency and accountability, high levels of corruption or the continued existence of oligarchies (see Note 7).

It should be stressed that both Pridham and Bobbio see a clear hierarchy between the two different forms of democracy. Pridham states 'that formal procedures are a necessary but not a sufficient condition for democracy' (See Note

4). It is the degree of substantive democracy that determines the quality of a democracy. Using a metaphor, if formal democracy (democratic institutions and processes) is the train which will lead us to 'rule by the people', the substantive democracy is the oil to grease the wheels of the train. If it is absent, no qualitative progress will be made towards democracy.

In the policy-world too, aspects of substantive democracy have gained in prominence, with international organizations putting more emphasis on the 'day-to-day experience of living democracy'.[12] The OSCE's Office for Democratic Institutions and Human Rights (ODIHR), for example, states: '... that it is "necessary to develop a democratic culture, on the local, regional and national level, in order to sustain new democratic institutions." In practice, democratization is a continuous dual effort of "fine-tuning" democratic structures and processes and nurturing a democratic culture based on respect for human rights, the rule of law, peace, and security. Democracy should not be restricted to one-off electoral events; it also requires democratic institutions that discharge their electoral mandate through consensus-driven, open, and transparent processes'.[13]

Criteria of good substantive democracy have been translated by various institutions into a wide array of principles, such as civil society involvement, inclusive participation, channels for dialogue and consultation, civic awareness, transparency of decision-making, access to information, accountability, absence of corruption, avoiding the abuse of immunities, and the diversity of free and critical media, including in ownership terms.[14]

In this contribution, we use Pridham's concepts of *formal democracy* and *substantive democracy* to refer to two forms of democracy. Formal democracy refers to institutional and procedural characteristics of a regime, guaranteeing a fair and free competition for the votes of the citizens as a basis for the attribution of public posts. Substantive democracy refers to principles and practical elements that allow for an ongoing societal control over policy processes and the distribution of power beyond the ruling elite. Rendering this concept more operational, we focus specifically on the acceptance and the implementation of principles of transparency, accountability and active participation in various policy processes.[15]

For our study of EU democracy promotion in Ukraine, this distinction is particularly relevant. The issue of societal participation has always been considered to be particularly crucial for the transition process in Central and Eastern Europe. After the collapse of communism, most former communist countries adopted liberal-democratic constitutions. Their civil societies, however, were weakly developed. As a result, some countries have developed purely political and formal democracies with the required formal institutions in place, but where a democratic culture is weak. This problem received considerable attention in the transition literature from the very early days of post-communism on,[16] but is also still relevant now in particular for some of the former Soviet states.[17]

In the following parts, the question will be raised which forms of democracy the EU promotes in Ukraine. Further, we will explore how the EU pursues the targets of both tracks of democratization, formal and substantive, and how success-ful it is in doing so.

Explaining success and failure of democracy promotion towards the Eastern neighbours

The EU has been described as a late democratizer.[18] It took until the Treaty of Maastricht of 1992 before a reference to democracy was included in the treaties and the EU was given a responsibility in promoting democracy in its foreign policy. Soon after, the European Council made democracy a formal admission condition at its meeting in Copenhagen in 1993. Also in its external cooperation, conditionality clauses on democracy appeared rather late. Only in the fourth Lomé Convention in 1989, development aid was made dependent on respect for human rights. Two years later, in 1991, a Council resolution would recognize the principle of human rights and democracy conditionality in development policy.[19] As appears from the many references in the European Neighbourhood Policy (ENP) Action Plans, the EU is not so much setting its own standards of formal democracy, but borrows them from other institutions, most notably the OSCE/ODIHR and the Council of Europe (including the Venice Commission). In other words, the EU's strategy of democracy promotion is mainly a reinforcement strategy. The EU does not create its own standards of democratization, but uses its bargaining power to back up the existing European organizations.

Though the EU has been credited for being a strong democratizer in the enlar-gement process, it appears as a 'reluctant debutante' in democracy promotion within its neighbourhood.[20] Most authors concur that the models of explaining the transfer of rules and norms under enlargement[21] cannot explain the much more limited rule transfer under the ENP and Eastern Partnership (EaP).[22] On the negative side, ENP rule transfer in general cannot be explained on the basis of conditionality. As the ENP excludes a membership prospect, it scores weakly on the incentives side. On the positive side, two interrelated factors may be impor-tant to explain the degree and the nature of (limited) rule transfer under the ENP/EaP, including the transfer of democratic rules.[23] The first factor is the *active legiti-macy-seeking of certain ENP countries*. States like Ukraine, who have made acces-sion to the EU a strategic priority, will try to appear to be the best pupil in the class by (selectively) adopting certain rules.[24] Even if membership is formally excluded under the ENP, these countries hope to create pressure on the EU in the longer term to put the door ajar for membership. The second factor is the *fit of ENP action points with domestic agendas*. The ENP Action Plans are used by certain actors as a menu for choice to legitimize domestic political preferences and strategies or as a platform for mobilization.[25] The transfer of EU rules to its Eastern neigh-bours is likely to increase as the rules are more in line with the reform preferences of influential domestic actors.

Building on this, in the following part, we will explore the hypothesis that active legitimacy-seeking and domestic preferences may lead to different outcomes in formal and substantive democracy promotion because of two reasons: the *visibility of reforms* and the *strategic behaviour of domestic actors*. It is hypothesized that an active legitimacy-seeking country, such as Ukraine, will opt for the most visible democratic reforms to prove itself a trustworthy potential EU candidate. This would suggest a higher emphasis on formal democracy, rather than on – less tangible – substantive democracy. It is hypothesized that in accepting democratic institutional reforms, elites will behave strategically in order to safeguard their power positions and to maintain existing opportunity structures to the maximum extent possible. Both factors fit with some key assumptions of the leverage model presented in this special issue. Opting for the most visible reforms, i.e. formal democratization, Ukraine fulfils what it perceives to be the most necessary conditions imposed by the EU. As will be illustrated in the next part, these are mainly conditions targeting the polity. The reward Ukraine seeks is increased legitimacy, which subjectively is perceived to lead to accession in the longer term. The introduction of visible, institutional democratic reforms inevitably creates considerable domestic adoption costs for those in power. These costs, however, can be compensated by restraining democratic reforms to the formal level and obstructing substantive democratic reforms. Domestic actors, who feel their power or privileges are threatened, are therefore expected to move strategically to safeguard 'deeper' opportunity structures and benefits, while accepting the procedures of a formal democracy.

The EU's two-track democracy promotion towards Ukraine

An analysis of the EU-Ukraine Action Plan indicates that the EU relies on a two-track approach in its democracy promotion, reflecting both formal democracy and substantive democracy. The emphasis, however, is clearly on the former. The first three 'priorities for action' in the EU/Ukraine AP refer to: 'Further strengthening the stability and effectiveness of institutions guaranteeing democracy and the rule of law; ensuring the democratic conduct of presidential (2004) and parliamentary (2006) elections in Ukraine in accordance with OSCE standards; ensuring the respect for the freedom of the media and freedom of expression'.[26]

The democracy chapter of the Action Plan refers predominantly to the strengthening of institutions (formal democracy) 'guaranteeing democracy and the rule of law' (see Note 26), human rights and the reform of the judicial apparatus. Reference in this field is made to 'international standards' and 'OSCE standards and OSCE/ODIHR recommendations' (see Note 26). The EU/Ukraine Association Agenda, which came to replace the Action Plan, confirms this image. The issues prioritized in the chapter on political dialogue refer mainly to the institutional framework of democracy: 'inclusive constitutional reform', 'checks and balances', 'independence of the judiciary' and 'human rights and fundamental freedoms'.[27]

The Action Plan also contains references to substantive democracy, most notably the fight against corruption, transparency and accountability of the administration (both under item 3), the development of civil society and the involvement of citizens in the decision-making process (item 5). Apart from that, most of the action points related to substantive democracy are dispersed throughout the Action Plan. There are many references (13) to transparency in economic and sectoral chapters, as well as to participation, usually coined in terms such as 'dialogue' or 'involving of civil society' (10 references). Again, the Association Agenda and the priorities formulated in 2010 confirm this image. References to substantive democracy feature in the document, but are secondary to formal democracy and dispersed throughout the text. In principle, elements of accountability, transparency and participation may also be found in sectoral arrangements between the EU and Ukraine. In the period since the launch of the ENP, however, fairly few sectoral agreements have been concluded between the EU and Ukraine.[28] Most of them are of a technical nature and contain few references to the principles of substantive democracy. When looking at specific projects and funding, the EU appears as a more active promoter of substantive democracy. Under Technical Assistance to the Commonwealth of Independent States and the European Initiative for Democracy and Human Rights, predating the ENP, the EU had limited funds available for the promotion of substantive democracy. The ENP Instrument has enhanced the budget destined to support democratic development and good governance.[29] Ukraine was also offered Twinning and Technical Assistance and Information Exchange programmes. Analysing current EU projects in Ukraine,[30] a limited number specifically targets issues of accountability, transparency and participation, most notably in the judicial sector. Others deal with the training of civil servants and indirectly promote substantive democracy. Richard Youngs, however, notes that 'many "democracy" projects [of the EU] are in practice concerned less with increasing the accountability and independence of technical bureaucratic bodies than they are with enhancing the effectiveness of decision-implementation'.[31]

This leads to a preliminary conclusion confirming the EU's two-track approach in its promotion of democracy in Ukraine, but indicates important asymmetries. At the political macro-level, formal democracy is most explicitly and prominently present. The benchmarks, with reference to the OSCE standards, are clear-cut. Substantive democracy is equally present, but tends to be more diffuse and scattered over the Action Plan. A call is made to respect the principles of transparency, accountability and participation, but clear benchmarks are lacking. At the micro-level of projects, substantive democracy features more prominently. The principles of participation and transparency are mainly translated into financial assistance or specific projects, such as twinning or training civil servants. On the basis of this distinction, we will now assess democratization in Ukraine in both areas – formal and substantive – and test how diverging outcomes can be explained on the basis of their different interference with the two factors introduced above: the visibility of reforms and the strategic behaviour of domestic actors.

Assessing democratization in Ukraine

The Orange Revolution of 2004 is widely regarded as a turning point in Ukraine's recent history. It closed the era of "managed democracy" under President Kuchma. The country's political system liberated itself from a number of semi-autocratic traits.[32] The changes were reflected in a number of constitutional amendments which came into force in 2006. Notwithstanding the changes introduced after the Orange Revolution, most authors agree that – even before the change of leadership in 2010 – 'significant problems remain'[33] and that Ukraine is far from an effective democracy. To assess to what extent Ukraine has effectively democratized between the constitutional amendments of 2006 and the presidential elections of January/February 2010 (the 'Orange years'), we divide our analysis along the two tracks of democracy promotion. We start from the findings of a number of international organizations on democratic progress in Ukraine, in particular the fact-finding mission of the Parliamentary Assembly of the Council of Europe (PACE) and the European Commission's Progress Report.[34] After that, we focus on the latest developments under Yanukovych's reign as president. As – at the time of writing – it is still early for final conclusions about the policies of the new government, we keep this separate from our analysis.

At the level of *formal democracy*, Ukraine is regarded by international organizations, such as the EU, the OSCE and the Council of Europe, to have made substantial progress in organizing free and fair elections.[35] The elections of 2007 were considered to be free and fair by international standards.[36] They have been praised as the 'third peaceful and democratic change of power in three years'.[37] On the other hand, during the period 2006–2009, important institutional issues which inhibited a smooth democratic process remained. This was most notably reflected in the existence of two centres of power in the executive branch, with an unclear division of authority between the President and the Government. The constitutional system failed to balance the power between both. Also, the political customs made a *co-habitation* between adversaries unlikely. As a result, Ukrainian politics found itself in an almost ongoing political crisis. Fierce competition led to recurring political instability and often paralysed decision-making and implementation. The PACE report mentions that 'the inherent flaws in the Ukrainian political system – constant sources of legal chaos and systemic constitutional crisis – have not been remedied. All political debates continue to be overshadowed by the internal tug of war over the redistribution of political authority, both inside the coalition and between different power institutions'.[38] The constitutional changes which came into force in 2006 were considered to be 'a shift to a parliamentary system, away from the semi-presidential system envisaged by the 1996 Constitution and the system which led to the abuse of power by President Kuchma'.[39] As Wolczuk argues, however, it has remained a semi-presidential system, in which an evolution towards a parliamentary system would depend 'on how the presidency behaves as a political actor'.[40]

While substantial progress has been made in the field of formal democracy, the situation remained – according to the same International Organizations – rather problematic in the field of *substantive democracy* in the same period 2006–2009. The Monitoring Committee of PACE in 2008, though recognizing the progress in organizing free and fair elections, was strikingly critical: 'regrettably, the political culture in Ukraine continues to be extremely low. Rather than playing by the rules, Ukrainian politicians keep on playing with the rules and stretch them as they wish. Ukrainian politics being primarily run by powerful businesses and their lobby groups does not help the situation'.[41] The report is particularly worried about: corruption in the parliament (par. 21); the end of state funding of political parties which is likely to foster political corruption (par. 27); the lack of reform of the judiciary in order to increase transparency and accessibility (par. 49); control over the appointment of judges (par. 53 and 54); the non-implementation of anti-corruption strategies (par. 59) and the lack of public participation in anti-corruption activities (par. 60); state-control over media and the lack of transparency of media ownership (par. 65 and 67).[42]

Corruption is an interesting case to test performance in substantive democracy, because it excludes per definition the key principles of transparency, accountability and participation by citizens and civil society organizations. A study by the Razumkov Centre on corruption[43] in Ukraine mentions similar principles as indispensable to combat corruption. The study concludes that 'political corruption in Ukraine has become all-embracing, "total": political corruption is inherent in all stages of formation and activity of the authorities and local self-government bodies, all state and political institutions without exception; the country has no "islets of honesty", both on the level of separate persons and structures or institutions'.[44] Also in the Corruption Perceptions Index of Transparency International, Ukraine scores badly: in the 2010 index, it ranks 134th out of 178 countries.[45] According to the study of the Razumkov Centre, the reasons quoted for this bleak picture range from the political situation, over the 'merger of business and power' to political culture.[46] The study mentions different reasons why the legal and institutional framework falls short of tackling corruption. A first set of reasons has to do with failure to adopt proper legislation creating accountability and transparency. An anti-corruption strategy was approved in 2006 ('On the road to integrity'), but very little changed on the ground.[47] The entering into force of a package of three anti-corruption laws has been deferred by the Verkhovna Rada from 2009 to January 2011.[48] A second set concerns the failing implementation of existing legislation or principles, such as 'publicity in the activity of government authorities'.[49] The third category relates to the lack of codes of administrative procedure. The study mentions explicitly the need for the 'development and implementation of sectoral anticorruption standards (codes)'.[50] All this indicates that the objectives set by the EU have not been met. Both intergovernmental efforts aiming at effective anti-corruption legislation through leverage and trans-governmental efforts to create more transparency and accountability through governance have not led to tangible results. Domestic factors appear to have inhibited success. If EU-funded projects at micro-level, aimed at fostering good governance in specific policy sectors, have yielded results for those involved, they appear to have failed in disseminating practices of substantive democracy to wider segments.

From this overview, we can conclude that progress has been made at the purely formal level of *formal democracy* through the successful reform of institutional procedures. This progress, however, has been counterbalanced by domestic political issues, blocking a solution to the problem of double authority in the executive. At the level of *substantive democracy*, progress has been limited or non-existent. As indicated above, substantive democracy in the form of participation, transparency and accountability in diverging areas is essential to give democracy real substance. As a result, one might argue that Ukraine's problems of substantive democracy (combined with the institutional deadlock) were so big that they undermined an effective democracy. Borrowing from Bobbio's critical analysis of the weaknesses of democracy, Ukraine suffered in particular from 'the survival of oligarchies'.[51] Also, after the Orange Revolution, Ukraine witnessed a 'continued oligarchization of power'.[52] Business oligarchs dominate economic life and are considered to be very influential in politics. Further, the problem of 'invisible power'[53] is very prominent, with non-accountable forces operating behind the scenes, often being the real decision-makers. This varies from invisible informal networks, over corruption, to organized crime. Corruption is arguably the biggest obstacle for effective democratization. Finally, there is the issue of 'limited space'.[54] Though civil society has undoubtedly gained in strength ever since the Orange Revolution, a democratic culture still fails to penetrate many spaces of society and non-political aspects of daily life.[55]

At the time of writing, it is still early for final conclusions on how the regime change of early 2010 will affect Ukraine's democratic record. However, there is a clear ambiguity. On the one hand, Ukraine was praised for organizing free elections and for a peaceful transition of power, notwithstanding heavy allegations within Ukraine from Tymoshenko, who narrowly lost the elections. Yanukovych's ascent to power was thus seen as a confirmation of Ukraine's progress in the field of formal democracy. Moreover, the change of power paved the way for solving the institutional deadlock between President and Government. On the other hand, a fierce debate broke out within Ukraine with opposition and civil society organizations accusing the new regime of setting back the clock. The new regime is accused to have taken small measures that constrain rights and liberties without giving them up altogether. In the field of substantive democracy, informal networks, corruption and media control are still colouring Ukrainian politics. So far, international organizations have been somewhat reluctant to express concerns over democratic developments in Ukraine. The EU has largely continued business as usual. However, for the first time since the presidential elections, the European Parliament raised a more critical voice in a resolution in November 2010. It expresses concerns about both the local elections in October and about infringements of rights and media freedom.[56] The draft report of a new fact-finding mission of PACE, presented in September 2010, sends mixed signals, but remains prudent. On the one hand, it noted that the presidential elections in 2010 have increased stability, but on the other hand, it urged the authorities 'to implement constitutional reforms that would create a robust and stable political framework with a clear separation between the different branches of power and an effective system of checks and balances between them'.[57] The report also expresses the 'concern about the increasing number of allegations that democratic freedoms, such as freedom of assembly, freedom of expression and freedom of the media, have come under pressure in recent months'.[58]

Explaining diverging results in both democracy tracks

To explain the diverging results in the promotion of formal democracy versus that of substantive democracy, this part introduces the two factors presented above: the visibility of reforms and strategic behaviour of domestic actors. It tests their explanatory value on the basis of interviews and discourse analysis. Semi-structured interviews were held with senior Ukrainian diplomats at the Foreign Ministry in Kyiv (21 June 2010) and at the Mission of Ukraine to the EU in Brussels (7 June 2010), and with a member of the Verkhovna Rada, the Ukrainian Parliament, in Kyiv (18 June 2010). All of the interviewees have a long-standing experience with Ukraine's European strategy and have been involved in negotiations with the EU. The main target of the interviews was to receive more information on perceptions among Ukrainian decision-makers on the role of the EU in democracy promotion and the role of domestic factors (in particular the perceived visibility of reforms and the strategic behaviour of domestic actors). A semi-structured interview was also held with an official of the Delegation of the European Commission in Kyiv (21 June 2010), aimed at receiving more detailed information of the EU's activities in the field. This information served to complement the information presented in official EU documents. Secondly a discourse analysis was done of speeches of some key decision-makers in the period 2006–2009 (presidential elections). The aim was to analyse how they formulated their policies vis-à-vis the EU and how they linked these policies to domestic reforms. Speeches were analysed of the following politicians:[59] Viktor Yushchenko (Prime Minister, December 1999–May 2001; President January 2005–February 2010), Yulia Tymoshenko (Prime Minister, January–September 2005; December 2007–March 2010), Boris Tarasyuk (Minister of Foreign Affairs 1998–2000 and 2005–2007) and Viktor Yanukovych (Prime Minister, November 2002–December 2004; August 2006–December 2007; President since February 2010). The discourse analysis followed a two-step method presented by Ruquoy.[60] The first stage is a static discourse analysis, revealing the semantic structural oppositions in the speech acts. These oppositions indicate how the author produces meaning by structurally opposing concepts. The second stage (dynamic discourse analysis) analyses the narrative through the actantial scheme of A.J. Greimas.[61] On the basis of the structural oppositions revealed in the first stage, this analysis reduces the narrative to three fundamental relations between 'actants': between Subject and Object (the quest or relation of desire), between

Helper and Opponent (relation of power) and between Sender and Receiver (relation of communication).

The discourse analysis reveals that one of the central narratives in the discourse of Ukraine's political leaders revolves around the concept of 'European choice', denoting Ukraine's priority of integrating into the EU. This was, of course, already the case before the Orange Revolution ever since the Kuchma regime made European integration a strategic priority,[62] though it should be noted that this objective resulted neither in substantial commitment nor in effective steps to the approximation of legislation.[63] Rather, Kuchma's European policy followed 'integration by declaration'.[64] Kubicek noted a contradiction between the declaratory statements about Ukraine's 'European choice' and authoritarian trends under Kuchma's rule.[65] After the Orange Revolution – which roughly coincided with the launch of the ENP – the new political elite was 'keen to inject dynamism into Ukraine's relations with the EU'.[66] In some fields, formal democracy most notably, the domestic reform agenda of the new regime largely overlapped with the priorities of the EU/Ukraine Action Plan and both would be interwoven in the new discourse. In other words, the 'European choice' narrative continued to be present in Ukrainian political discourse, not only on foreign policy but also domestically, but was more explicitly linked to the programme of democratic reforms. There is a large consensus in Ukraine on joining the EU. This objective is shared by all political parties and the most influential business people.[67]

The analysis of speeches by the four key players between 2006 and 2009 (President Yushchenko, Prime Ministers Tymoshenko and Yanukovych and Foreign Minister Borys Tarasyuk) reveals a considerable number of references to the necessity to carry out reforms in the interest of the country's 'European choice' (i.e. the strategic priority to become a member of the EU) in the field of formal democracy. The need to democratize the state's institutions and procedures in order to guarantee a fair and free electoral process and a stable separation of powers is legitimized both on purely domestic grounds and in terms of Ukraine's 'European choice' and the possible prospects of membership. When it comes to substantive democracy and procedures to distribute power beyond the ruling elite, there are very few references linking it to the country's 'European choice'. Also, speeches by Yushchenko and Tymoshenko reveal a high frequency of the term 'European choice' of which the speakers claim to be the main guarantors. Institutional changes in formal democracy (or the need for such) are legitimized in terms of this strategic objective.[68] In his speech proposing constitutional reform, President Yushchenko refers to the 'example of democratic models widely applied these days in many EU countries', linking domestic reforms to Ukraine's strategic goal of EU membership.[69] Also, Yanukovych, when serving as Prime Minister, regularly referred to Ukraine's European choice. However, he tends to link it to a broader reform package, of which democratic reforms are one aspect.[70] Formulated in terms of the 'actantial scheme', all key players use a similar narrative. The Subject is Ukraine, aspiring to become a member of the EU (Object). This aspiration will be realized if institutional reforms take place (Helper), it will be blocked if it fails to carry out such reforms (Opponent). The speakers also associate themselves and/or the political forces they represent, with the Helper actant, presenting themselves as the guarantors of formal democratic reforms. The strategic objective of EU accession is legitimized by both domestic necessity and the 'European choice' made by Ukraine (Sender). It is communicated to the politicians carrying responsibility for implementing reforms (Receiver). Aspects of substantive democracy, such as transparency and accountability, are notably absent in the narrative on Ukraine's strategic objective of EU membership. The Helper category is limited to the democratic reform of the institutions and the electoral process.

All Ukrainian interviewees confirm the centrality of the objective of EU accession in the policy of reforms. All claim that domestic reforms are to a large extent – though not exclusively – determined by the objective of joining the EU. They share the belief that the visibility of reforms played a prominent role in establishing a domestic consensus within the country. The acceptance of the principles of formal democracy is considered to be the most crucial way to prove the trustworthiness of Ukraine as a potential candidate member state.[71] Democratic institutions and procedures are considered to be the most important benchmarks, but can only be achieved if there is no opposition from veto-players. At several points, Ukraine has actively tried to get clear guidelines from the EU on the prioritized reforms, hoping this would pave the way to an accession prospect. In certain areas, the EU has even drafted laws for Ukraine, though they often got amended in the course of the decision-making process.[72] Two interviewees also confirmed that Ukraine claims a clause offering a prospect of accession in the Association Agreement, which is under negotiation.[73] These elements confirm that Ukraine actively seeks legitimacy by prioritizing the most prominent reforms, hoping this will increase its longer term chances of EU membership.

The internal developments in Ukraine in general, and in the field of formal democracy reforms specifically, are regarded as 'determining for future membership'.[74] Most interviewees agree that the EU had a substantial effect as democracy promoter and will continue to do so.[75] They consider the EU as democracy promoter, but largely confined to the field of democratic institutions and fair elections. Particularly interesting in this respect is the attitude of the interviewees towards the Füle matrix. During his visit to Kyiv in April 2010, Commissioner Füle presented a list of priority areas for reforms.[76] The matrix contained concrete goals and deadlines in the short term (6 months), mid-term (6–18 months) and in the longer term (over 18 months).[77] One of the priority areas of the Füle matrix was formal democracy. One of the interviewees stated that 'the Ukrainian government welcomes and agrees with the Füle matrix'.[78] The matrix was appreciated as providing clear and explicit guidelines on the EU's expectations towards Ukraine. It was seen as confirming the importance of progress in the field of formal democracy, with little or no emphasis on aspects of substantive democracy. The latter are considered by the interviewees to be of secondary importance: they are perceived as less determining for Ukraine's long-term chances of accession, while at the same time being complex to achieve. When formal democracy reforms fail, most interviewees blame that on the political stalemate and conflicting agendas between the key policy makers, who are scared to see their power decline. Clinging to power, at all levels of politics and administration, is regarded as the main reason why it is hard to tackle obstacles for substantive democracy, such as corruption.

In sum, we have seen a threefold development between the Orange Revolution and the presidential elections of 2010. First, institutional changes have been adopted at state level, allowing a procedurally 'free and fair' electoral process. Several institutional issues remain, in particular the unclear division of authority between the President and the Government, creating de facto political instability. Problems in the field of substantive democracy continue to disrupt daily democratic practice: lack of participation, lack of accountability, lack of transparency, a considerable degree of corruption, strong oligarchies and invisible power networks and lack of democratic culture in policy processes.

The discourse analysis and interviews thus confirm that formal democratic changes have been made – at least partly – to gain legitimacy with the EU. Especially after the Orange Revolution, Ukraine, which had been a laggard in democratization in the 1990s, felt a strong need to affirm its new identity through highly visible changes at the institutional level. Domestic support from the relevant players, however, was a necessary condition for introducing these institutional changes. This is precisely the reason why Ukraine managed to democratize the electoral process, but failed to introduce a new institutional balance of power between President and Government. Agreement on the latter was lacking within the broad Orange coalition. The intense conflict and fierce accusations between Yushchenko and Tymoshenko would lead to a complete stalemate on further reforms in formal democracy. The visibility of reforms is generally much weaker in the field of substantive democracy. Inevitably, this is a much more complicated process, requiring the internalization of principles of accountability, transparency and participation. The poor results in this area indicate that so far this has not reached the heart of the political-administrative system.

The interviews, as well as concrete examples, indicate that the poor results in substantive democracy and the progress in the reform of formal democracy are interconnected. Substantive democracy reforms were precisely obstructed because elites feared that the reforms in the field of formal democracy would otherwise affect their power positions. In order to avoid changes in the existing opportunity structures, they resisted more substantive democratic reforms. In other words, they allowed for the institutional democratic facade to be renovated, because this would increase Ukraine's trustworthiness as a partner of the EU, but were reluctant to accept changes in the deeper underlying structures. The incapacity to solve the institutional deadlock can be explained by the same fear of losing power.

Conclusion

In its external policy, the EU promotes two types of democracy. Borrowing Pridham's concepts, we have labelled these types as formal democracy (institutional and procedural characteristics of a regime, guaranteeing a fair and free competition for the votes of the citizens as a basis for the attribution of public posts) and substantive democracy (principles and mechanisms that allow for an ongoing societal control over policy processes and the distribution of power beyond the ruling elite). The research presented allows us to answer three questions. First, which models prevail in the EU's promotion of democracy towards Ukraine? Secondly, how can we explain the diverging outcomes of both tracks of democracy promotion against the background of the leverage model? Thirdly, which conclusions can we draw concerning the effectiveness of the EU's democracy promotion?

First, studying the case of Ukraine during the Orange years, we have found that the EU promotes formal democracy through intergovernmental channels, targeting the polity. Substantive democracy is promoted to a more limited extent through transgovernmental channels, but mainly restricted to specific EU-funded projects rather than through sectoral agreements. As illustrated by the case of corruption, the effects of these projects fail to disseminate to different sectors. In a much weaker form, substantive democracy is also promoted through intergovernmental channels. Aspects of transparency, accountability and participation feature, for example, in the EU/Ukraine Action Plan, but play a fairly marginal role.

This illustrates the dominance of the *leverage model* in the EU's democracy promotion towards Ukraine. Seeking to induce democratic change at polity level, the EU formulates guidelines for democratic reforms at institutional and procedural levels. It reflects an asymmetrical relation. Ukraine seeks legitimacy with the EU, a symbolic reward, which it perceives to increase chances of accession in the longer term. The EU may grant or withhold the legitimacy, as well as material forms of assistance. The criteria for formal democracy, presented by the EU, offer clear guidelines to the Ukrainian elites, allowing them to detect the most necessary reforms, i.e. those necessary to gain legitimacy. The reforms imply considerable adoption costs, which elites will seek to reduce.

Secondly, when looking at the *outcomes* of the EU's two-track democracy promotion, we see a striking discrepancy, with considerable progress in the field of formal democracy, but little progress in the field of substantive democracy. The heavier emphasis the EU puts on formal democracy can only partly be held responsible for this discrepancy. Discourse analysis and interviews held by the author have indicated that among the Ukrainian elites, both democratization strategies serve contradictory instrumental purposes. Again, this can be explained in terms of the leverage model.

First, in order to create legitimacy with the EU, Ukrainian elites have been willing to adopt formal democratic reforms. Diplomats and policy-makers consider *formal democracy* as the litmus test of Ukraine's trustworthiness as a potential candidate member state. They believe that visible reforms in this field will increase the chances of Ukraine to join the EU in the longer term and legitimize democratic reforms in these terms. Active legitimacy seeking with the EU was an important factor in creating domestic support for introducing highly visible reforms in the field of formal democracy. Although conditionality is not the central mechanism explaining rule transfer under the ENP, we could speak of *self-imposed condition-ality*: Ukraine perceives respect for the procedures of formal democracy as the benchmark par excellence to gain legitimacy with the EU and to enhance its chances of membership. The lack of domestic consensus on the division of authority of the executive power (President versus Government) during the Orange years has, however, constrained these reforms mainly to the electoral process. Of course, this implies that success in the promotion of formal democracy is dependent on Ukraine continuing its European strategy. Doubts have been raised about President Yanukovych's real intentions,[79] but at the time of writing, there is no official change in the country's policy.

Secondly, fearing the loss of power that may follow from institutional democratic reforms, Ukrainian elites have obstructed reforms in the field of substantive democracy. The adoption and implementation of principles and rules of *substantive democracy* are perceived to be less urgent as they contribute fairly little to the search for legitimacy. They are less visible for external democracy promoters, but also require complex processes of adaptation and internalization. On the contrary, obstructing substantive democracy is a way for certain elites to retain the power positions and privileges they would lose if a full-fledged substantive democratization would take place. We could speak of a *compensation strategy*: some elites are inclined to compensate for the power they lost as a result of formal democratic reforms. This compensation strategy is facilitated because of the EU's one-sided promotion of formal democracy over substantive democracy, which could consolidate a more qualitative democracy.

To conclude, what does this teach us about the *effectiveness* of democracy promotion? First, the outcome of democracy promotion remains strongly dependent on domestic factors. In the case of Ukraine, in a context of weak conditionality outside the accession framework, leverage may only succeed at inducing formal democracy reforms if a country 'exposes' itself to the external pressure and creates some form of self-imposed conditionality.

Secondly, the compensation strategy of elites has indicated that asymmetrical democracy promotion may undermine the effectiveness of democratization efforts. To be effective, formal and substantive democracy should be promoted simultaneously, with equal emphasis, through different channels. In case of imbalance, weak performance in creating a substantive democracy risks to erode democratization efforts. The EU should thus be more active in fostering forms of substantive democracy, if it wants to create a fertile ground for a qualitative democracy.

Finally, as elites try to compensate the power they lost in formal democratic reforms by obstructing deeper democratic reforms, substantive democracy promotion has better chances of being effective when it empowers non-elite actors. They are not susceptible to a similar 'compensation strategy'. Outside the accession context, deeper democratization is not to be expected from elites at polity or sectoral level. Pressure for reforms 'can only come from civil society'.[80] Only this pressure, in combination with the necessary institutional procedures, can guarantee that substantive democracy spreads beyond islands in specific sectors. In other words, the

EU has to think creatively how it can integrate both tracks of democracy promotion, so that substantive and formal democracy promotion reinforce rather than obstruct one another. If deep democratization is mainly resisted by elites, such a strategy should target non-elite and civil society actors more strongly.

Notes

1. Pridham, *Dynamics of Democratization*, 4–5.
2. Several authors have pointed out that the EU concentrates less on civil society groups and transnational democracy promotion. Programmes target primarily government and state bureaucracies (See, for example, Baracani, 'US and EU Strategies', 310, for the EU's democracy promotion in general and for Ukraine specifically: Solonenko and Jarabik, 'Ukraine', 93; Gawrich, Melnykovska, and Schweickert, 'Neighbourhood Europeanization through ENP', 1212).
3. Rose, 'Evaluating Democratic Governance', 253.
4. Pridham, *Dynamics of Democratization*, 4.
5. Beetham, *Democracy and Human Rights*, 90.
6. Pridham, *Dynamics of Democratization*, 5.
7. Bobbio, *Future of Democracy*.
8. I prefer to use the term 'societal democracy' for Bobbio's Italian term 'democrazia sociale', rather than the term 'social democracy' used in Roger Griffin's translation (Bobbio 1987). The latter is confusing because it may be associated with the ideology of social democracy.
9. Bobbio, *Future of Democracy*, 55.
10. Bobbio, *Democracy and Dictatorship*, 156.
11. Similar ideas about the role of social organizations can be found in the work of Robert Putnam. He regards a civic community as one of the crucial conditions for 'strong, responsive, effective representative institutions' (Putnam, *Making Democracy Work*, 6).
12. OSCE, 'Human Dimension Seminar 2004', 1. The OSCE refers to this as 'democratic governance'.
13. ODIHR, 'Democratic Governance'. The UNDP uses a similar concept of democratic governance: 'people should govern themselves through the systems they choose through open and transparent participatory processes. Democratic governance means that people have a say in the decisions that affect their lives and that they can hold decision-makers accountable'. (UNDP, *Guide to Democratic Governance*, 15).
14. UNDP, *Guide to Democratic Governance*; ODIHR, 'Democratic Governance'; OSCE, 'Human Dimension Seminar 2004'; OSCE, 'Best Practices'; OSCE, 'Human Dimension Seminar 2007'.
15. See also Héritier, 'Elements of Democratic Legitimation'; Freyburg, Skripka, and Wetzel, 'Democracy Between the Lines', 14. Note that, contrary to Freyburg, we do not limit the term democratic governance to specific sectoral policies.
16. See, for example, early texts such as Miszlivetz, 'Unfinished Revolutions of 1989'; Kolarska-Bobinska, 'Changing Face of Civil Society'.
17. Howard, *Weakness of Civil Society*; On the state of civil society in Ukraine, see Gromadzki et al., *Beyond Colours*, 64–67.
18. Baracani, 'US and EU Strategies'.
19. Dimier, 'Constructing Conditionality', 263. Several authors have indicated that strategic considerations, reflecting the EU's interests, have in practice often prevailed over its proclaimed commitment to export democratic values (e.g. Warkotsch, 'European Union and Democracy Promotion'; Youngs, 'Normative Dynamics and Strategic Interests').

20. Emerson, Aydin, Noutcheva, Tocci, Vahl, and Youngs, 'Reluctant Debutante'
21. Schimmelfennig and Sedelmeier, 'Governance by Conditionality'.
22. Magen, 'Shadow of Enlargement'; Schimmelfennig and Scholtz, 'EU Democracy Promotion'.
23. This is based on interviews and research of which the results were published in: Casier, 'To Adopt or Not to Adopt'.
24. See Bauer, Knill, and Pitschel, 'Differential Europeanization'; Magen, 'Shadow of Enlargement'. Also, the concept of isomorphism explains institutional adaptation in terms of legitimacy. See DiMaggio and Powell, 'The Iron Cage'.
25. For the EU's Eastern neighbours, see Sasse, 'European Neighbourhood Policy, 303. In the case of the EU's Southern neighbours, see Cavatorta, Gomez Arana, Kritzinger, and Chari, 'EU External Policy-Making', 362.
26. European Union, 'EU/Ukraine Action Plan'.
27. European Commission, 'EU-Ukraine Association Agenda'; European Commission, 'List of the EU-Ukraine Association Agenda Priorities'.
28. For an overview of EU-Ukraine treaties, see the EU Treaty Office.
29. Solonenko and Jarabik, 'Ukraine', 93.
30. For an overview of running EU-funded projects in Ukraine, see EEAS, 'List of Projects', http://eeas.europa.eu/delegations/ukraine/projects/list_of_projects/projects_en.htm (accessed November 1, 2010).
31. Youngs, 'Democracy Promotion as External Governance', 902.
32. Wolczuk, 'Domestic Politics and European Integration'.
33. Kubicek, 'Problems of post-communism', 323.
34. PACE, 'Functioning of Democratic Institutions – 2008'; European Commission, Progress Report.
35. European Commission, Progress Report.
36. PACE, 'Functioning of Democratic Institutions – 2008'.
37. Ibid., art. 9.
38. Ibid., par. 6.
39. Wolczuk, 'Domestic Politics and European Integration', 13.
40. Ibid., 13.
41. Ibid., par. 19.
42. Ibid., different paragraphs.
43. Corruption is defined in the study as 'illegitimate use by political actors and bearers of public power of their capabilities and powers with the purpose of getting personal or group benefits' (Razumkov Centre, 'Political Corruption in Ukraine', 40).
44. Ibid., 34.
45. http://www.transparency.org/policy_research/surveys_indices/cpi/2010.
46. Razumkov Centre, 'Political Corruption in Ukraine', 34.
47. PACE, 'Functioning of Democratic Institutions – 2008', par. 59.
48. PACE, 'Functioning of Democratic Institutions – 2010', 15.
49. Razumkov Centre, 'Political Corruption in Ukraine', 41.
50. Ibid., 41.
51. Bobbio, Future of Democracy, 30. Bobbio's critique deals with Western liberal-democracies, Italian democracy in the first place. All democracies are thus seen to suffer from important weaknesses.
52. Hoshovsurka, quoted in Kubicek, 'Problems of Post-communism', 332.
53. Bobbio, Future of Democracy, 33.
54. Ibid., 32.
55. Solonenko, 'EU's Transformative Power'.
56. European Parliament, 'European Parliament Resolution of 25 November 2010 on Ukraine'. P7_TA(2010)0444, http://www.europarl.europa.eu/sides/getDoc.

do?type=TA&reference=P7-TA-2010-0444&language=EN&ring=P7-RC-2010-0650 (accessed February 1, 2011).
57. PACE, 'Functioning of Democratic Institutions – 2010', 17.
58. Ibid., 4.
59. See Yushchenko, 'Ukraine needs constitutional change'; Tymoshenko, 'Address on the Political Situation in Ukraine', 'Address on the Political and Economic Situation in Ukraine'; Tarasyuk, 'Speech of Minister for Foreign Affairs of Ukraine'; and Yanukovych, 'Where Ukraine is Heading' for details.
60. Ruquoy, 'Analyse structurale'.
61. Greimas, *Structural Semantics*.
62. Kuchma, 'Decree by the President of Ukraine'.
63. See Wolczuk, 'Implementation Without Coordination', 193–195.
64. Sherr, quoted in ibid., 197.
65. Kubicek, 'The European Union and Democratization in Ukraine'.
66. Wolczuk, 'Implementation Without Coordination', 197.
67. Copsey and Shapovalova, 'Ukrainian Views of European Integration'.
68. See, for example, Tymoshenko, 'Address on the Political Situation in Ukraine'; Tymoshenko, 'Address on the Political and Economic Situation in Ukraine'.
69. Yushchenko, 'Ukraine Needs Constitutional Change'.
70. Yanukovych, 'Where Ukraine is Heading'.
71. See also Bobitski, 'Do Ut des'.
72. Interview with an official of the Delegation of the European Commission in Kyiv, 21 June 2010. All interviews were conducted in confidentiality, and the names of the interviewees are withheld by mutual agreement.
73. Interview with senior diplomat at the Ukrainian Mission to the EU, 7 June 2010; interview with member of Verkhovna Rada, 18 June 2010.
74. Interview with member of Verkhovna Rada, 18 June 2010.
75. Interview with member of Verkhovna Rada, 18 June 2010; interview with senior diplomat at the Ministry of Foreign Affairs, 21 June 2010.
76. The Füle matrix was not a public document, but found its way to the Ukrainian press. It is also mentioned in Solonenko, 'EU's Transformative Power', 11.
77. Interview with an official of the Delegation of the European Commission in Kyiv, 21 June 2010.
78. Interview with a senior diplomat at the Ministry of Foreign Affairs, 21 June 2010.
79. See Sherr 'Mortgaging of Ukraine's Independence'.
80. Solonenko, 'EU's Transformative Power', 26.

Notes on contributor

Tom Casier is Director of Research Studies and Convener of the MA in International Relations and the MA in European Public Policy at the Brussels School of International Studies, University of Kent. His research interests include EU-Russia relations, Russian and EU foreign policy and European Neighbourhood Policy / Eastern Partnership. Currently he is completing the book 'Europe and the World. Redefining Europe's Role in a Changing World' with Sophie Vanhoonacker (to be published with Palgrave).

Bibliography

Baracani, Elena. 'US and EU Strategies for Promoting Democracy'. In *The Foreign Policy of the European Union. Assessing Europe's Role in the World*, ed. Federiga Bindi, 303–18. Washington, DC: Brookings Institution Press, 2010.

Bauer, Michael, Christoph Knill, and Diana Pitschel. 'Differential Europeanization in Eastern Europe: The Impact of Diverse EU Regulatory Governance Patterns'. *Journal of European Integration* 29 (2007): 405–23.

Beetham, David. *Democracy and Human Rights*. Cambridge: Polity, 1999.

Bobbio, Norberto. *Democracy and Dictatorship. The Nature and Limits of State Power* Cambridge: Polity, 1989.

Bobbio, Norberto. *The Future of Democracy. A Defence of the Rules of the Game* Minneapolis: University of Minnesota Press, 1987.

Bobitski, Nazar. 'Do Ut Des? The Need for True Reciprocity in the European Neighbourhood Policy'. *European Foreign Affairs Review* 13 (2008): 449–72.

Casier, Tom. 'To Adopt or Not to Adopt. Explaining Selective Rule Transfer under the European Neighbourhood Policy'. *Journal of European Integration* 33 (2011): 37–53.

Cavatorta, Francesco, Arantza Gomez Arana, Sylvia Kritzinger, and Raj S. Chari. 'EU External Policy-Making and the Case of Morocco: 'Realistically' Dealing with Authoritarianism'. *European Foreign Affairs Review* 13 (2008): 357–76.

Copsey, Nathaniel, and Natalya Shapovalova. 'Ukrainian Views of European Integration'. *SIPU Report*, April 30, 2008, http://www.wider-europe.org/files/Ukrainian% 20Views%20of%20EU%20Integration.pdf (accessed September 1, 2010).

DiMaggio, Paul, and Walter Powell 'The Iron Cage Revisited: Institutional Isomorphism and Collective Rationality in Organizational Fields'. *American Sociological Review* 48 (1983): 147–60.

Dimier, Véronique. 'Constructing Conditionality: The Bureaucratization of EC Development Aid'. *European Foreign Affairs Review* 11 (2006): 263–80.

EEAS. 'List of Projects', http://eeas.europa.eu/delegations/ukraine/projects/list_of_ projects/projects_en.htm (accessed November 1, 2010).

Emerson, Michael, Senem Aydin, Gergana Noutcheva, Nathalie Tocci, Marius Vahl, and Richard Youngs. 'The Reluctant Debutante. The European Union as Promoter of Democracy in its Neighbourhood'. *CEPS Working Document*, No. 223, July 2005.

European Commission. 'EU-Ukraine Association Agenda to Prepare and Facilitate the Implementation of the Association Agenda' (2009). European Union. http://eeas. europa.eu/ukraine/docs/2010_eu_ukraine_association_agenda_en.pdf (accessed November 1, 2010).

European Commission. Progress Report Ukraine (2008). SEC(2008)402. European Union. http:// ec.europa.eu/world/enp/pdf/progress2008/sec08_402_en.pdf (accessed April 1, 2009).

European Commission. 'List of the EU-Ukraine Association Agenda Priorities for 2010' (2010). European Union. http://eeas.europa.eu/ukraine/docs/2010_association_agenda_priorities_ en.pdf (accessed November 1, 2010).

European Parliament. 'European Parliament Resolution of 25 November 2010 on Ukraine'. P7_TA(2010)0444. http://www.europarl.europa.eu/sides/getDoc.do?type=TA&reference= P7-TA-2010-0444&language=EN&ring=P7-RC-2010-0650 (accessed February 1, 2011).

European Union. 'EU/Ukraine Action Plan'. http://ec.europa.eu/world/enp/pdf/action_ plans/ukraine_enp_ap_final_en.pdf (2005) (accessed September 1, 2010).

EU Treaty Office. 'List of Treaties by Country: Ukraine', http://ec.europa.eu/world/agreements/ searchByCountryAndContinent.do?countryId=3856&countryName=Ukraine (accessed November 1, 2010).

Freyburg, Tina, Tatiana Skripka, and Anne Wetzel. 'Democracy Between the Lines? EU Promotion of Democratic Governance via Sector-Specific Co-operation'. *NCCR Democracy, Working Paper*, 5, 2007. http://www.nccr-democracy.uzh.ch/publications/ workingpaper/pdf/WP5.pdf (accessed April 1, 2009).

Gawrich, Andrea, Inna Melnykovska, and Rainer Schweickert. 'Neighbourhood Europeanization through ENP: The Case of Ukraine'. *Journal of Common Market Studies* 48 (2010): 1209–35.

Greimas, Algirdas J. *Structural Semantics: An Attempt at a Method*. Lincoln: University of Nebraska Press, 1984.
Gromadzki, Grzegorz, Veronika Movchan, Mykola Riabchuk, Iryna Solonenko, Susan Stewart, Oleksandr Sushko, and Kataryna Wolczuk. *Beyond Colours: Assets and Liabilities of 'Post-Orange' Europe*. Kyiv: International Renaissance Foundation and Warsaw: Stefan Batory Foundation, 2010.
Héritier, Adrienne. 'Elements of Democratic Legitimation in Europe: An Alternative Perspective'. *Journal of European Public Policy* 6 (1999): 269–82.
Howard, Marc. *The Weakness of Civil Society in Post-communist Europe*. Cambridge: Cambridge University Press, 2002.
Kolarska-Bobinska, Lena. 'The Changing Face of Civil Society in Eastern Europe'. *Praxis International* 10 (1991): 324–36.
Kubicek, Paul. 'Problems of Post-communism: Ukraine after the Orange Revolution'. *Democratization* 16 (2009): 323–43.
Kubicek, Paul. 'The European Union and Democratization in Ukraine'. *Communist and Post-Communist Studies* 38 (2005): 269–92.
Kuchma, Leonid. 'Decree by the President of Ukraine on Approvement the Strategy of Ukraine's Integration to the European Union. [Includes the Strategy of Ukraine's Integration to the European Union, Approved by the Decree of the President 615/98 on June 11, 1998]'. Ukraine Ministry of Foreign Affairs. http://www.ukraine-eu.mfa.gov.ua/eu/en/publication/content/1999.htm (accessed April 1, 2009).
Magen, Amichai. 'The Shadow of Enlargement: Can the European Neighbourhood Policy Achieve Compliance?'. *Columbia Journal of European Law* 12 (2006): 383–427.
Miszlivetz, Ferenc. 'The Unfinished Revolutions of 1989: The Decline of the Nation-State?'. *Social Research* 58 (1990): 781–804.
ODIHR. 'Democratic Governance'. ODIHR. http://www.osce.org/odihr/43612 (accessed April 1, 2009).
OSCE. 'Best Practices in Combating Corruption'. OSCE. http://www.osce.org/files/documents/9/a/13738.pdf (2004) (accessed April 1, 2009).
OSCE. 'Human Dimension Seminar. Effective Participation and Representation in Democratic Societies'. OSCE. http://www.osce.org/odihr/28103 (2007) (accessed April 1, 2009).
OSCE. 'Human Dimension Seminar on Democratic Institutions and Democratic Governance. Consolidated Summary'. OSCE. http://www.osce.org/odihr/37750 (2004) (accessed April 1, 2009).
PACE. 'The Functioning of Democratic Institutions in Ukraine. Report. Committee on the Honouring of Obligations and Commitments by Member States of the Council of Europe'. AS/Mon(2008)06 rev., March 18, 2008. Council of Europe. http://assembly.coe.int/CommitteeDocs/2008/20080318_amondoc06r.pdf (accessed September 1, 2010).
PACE. 'The Functioning of Democratic Institutions in Ukraine. Report. Committee on the Honouring of Obligations and Commitments by Member States of the Council of Europe'. Doc. 12357, September 20, 2010. Council of Europe. http://assembly.coe.int/main.asp?Link=/documents/workingdocs/doc10/edoc12357.htm (accessed November 1, 2010).
Pridham, Geoffrey. *The Dynamics of Democratization. A Comparative Approach*. London: Continuum, 2000.
Putnam, Robert D., Roberto Leonardi, and Rafaella Y. Nanetti. *Making Democracy Work: Civic Traditions in Modern Italy*. Princeton: Princeton University Press, 1994.
Razumkov Centre. 'Political Corruption in Ukraine: Actors, Manifestations, Problems of Countering'. Special issue, *National Security and Defence* no. 7 (2009): 1–84.

Rose, Richard. 'Evaluating Democratic Governance: A Bottom-up Approach to European Union Enlargement'. *Democratization* 15 (2008): 251–71.

Ruquoy, Danielle. 'Les principes et les procédés méthodologiques de l'analyse structurale'. In *Méthodes d'analyse de contenu et sociologie*, ed. Jean Remy and Danielle Ruquoy, 93–109. Brussels: Facultés universitaires Saint-Louis, 1990.

Sasse, Gwendolyn. 'The European Neighbourhood Policy: Conditionality Revisited for the EU's Eastern Neighbours', *Europe-Asia Studies* 60 (2008): 295–316.

Schimmelfennig Frank, and Hanno Scholtz. 'EU Democracy Promotion in the European Neighbourhood. Political Conditionality, Economic Development and Transnational Exchange'. *European Union Politics* 8 (2008): 187–215.

Schimmelfennig, Frank, and Ulrich Sedelmeier. 'Governance by Conditionality: EU Rule Transfer to the Candidate Countries of Central and Eastern Europe'. *Journal of European Public Policy* 11 (2004): 661–79.

Sherr, James. 'The Mortgaging of Ukraine's Independence'. *Chatham House Briefing Paper*, REP BP 2010/01.

Solonenko, Iryna. 'The EU's "Transformative Power" Towards the Eastern Neighbourhood: The Case of Ukraine'. *SPES Policy Papers*, August 2010.

Solonenko, Iryna, and Balazs Jarabik. 'Ukraine'. In *Is the European Union Supporting Democracy in its Neighbourhood?* ed. Richard Youngs, 81–98. Madrid: FRIDE, 2008.

Tarasyuk, Borys. 'Speech of Minister for Foreign Affairs of Ukraine Borys Tarasyuk at the Ceremony of Opening of the Academic Year at the Diplomatic Academy of the Ministry of Foreign Affairs of Ukraine on September 1, 2006'. Ministry of Foreign Affairs Ukraine. http://www.mfa.gov.ua/mfa/en/publication/content/6748.htm (accessed September 1, 2010).

Tymoshenko, Yulia. 'Address on the Political and Economic Situation in Ukraine'. October 20, 2008. Ukrainian Government. http://www.kmu.gov.ua/control/en/publish/article?art_id=165465436&cat_id=32606 (accessed April 1, 2009).

Tymoshenko, Yulia. 'Address on the Political Situation in Ukraine'. September 4, 2009. Ukrainian Government. http://www.kmu.gov.ua/control/en/publish/article?art_id=156262492&cat_id=32606 (accessed April 1, 2009).

UNDP. 'A Guide to UNDP Democratic Governance'. UNDP. http://www.undp.org/governance/ (accessed September 1, 2010).

Warkotsch, Alexander. 'The European Union and Democracy Promotion in Bad Neighbourhoods: The Case of Central Asia'. *European Foreign Affairs Review* 11 (2006): 509–25.

Wolczuk, Kataryna. 'Domestic Politics and European Integration in Ukraine'. *The International Spectator* 4 (2006): 7–24.

Wolczuk, Kataryna. 'Implementation Without Coordination: The Impact of EU Conditionality on Ukraine under the European Neighbourhood Policy'. *Europe-Asia Studies* 61 (2009): 187–211.

Yanukovych, Viktor. 'Speech by Prime Minister of Ukraine Viktor Yanukovych at On-Line Conference in Davos "Where is Ukraine heading"'. January 27, 2007. Ukrainian Government. http://www.kmu.gov.ua/control/en/publish/article?art_id=65899552&cat_id=32606 (accessed April 1, 2009).

Youngs, Richard. 'Democracy Promotion as External Governance?'. *Journal of European Public Policy* 16 (2009): 895–915.

Youngs, Richard. 'Normative Dynamics and Strategic Interests in the EU's External Identity'. *Journal of Common Market Studies* 42 (2004): 415–35.

Yushchenko, Viktor. 'Ukraine Needs Constitutional Change. [Speech]'. April 7, 2009. Ministry of Foreign Affairs Ukraine. http://www.ukraine-eu.mfa.gov.ua/eu/en/publication/content/29692.htm (accessed April 1, 2009).

The promotion of participatory governance in the EU's external policies: compromised by sectoral economic interests?

Anne Wetzel

Centre for EU Studies, Ghent University, Belgium

Besides the more conventional top-down leverage and bottom-up linkage approach, the European Union (EU) uses a third way to promote democracy in third countries: promotion of democratic governance through functional cooperation in policy sectors. This governance model of democracy promotion has so far been studied only with regard to its effectiveness in target countries. In contrast to earlier research, this contribution takes an 'input' perspective and asks whether adverse sectoral economic interests prevent the EU from consistent democratic governance promotion. Based on three case studies from the two policy sectors of environmental and fisheries policy, the contribution concludes that EU democratic governance promotion is indeed inconsistent when sectoral economic interests are at stake. The governance model is thus subject to the same pattern of inconsistency as the leverage and linkage model with regard to economic interests.

Introduction

The last years have not only seen the emergence of extensive European Union (EU) external governance[1] but also of an EU democracy promotion strategy that is directly connected to it. This strategy aims at deliberately making use of the functional ties established under the external governance agenda with third countries by transferring norms of democratic governance through sectoral cooperation. It was first outlined as one instrument among others in the 2001 European Commission's Communication on human rights and democracy promotion. There, the Commission acknowledged the potential of a sectoral approach to democracy promotion:

To promote human rights and democratisation objectives in external relations, the EU draws on a wide-range of instruments [. . .] Some are more innovative, and potentially underused, namely *Community instruments in policy areas such [as] the environment, trade, the information society and immigration which have the scope to include human rights and democratisation objectives*. These tools should be used in a coherent manner, to achieve synergy and consistency and to ensure maximum effective use of resources to promote sustainable development and respect for human rights and democratisation world-wide.[2]

The Commission's approach was subsequently supported by the Council.[3]

Shortly after the launch of the European Neighbourhood Policy (ENP), which can be regarded as the EU's most ambitious external governance project, the Commission stated that one of the goals regarding the participating countries is 'introducing sectoral reforms [. . .] in order to improve management and *encourage the authorities to account for their decisions to those they administer*'.[4] Thus, the aim is not only to make sectoral governance in third neighbouring countries more effective, as standards of good governance would emphasize.[5] By stressing the notion of accountability these reforms are also intended to make sectoral governance more democratic through the enhancement of popular control.[6] As the Council and the Commission jointly pointed out, in the ENP Action Plans 'democracy building and support' do not only feature in the 'political section' but are also components of the other, i.e. the sectoral sections.[7] There they are part of solutions for sectoral policy problems.

The goal of democratic governance promotion through functional cooperation is not restricted to the ENP. With regard to developing countries, the Commission outlined a similar approach by stressing the importance of mainstreaming democratic governance objectives into sectoral cooperation:

Democratic governance is to be approached holistically, taking account of all its dimensions (political, economic, social, cultural, environmental, etc.). [. . .] Accordingly, the concept of democratic governance has to be integrated into each and every sectoral programme.[8]

Again, democratic governance is acknowledged as a goal of cooperation. The intention is that it should form part of the sectoral cooperation that is in the first place directed at objectives such as reaching the Millennium Development Goals. Thus, the basic idea in both the ENP as well as in the approach towards developing countries is to 'use' sectoral functional cooperation, however motivated in the first place, in order to encourage the development of norms of democratic governance in third countries.

In order analytically to grasp this new approach – which complements the more traditional bottom-up and top-down external democratization strategies – the literature has introduced the governance model of democracy promotion.[9] Democratic governance promotion represents a more horizontal approach based on functional, transgovernmental cooperation in policy sectors. Through such cooperation, the sector-specific rules of democratic governance embodied in the EU's *acquis communautaire* are promoted in the third country as parts of solutions for policy problems. The target actors are neither the third countries' governments nor civil society but sub-units of the state administration. In contrast but not in opposition to democracy proper, which relates to the level of the polity and is often connected to certain institutional features such as general elections, the notion of democratic governance is defined at a sectoral level and comprises the three main principles of transparency, accountability, and participation.[10] So far, it has been shown that the EU is fairly successful in promoting the formal adoption of rules of democratic governance in third countries.[11] However, it has not been asked under what conditions the EU engages in democratic governance promotion in the first place. In particular, we do not know yet whether EU democratic governance promotion follows the same pattern of inconsistency that can be found in the top-down[12] and bottom-up approaches[13] to democracy promotion.

This contribution responds to the call for more empirical analysis of the EU's commitment to normative foreign policy goals in specific policy sectors.[14] In particular, it will examine whether adverse sectoral economic interests have an influence on the promotion of public participation, as one element of democratic governance. In order to seek to answer the question, the consistency of EU promotion of public participation in third countries will be analysed in three cases from the EU's external environmental and fisheries policy that are characterized by varying degrees of adverse sectoral economic interests. The contribution follows participatory democratic theories that stress the democratizing potential of public participation procedures.[15] Participatory governance will here be generally understood as interaction of the public with institutions of the political system in the process of making binding decisions with the aim of influencing these decisions.[16] While public participation is not necessarily successful it must be meaningful, i.e. participatory governance does not include instances of (merely) 'ceremonial' or 'pseudo' participation.[17]

The contribution proceeds in the following way. The next part deals with the explanations that have been offered in the literature in order to account for the EU's inconsistent democracy promotion through the intergovernmental and transnational channels. This provides the basis for case selection. In the subsequent empirical part, the three case studies – cooperation on genetically modified organisms (GMO) and water governance with the Eastern European ENP countries[18] and cooperation on fisheries policy under Fisheries Partnership Agreements (FPA) – will be presented and the EU's democratic governance promotion activities will be analysed. The contribution concludes that EU democratic governance promotion is inconsistent when important sectoral interests are concerned.

Consistency of EU democracy promotion

In a review of the existing literature regarding the consistency of EU general democracy promotion, Frank Schimmelfennig comes to the conclusion that '[d]espite the pervasive political and legal rhetoric of democracy and human rights promotion, actual policy seems to match rhetoric only when consistency is "cheap"; otherwise, it is driven by a host of other – geopolitical, economic or security – interests'.[19] More particularly, authors have demonstrated that in cases where (soft) security issues arise the EU foregoes democracy promotion.[20] It is also suggested that 'conflicting functional goals' may have led to a less consistent application of (positive) conditionality.[21] Furthermore, authors indicate that inconsistency in the EU's reaction to third states' non-compliance with democratic standards is mainly due to self-regarding concerns.[22] With regard to democracy promotion through linkage it has been pointed out that the rather unsuccessful implementation of the bottom-up approach in the Southern Mediterranean countries can in part be attributed to EU Member States' (in particular, French and Spanish) 'political objections to a strengthening of the EU's democratization policy in the Mediterranean'.[23]

Existing studies on EU external democracy promotion provide different explanations for the observed inconsistencies. The most pervasive argument is that economic and security interests override democratization objectives.[24] Another, related explanation is interdependence, which, if asymmetrical in favour of the third country, is assumed to lead to a decrease in democracy promotion.[25] Taking into account that democratization may lead to instability and war,[26] the EU's reluctant democracy promotion has also been explained with the democracy-stability dilemma.[27]

EU democracy promotion has also been found to be dependent on target countries' geographic proximity. Starting from a democratic peace proposition – that is, that democracies are more prone to seek peace among each other than non-democracies – and the EU's strategy to gain regional influence through integration, Warkotsch argues that 'the EU possesses a weighted utility function where its benefits from democracy in a neighbouring country are weighted more heavily than anywhere else'.[28] Similarly, constructivist approaches often highlight the same issue.[29] Identity-based values and norms are supposed to 'become the more politically relevant in relations with external countries the closer these countries move toward membership'.[30] Finally, according to Kochevov, the ambiguity of the template for democracy promotion is a reason for inconsistent application of standards.[31]

Which expectations can we derive from the existing literature for democratic governance promotion? Given the strong emphasis that the literature puts on overriding interests, we can assume that 'only if no other concerns [...] are important in a given situation'[32] will the EU promote democratic governance. Which concerns should be considered as being 'important'? The preset contribution employs a liberal view on democratic governance promotion in that it takes a '"bottom-up" view of politics'.[33] It thus follows several recent empirical studies that have collectively provided evidence for the influence of domestic sectoral interests on the EU's external relations in the fields of environment, development and trade.[34] Since democratic governance promotion proceeds at a sectoral level, it can be expected that countervailing influential sectoral economic interests are an obstacle to it and that the EU's external relations 'in a given issue area will aim at achieving the material or immaterial goals which are pursued by the most influential domestic actors'.[35] Thus, it can be hypothesized that the more salient domestic interests are connected to the external dimension of the policy sector that would be hurt by the promotion of democratic governance the more likely it is that the EU forgoes this goal.

In this contribution, I will examine whether the presence of adverse sectoral economic interests has an influence on democratic governance promotion. In order to do so, I will combine a most similar case design with comparison of a case of the same type. Whereas the controlled comparison reveals the outcome of the key independent variable on the dependent variable, the latter may reveal whether causal paths are similar and increase confidence in generalization.[36] The EU's policy will first be analysed in the environmental sector with regard to cooperation with Eastern European ENP countries on GMO and water issues. I have chosen environmental cooperation with Eastern European countries because it allows keeping other explanatory variables stable for cases with different values on the key independent variable. Furthermore, according to the above mentioned explanations the context is rather favourable for democratic governance promotion. First, the environmental sector has a comparatively well-developed *acquis* on participatory governance. There are even issue-specific templates that the EU could promote in third countries. Thus, ambiguity of standards is low. The templates are also embedded in international law and their promotion can thus be seen as legitimate.[37] Furthermore, there is a 'misfit' insofar that the Eastern European ENP countries have not yet established comprehensive participatory arrangements in environmental decision making. Interdependence with regard to the two policy sectors and overall interdependence is not to the detriment of the EU. Environmental policy can generally be regarded as 'low politics', which excludes security interests as sources of inconsistency. Finally, although they are not on the way to accession, the Eastern European ENP countries are geographically close to the EU. Furthermore, they are part of an 'expanding system of functional regional integration'.[38] Thus, overall, the conditions for democratic governance promotion are very favourable. However, with the field of GMO the sector contains an issue that is highly disputed and where economic interests are at stake. As will be shown in more detail below, some economic interests are not particularly compatible with democratic governance promotion. Since there are no comparably strong economic interests with respect to water governance, the cases vary with regard to the key independent variable.[39]

The third case in the comparison – cooperation on fisheries policy under the FPAs – is similar to the GMO case. Since the cooperation on sectoral policy reform in third countries is part of a commercial arrangement there is a tension between commercial goals such as access to the resource and the promotion of governance objectives in order to enhance sustainability. At the same time, this case can also be regarded as low politics. Interdependence is not disadvantageous for the EU. There are EU internal and international templates on participatory governance in the fisheries sector.[40] Geographically, however, the case is more diverse since it covers countries belonging to the African, Caribbean and Pacific Group of States (ACP), and also the ENP country Morocco (Table 1).

EU promotion of participatory governance
Environmental policy

The issue of public participation entered European environmental policy in the early 1990s. Today, the EU *acquis* on participative governance is well developed. This is true for general provisions such as the ones on Environmental Impact Assessment,[41] but there are also sector-specific rules as will be outlined below. The EU's environmental policy has developed a very ambitious and multifaceted external dimension. One priority of the EU is the promotion of environmental cooperation with neighbouring countries and regions.[42] With the Eastern European ENP countries, cooperation takes place in different frameworks, among others under the ENP sub-committees, but also in international fora such as the United Nations Economic Commission for Europe (UNECE). One of the overall aims of environmental cooperation with Eastern Europe is the improvement of environmental governance, which includes public participation in environmental decision-making.

Genetically modified organisms

Compulsory rules for public participation with regard to the deliberate release of GMO can be found in Article 9 of Directive 2001/18 that entered into force on 17 April 2002 and repealed an earlier Directive with non-binding rules on public participation. Similarly, the Regulation 1829/2003 on genetically modified food and feed includes provisions on access to information and in Arts. 6(7) and 18(7) gives the public an opportunity to make comments on the opinion of the Authority that deals with an application for authorization.

While codifying participation rules in GMO matters internally, the EU is rather reluctant to promote them in Eastern European ENP countries. Although the Sixth Environmental Action Programme mentioned 'supporting the build up of regulatory frameworks in third countries where needed through technical and financial assistance' as a priority action regarding GMO[43] the EU is not very active on this issue with regard to this particular region. Despite the fact that legislation on GMO and biosafety was still underdeveloped in the Eastern European ENP countries in the early and mid-2000s, cooperation on this issue was – in contrast to issues such as water quality, waste management and air pollution – not foreseen in the ENP strategy paper[44] and is not mentioned in any of the ENP Action Plans with Eastern neighbours.[45]

Cooperation on participation regarding GMO issues is not only neglected but the EU has even deliberately obstructed attempts to promote participation rules related to GMOs in the Eastern European ENP countries. In the early 2000s, several countries in transition explicitly demanded an internationally binding template for participation rights in GMO matters in order to introduce respective rules 'at home'. For that reason, they suggested to amend the Convention on Access to Information, Public Participation in Decision-making and Access to Justice in Environmental Matters (Aarhus Convention) which hitherto contained only a very weak provision on public participation regarding GMO issues.[46] For the EU as a signatory and party to the Aarhus Convention[47] and an actor that officially wants to 'work towards strengthening international environmental governance',[48] this would have been an ideal opportunity to aim at the transfer of the related *acquis* rules to third countries.

In fact, in the discussions on the EU negotiating mandate, several EU countries, in particular Belgium, Italy, Hungary, Portugal, Slovenia, and Finland, supported a 'clear signal in favour of [...] detailed provisions on public participation in decision-making on GMOs consistent with existing Community legislation'.[49] This opinion was, however, rejected by another group of member states, led by France. The latter explicitly favoured a non legally binding option or a rather general obligation to promote, i.e. not guarantee, public participation. A similar conservative stance was taken by the European Commission.[50] Given the conservative position of important EU member states, such as France and Germany, and the diversity of views within the EU, the negotiations proved to be extremely difficult and polarized. A final compromise on legally binding rules for participation on GMO issues was reached at last minute at the second meeting of the Parties in Almaty, Kazakhstan, in 2005.

The reluctant EU position has been ascribed to two main factors. It was on the one hand seen as 'service to the GMO industry and the governments that support it'. On the other hand, observers pointed to pressure from the US government.[51] One observer named a 'coalition of the biotechnology and trade lobby' as the source of the EU's tough stance.[52] What is at stake regarding the promotion of public participation rules in GMO issues? In the EU, the field of GMO is characterized by rather strict regulation and a sceptical public opinion. The former has led large biotech companies to relocate research activities, field trials, and commercialization outside the EU.[53] In parallel with the growing scepticism of Western European public opinion on GMO in the 1990s, transnational corporations such as Monsanto and Pioneer began to focus on Central and Eastern Europe and the Newly Independent States where public awareness regarding this issue was much lower. Since agriculture is still a major economic sector in this region, the Western agricultural industry finds is attractive to start with field trials as a first step towards subsequent commercialization. Furthermore, the levels of regulation were very weak, in particular when compared with those of the EU.[54] Since most of these countries lacked well-developed laws on this issue, there were hardly any hurdles to companies' activities. Transparency on field trials was often rather low. Lack of public protest was even seen as to be a market advantage.[55] This provided a rather favourable environment for biotechnology corporations since they usually have a preference for low regulation.[56]

In the EU, the big member states – including, Germany, United Kingdom, and France – are leading players in biotechnology.[57] The EU itself is a target of lobbying activities of transnational bioindustry associations such as EuropaBio, founded in 1997, which enjoys 'good working relations with the Commission',[58] and are reported to have an influence on decision making.[59] In 2003, the Commission appointed the Competitiveness in Biotechnology Advisory Group with Industry and Academia. It comprises 'representatives from all the various industry segments and from companies at every stage of company development together with entrepreneurial academics'.[60] Besides the good access, internal unity of the European biotech sector has strengthened considerably during the 1990s. Companies – such as Bayer, Monsanto, or Syngenta – tend to enter into large coalitions and there is a trend for mergers within the sector.[61] The global biotechnology industry structure is characterized by high concentration and internationalization where regional differences of interests disappear. For Falkner and Bernauer, such a high concentration is assumed to be conductive to successful companying lobbying against strict regulations.[62]

With regard to the amendment of the Aarhus Convention, the world's largest biotechnology organization, the Biotechnology Industry Organization, which enjoys strong (financial) support of major biotech firms, maintains close relationships with the US regulatory agencies[63] and has EuropaBio among its members, expressed its discontent with new legally binding solutions.[64] The same opinion was voiced by CropLife International.[65] This global federation represents the plant science industry and also represents EuropaBio as one of its members. It was represented by two to three people in the negotiations, who actively expressed 'conservative' standpoints. European Environmental non-governmental organizations (NGO), including NGOs from Eastern Europe, on the other hand, have from the beginning of the amendment process called on EU environmental ministers to support the introduction of legally binding participation rules into the Convention[66] and 'not to continue moving down a path of promoting weak biosafety frameworks in the non-EU region'.[67] NGO[68] representatives report that democratic governance issues related to GMO are in general weakly financed in EU and for NGOs it is difficult to receive funding. In the Eastern neighbourhood countries the situation is said to be even worse. Obviously, the coalition of environmental agents that has profited from and was carried by a strong negative public perception of agri-biotechnology and that 'succeeded in stemming the demand for deregulation and induced a strengthening of European GMO policy'[69] has much less influence when it comes to external relations. This can be explained by the lack of 'public outrage', i.e. the 'fear or anger a particular risk generates among a relatively large part of a country's population'[70] and the resulting decline of collective action capacity.

As a result of this case study an additional factor emerged as potentially important for the outcome. Besides the biotech companies' and their business associations' initiatives, it must be kept in mind that GMO issues are subject to 'regulatory polarization' between the US and the EU with the US on the 'pro-agri-biotech' side and the

EU on the other.[71] US initiatives massively back the industry's activities in Eastern Europe.[72] Moreover, it needs to be noted that in 2003, after years of threatening to do so, the government of the USA, responding to domestic interests, and other GMO exporters filed suit against the EU before the World Trade Organization on GMO crops and food.[73] There was thus severe transatlantic tension over this issue. While one of the Commission's answers to this crisis was to signal an end of the unofficial moratorium on GMO release, the conservative stance in the Aarhus amendment negotiations can also be interpreted as a strategy to appease the US government that was very much against the amendment. Eventually, the Commission's stance reflected very much the position of DG Trade (see footnote 52).

Water governance

With the adoption of the Water Framework Directive in 2000, the EU established a framework for water protection and management whose success is seen to be dependent 'on information, consultation and involvement of the public'.[74] Article 14 of this directive is dedicated to public information and consultation and demands that 'Member States shall encourage the active involvement of all interested parties in the implementation of this Directive, in particular in the production, review and updating of the river basin management plans'. More concretely, they shall ensure that 'they publish and make available for comments to the public, including users' certain specified documents related to a new or updated river basin management plan, and 'shall allow at least six months to comment in writing on those documents in order to allow active involvement and consultation'. River basin management plans in turn have to include 'a summary of the public information and consultation measures taken, their results and the changes to the plan made as a consequence'.[75]

In contrast to the issue of GMO, water governance in Eastern European ENP countries is not connected to comparably strong commercial interests that would be incompatible with the promotion of public participation. On the one hand, the water sector is an example that 'challenged the notion that the civil society sector acts only as a counterpart to the private sector'.[76] In particular with regard to the issues of water pricing and full cost recovery environmental NGOs have joined the pro-pricing position of the water industry in the past. Furthermore, the preferences of stakeholders from the industry regarding the regulation of water issues are not necessarily the same but may even be contradictory, e.g. between agriculture and private water companies.[77] On the other hand, most Eastern European ENP countries are rather unattractive for international private water operators. Investments are seen to be risky due to the economic and political situation, weak regulatory frameworks, comparatively poor revenue streams due to low tariffs that are usually below operational costs and do not meet requirements of full cost-recovery, and a lack of political will to involve the private sector. Thus, Public–Private Partnerships in Eastern Europe, Caucasus and Central Asian (EECCA) countries with international participation remain at a low level.[78]

Public participation is one of the central themes of EU environmental cooperation with the Eastern neighbours and takes place in different frameworks. The EU does not hide its attempt to promote participative water governance in Eastern European ENP countries. On the contrary, the enhancement of public participation is regularly a component in water-related projects. The 2007 Regional Indicative Programme for Eastern Europe expects as results of the planned activities among others the '[e]nhanced implementation of the EU Water initiative' and '[i]ncreased environmental awareness and civil society cooperation'.[79] For example, the EU-financed project on 'Environmental Collaboration for the Black Sea' (2007–2009), which comprised Georgia, Moldova, and Ukraine, on the one hand aimed to improve national legislation taking into account the water-related EU *acquis* and, on the other hand, explicitly included the improvement of public participation as one project goal. Adoption and implementation of water-related legislation is also the aim of another EU-financed project on 'Water Governance in the Western EECCA Countries' (2008–2010), which involves Belarus, Moldova and Ukraine, Armenia, Azerbaijan, and Georgia. The work on these countries' legislation is seen as 'part of the process of convergence with EU environmental legislative and implementation principles'. As such, the project also intends to support public participation in decision-making processes.[80] Thus, with regard to water governance, we see a clear intention of the EU to promote its norms on public participation which translates into concrete action.

Fisheries policy

Governance has recently become a major topic in the EU's Common Fisheries Policy (CFP). Regarding participation in fisheries policy the basic Council Regulation for the reformed CFP, EC 2371/2002 now defines in Article 2.2 that fisheries policy 'shall be guided by [...] broad involvement of stakeholders at all stages of the policy [...]'.[81] The topic of participatory governance was not only raised at a rhetorical level but concrete measures have been taken in order to substantiate it, in particular with the renewal of the Advisory Committee for Fisheries and Aquaculture (ACFA) in 1999 and the establishment of Regional Advisory Councils in 2002. Furthermore, there exists a Sectoral Dialogue Committee on sea fisheries.

The EU's CFP has developed an external dimension. Clearly, the fisheries agreements are its most important aspect.[82] The present design of the 'Southern agreements', which are mainly concluded with ACP countries, is the result of a reform process which began in 2002. This reform aimed at a new approach towards third countries. In contrast to the much criticized 'pay, fish and go' approach of the existing fishing agreements, new partnership agreements were designed with a 'focus on cooperation to promote sustainable fishing, just as in our own waters'.[83] With their inclusion of dialogue and the setting aside of a share of the EU's financial contribution in order to 'to support the sectoral fisheries policy in the third country with a view to introducing responsible and sustainable fishing'[84] the agreements have a dual aim. Besides the commercial dimension there is the objective of 'projecting the Community "acquis" in multilateral and bilateral arenas'.[85]

The new external dimension of the CFP has been implemented since 2003. Today, all fisheries agreements with financial compensation are FPAs and in all of them, a percentage of the EU's financial contribution is earmarked for fisheries sector support in the respective third country. The third countries' progress with sector reforms is regularly discussed in Joint Committees on the basis of a country-specific 'sectoral matrix' (*matrice sectorielle*). An analysis of the available minutes of the Joint Committees[86] shows that issues of participation do not play a role in these meetings. In no instance did the EU refer to or even demand the enhancement of stakeholder participation with regard to fisheries in the third country. This is also acknowledged by interview partners. The same picture emerges from the sectoral matrices that the author was able to obtain. This does not imply that single matrices do not refer to arrangements to extend stakeholder participation. For example, the matrix of Guinea-Bissau makes a reference to the strengthening of participative management committees (*comités de gestion participative*). However, as interview partners confirmed, there is no systematic attempt by the EU to encourage third countries to establish such arrangements.[87] On the contrary, the EU explicitly rejects the promotion of governance norms through FPA: 'Some of the expectations placed on FPAs are unreasonable: they are there to support and assist, but they are not a tool for imposing what we think are the "right" policies or governance systems on our partners. Their sovereignty is paramount.'[88]

At first sight this statement seems to point to conflicting norms, i.e. democratic governance promotion *vs* non-interference into the affairs of a sovereign state. However, even though the EU might have some leverage in some of the FPA countries, there would be no possibility to 'impose' governance reforms. Eventually, the third countries are free to spend the compensation from the FPAs as they want. Furthermore, given that the EU has an official democracy promotion policy in place which explicitly rejects the imposition of democracy from the outside[89] and has democracy and human rights clauses in all its general agreements with third countries the reluctance to participatory governance promotion can rather be attributed to the opinion that it would make matters much more complicated as one interviewee judged. Fisheries agreements first and foremost remain commercial agreements. They are the result of negotiations on quota and financial compensation and there are diverse interests connected to them. The 2002 Commission Communication on FPAs states that apart from the overall aim of promoting sustainable fisheries, the specific objective of the CFP with regard to the fisheries agreements is 'to maintain the European presence in distant fisheries and to *protect European fisheries sector interests*'.[90] The Council endorsed this objective with a view to employment and those European regions that are highly dependent on fisheries.[91]

The FPAs in their present form mainly serve the catching sector's interests, with particulary fleets from Spain, Portugal, Italy, and France benefiting from them. At EU level, these interests are represented by *Europêche* as the 'vehicle through which the national fishermen's organizations agree their official representation vis-à-vis the Commission'.[92] In its position on the 2002 sector reform this group attached 'utmost importance' to the CFP's external dimension and pointed to 'the essentially commercial character' of fisheries agreements.[93] In 2009, *Europêche* rejected any change of the CFP's external objectives and stated that the external dimension 'must continue to target upholding Community fishing fleets' interests in third countries'.[94] The French *Union of the Armateurs à la Pêche* demanded in 1998 that the EU should pursue 'an aggressive, dynamic and expansionist policy in the matter of fishing agreements. It no longer suffices to safeguard what already exists, [the EU] should develop what could be'.[95] The catching sector was the dominant pressure group in the early 2000s and still is rather influential. There are strong informal contacts between fisheries lobbyists and some national Council delegations. Partly, these circles have evolved through a common university education of its members and now persist. In general, the CFP is characterized as 'rather strong horizontal coordinating governance arrangement [. . .] between policymakers, fisheries managers and the fisheries sector' where the inner circle is made up of a limited number of actors, i.e. fishers and policymakers.[96] Fishing interests have also long been organized at the national level and are viewed to be even more influential on CFP development than European organizations.[97] They enjoy a high level of political salience that does not necessarily match statistical indicators.[98] In contrast to the GMO case, external sectoral interests are not involved in the fisheries case.

Calls on the EU to promote participatory governance come from European NGOs, including the Coalition for Fair Fisheries Arrangements, as well as some members of the European Parliament, and – from outside the EU – some third country fisheries organizations.[99] They are often part of a more comprehensive development agenda for the third countries. However, these demands are not reflected in the EU's policy. This is not least due to the worse access points for these actors: 'in an area of Commission competence, where DG fisheries is in the lead [and DG Development marginalized], and where Council considerations are focused on fish rather than development, there is little formal opportunity for development inputs to be made'.[100] Interestingly, however, the ACFA as the official consultative committee of the Commission on fisheries that includes representatives from industry but – since its reform in 1999 – also environmental and development NGOs has recently suggested that through the FPAs 'the EU should promote transparency and stakeholder participation, two important aspects recognized by the code of conduct for responsible fishing of the FAO'.[101] It remains to be seen whether this position will finally be reflected in the future EU policy on cooperation under the FPAs.

Conclusions

The promotion of democratic governance through sectoral cooperation offers the EU a third, alternative way to further democratization objectives in third countries. In particular in contexts where top-down leverage and bottom-up linkage strategies reach their limits[102] the governance approach with its focus on the transfer of functional solutions for policy problems opens a 'back door' for democracy promotion. Whereas research has shown that the EU is able to induce the adoption of rules of democratic governance in third countries[103] this contribution has demonstrated that it does not always make use of this potential. After investigating EU democratic governance promotion in three cases with different levels of adverse interests, it can be concluded that the governance model is subject to the same pattern of inconsistency as the linkage and leverage model (Table 1).

In cases such as cooperation on water governance with Eastern European ENP countries where no significant interests of EU domestic actors or other important external actors are hurt by the promotion of rules of democratic governance, the EU puts emphasis on them. The two cases of cooperation on GMO with Eastern European ENP countries and cooperation on fisheries policy under FPAs, however, show that the EU does not only neglect democratic governance promotion when sectoral interests would be hurt but even actively rejects such demands. While in the GMO case there are also strong external sectoral interests that may have influenced the result, no such interests are present in the fisheries case. Thus, strong external sectoral interests do not seem to be decisive for the inconsistency of EU democratic governance promotion.[104] Summing up, the EU's democratic governance promotion policy is likely to be inconsistent when significant adverse sectoral economic interests are at stake.

Table 1.   EU participatory governance promotion.

	GMO – Eastern European ENP countries	Water – Eastern European ENP countries	Fisheries – FPA
Acquis	Issue-specific, internationally embedded	Issue-specific, internationally embedded	Issue-specific, internationally embedded
Interdependence	Not unfavourable for EU	Not unfavourable for EU	Not unfavourable for EU
Security	Low politics	Low politics	Low politics
Proximity	Close	Close	Close/Distant
Interests	Agri-biotech industry Trade lobby (*vs.* Environmental NGOs) (external actors)	No significant adverse interests	Catching sector (*vs.* development NGOs)
Participatory governance promotion	–	+	–

Acknowledgements

The research for this contribution has been undertaken within the National Center of Competence in Research (NCCR) Democracy. Financial support by the Swiss National Science Foundation is gratefully acknowledged. The author thanks Sandra Lavenex, Frank Schimmelfennig, Ulrich Sedelmeier, Tina Freyburg, the European politics research group at ETH Zurich, the participants of the Oxford Politics & IR Graduate Research Workshop 2009, the panel participants and audience at the 2010 ISA Annual Convention, in particular Thomas Legler, two anonymous reviewers and the journal editors for the valuable comments. The empirical parts of the contribution are partly based on interviews conducted with officials of the European Commission in Brussels, in particular DG Environment, DG MARE and DG Development; the Council Secretariat in Brussels; Directorate Agriculture and Fisheries; and representatives from non-governmental organizations based in Belgium, Ukraine, and Moldova, between 2007 and 2011.

Notes

1. Lavenex, 'EU External Governance'.
2. European Commission, 'European Union's Role in Promoting Human Rights and Democratisation', 6, emphasis added.
3. Council, 'Conclusions on Human Rights and Democratisation', III, IV.
4. European Commission, 'Governance in the European Consensus on Development', 16, emphasis added.
5. Kaufmann, Kraay, and Mastruzzi, 'Governance Matters VIII', 6.
6. Beetham, *Democracy and Human Rights*, 155–6.
7. European Commission and Council, 'Democracy building', 26.
8. European Commission, 'Governance in the European Consensus', 6.
9. Freyburg et al. 'EU Promotion of Democratic Governance'.
10. Freyburg, Skripka, and Wetzel, 'Democracy between the Lines'.
11. Freyburg et al. 'Democracy Promotion', in this volume.
12. Maier and Schimmelfennig, 'Shared Values'; Olsen, 'Promotion of Democracy'; Olsen 'The European Union'; Smith, European Union Foreign Policy, 165–7; Warkotsch, 'Non-Compliance'.
13. Crawford, 'The European Union'; Jünemann, 'From the Bottom to the Top'; Youngs, 'The European Union', 56–7.
14. Orbie 'Civilian Power Europe', 126.
15. Held, *Models of Democracy*, 209–15, Schmidt, *Demokratietheorien*, 236–53.
16. Friedrich, 'Old Wine', 5; Schmitter, 'Participation', 56.
17. Verba, 'Democratic Participation', 55–56; Verba, Small Groups, 220–1.
18. Armenia, Azerbaijan, Georgia, Moldova, Ukraine; all of them are considered to be 'European' countries by the European Commission, see http://europa.eu/abc/european_countries/others/index_en.htm (01.12.2010).
19. Schimmelfennig, 'Europeanization beyond Europe', 15.
20. Olsen, 'Promotion of Democracy'; Olsen 'The European Union'.
21. Maier and Schimmelfennig, 'Shared Values', 40.
22. Warkotsch, 'Non-Compliance'.
23. Jünemann, 'From the Bottom to the Top', 102.
24. Schraeder, 'State of the Art', 33–34; Jünemann and Knodt, 'Explaining EU Instruments', 353–355; Olsen, 'Promotion of Democracy', 163.25.
25. Jünemann and Knodt, 'Explaining EU Instruments', 357–8.
26. Snyder, *From Voting to Violence*.

27. The dilemma is that democratization processes may (temporarily) lead to instability, the empowerment of radical parties and even civil war. Seen from a role theory perspective, the EU faces an internal role conflict: as a democracy promoter it should prioritize democracy even when it is risky, as a security actor, however, the EU has to take these risks into account. Jünemann, 'Externe Demokratieförderung', 164; see also Powel, 'A clash of Norms'; Andrés Viñas, 'EU's Democracy Promotion Policy'.
28. Warkotsch, 'Non-Compliance', 230–1.
29. Schimmelfennig, 'Community Trap', 58–61.
30. Maier and Schimmelfennig, 'Shared Values', 45.
31. Kochenov, 'Behind the Copenhagen Façade'.
32. Olsen, 'Promotion of Democracy', 144.
33. Moravcsik, 'Taking Preferences Seriously', 517.
34. Falkner, 'Political Economy'; Dür, 'Bringing Economic Interests Back'; Elgström, 'Trade and Aid'.
35. Bienen, Freund, and Rittberger, 'Societal Interests', 3.
36. George and Bennett, Case Studies, 81–83; Yin, Case Study Research, 47.
37. For provisions on participation in environmental policy: Principle 10 of the 1992 Rio Declaration on Environment and Development (non-binding), UNECE Convention on Access to Information, Public Participation in Decision-making and Access to Justice in Environmental Matters 1998 (binding, including weak participation provisions on GMOs in Art. 6.11); in particular with regard to GMOs (transboundary movement): Art. 23 of the 2000 Cartagena Protocol (binding); in particular with regard to water: Protocol on Water and Health to the 1992 Convention on the Protection and Use of Transboundary Watercourses and International Lakes (binding).
38. Lavenex, 'A Governance Perspective', 939.
39. King, Keohane, and Verba, *Designing Social Inquiry*, 140.
40. For (non-binding) provisions on participation in fisheries policy: FAO Code of Conduct for responsible fisheries 1995: 'States, in accordance with appropriate procedures, should facilitate consultation and the effective participation of industry, fishworkers, environmental and other interested organizations in decision-making with respect to the development of laws and policies related to fisheries management, development, international lending and aid.' (6.13); 'Within areas under national jurisdiction, States should seek to identify relevant domestic parties having a legitimate interest in the use and management of fisheries resources and establish arrangements for consulting them to gain their collaboration in achieving responsible fisheries' (7.1.2).
41. European Parliament and Council, 'Directive 2003/35/EC'.
42. European Parliament and Council, 'Decision No 1600/2002/EC', Art. 9.2(i).
43. Ibid., Art. 6.2(i).
44. European Commission, 'European Neighbourhood Policy'.
45. One interview partner mentioned that the European Commission provides comments under the WTO TBT notification procedure on Ukraine (G/TBT/N/UKR/45). There is also some cooperation in TAIEX workshops (e.g. planned TAIEX workshop AGR 42006 on 'Harmonisation of GMO analysis', which, however, does not deal with public participation). UNECE, 'Report', 3.
46. The European Commission signed the Aarhus Convention for the European Community on 25 June 1998. Ratification took place on 17 February 2005.
47. European Parliament and Council, 'Decision No 1600/2002/EC', Art. 9.2c.
48. Council, 'Note from Council Secretariat', 2.
49. Ibid.
50. Ibid.
51. Silina and Hontelez, 'Aarhus Convention', 2.

52. Personal interview, Brussels, 4 February 2011.
53. Rosendal, 'Governing GMOs', 90.
54. Today, the situation has somewhat changed. For example, Ukraine has passed the law 'On the State System of Biosafety at the Time of Creating, Testing, Transporting, and Using Genetically Modified Organisms' (Law of Ukraine of 31.05.2007 No. 1103-V) and other new legislation. Nevertheless, 'the Biotech regulatory system in Ukraine is still under development' (for this assessment and an overview of legislation see USDA, 'GAIN Report Ukraine'). National Biosafety Frameworks have been developed as part of a respective UNEP-GEF project in Armenia, Azerbaijan, Belarus, Georgia, Moldova, and Ukraine.
55. Kruszewska, 'Der Wilde Osten'; Zoeller, 'CEE's Experimental Fields'.
56. Bernauer, *Genes*, 83; Falkner, *Business Power*, 153.
57. European Commission, 'Innovation and Competitiveness', 32–3; Ramani, 'Creating Incentives', 1996.
58. Rosendal, 'Governing GMOs', 93.
59. Friends of the Earth Europe, 'Too Close'.
60. European Commission, 'Life Sciences', 7.
61. Rosendal, 'Governing GMOs', 91–3.
62. Falkner, *Business Power*, 159–160; Bernauer, *Genes*, 81.
63. Bernauer, *Genes*, 95.
64. Val Giddings, 'Letter'.
65. Verschueren, 'Letter'.
66. Hontelez, 'Letter'.
67. European Eco-Forum and other Civil Society organizations of the UN-ECE region 'Almaty Action Statement'.
68. NGO Eco-Tiras, Moldova.
69. Rosendal, 'Governing GMOs', 100.
70. Bernauer, *Genes*, 69.
71. Ibid., 8.
72. Kruszewska, 'Der Wilde Osten', Higgins, H. 'Romania', 3.
73. Pollack and Shaffer, *When Cooperation Fails*, 177–234.
74. European Parliament and Council, 'Directive 2000/60/EC', Preamble. The following quotes refer to this Directive.
75. Ibid., Annex VII: A9.
76. Partzsch, 'European Union Water Policy', 243.
77. Page and Kaika, 'EU Water Framework Directive', 334–35.
78. Martin, 'Position Paper'.
79. European Commission, 'European Neighbourhood and Partnership Instrument', 11.
80. Mott MacDonald, 'Water Governance', A-3.
81. Council Regulation (EC) No 2371/2002 of 20 December 2002 on the Conservation and Sustainable Exploitation of Fisheries Resources under the Common Fisheries Policy.
82. Currently, there are two major types of fisheries agreements. First, there are the agreements based on reciprocal access to the resource (the so-called 'Northern agreements', with the exception of Greenland). Second, there are the agreements where access to the resource is granted in exchange for financial compensation from the EU budget. Such agreements exist mainly with ACP countries but also with Morocco and Greenland ('Southern agreements'). After the 2002 CFP reform, these are called 'Fisheries Partnership Agreements'. A third type of agreement existed with Argentina but remained the only of its kind (Lequesne, *The Politics of Fisheries*, 137–138). This article focuses on the agreements of the second type.
83. Borg, 'A Partner in Global Fisheries'.

84. European Commission, 'Commission Staff Working Paper SEC(2007) 1202', 86.
85. European Commission, 'Reflections on Further Reform', 2.
86. (European Commission/Guinea Bissau, 2008a, 2010; European Commission/Mozambique, 2008; European Commission/Cape Verde, 2009; European Commission/Comoros, 2008; European Commission/Greenland, 2008, 2009; European Commission/Ivory Coast, 2008, 2009; European Commission/Madagascar, 2008; European Commission/Mauritania, 2008, 2010; European Commission/Morocco, 2009, 2010; European Commission/São Tomé et Príncipe, 2007; European Commission/Seychelles, 2009b, 2009a), http://ec.europa.eu/fisheries/cfp/international/agreements/joint_committees/index_en.htm, last access 15 June 2010.
87. Personal interviews Council Secretariat, Brussels, 24 March 2009; European Commission, DG Fisheries, Brussels, 26 March 2009.
88. European Commission, *The Common Fisheries Policy*, 25.
89. Council, 'Conclusions on Democracy Support', 1; European Commission, 'European Union's Role in Promoting Human Rights and Democratisation'.
90. European Commission, 'Integrated Framework for Fisheries', 5, emphasis added.
91. Council, 'Fisheries Partnership Agreements', Art. 2, p. 15; Council, 'Regulation (EC) No 861/200 ', Art. 7.
92. Lequesne, 'Fisheries Policy', 373 and 361.
93. Europêche and COGECA, 'Position', 13.
94. Europêche and COGECA, 'Answers', 25.
95. Quoted in Lequesne, 'Fisheries Policy', 373.
96. Van Hoof and van Tatenhove, 'EU Marine Policy', 728–29.
97. Churchill and Owen, *EC Common Fisheries Policy*, 28.
98. Lequesne, 'Fisheries Policy', 258.
99. Gorez, 'The Future of Fisheries Partnership Agreements'; West African Artisanal Fisheries' Organisations Representatives, 'Nouakchott Declaration'; European Parliament, 'Report', 17.
100. Hudson, 'Case Study', 127–128.
101. ACFA, 'ACFA Opinion', 18.
102. Schimmelfennig and Scholtz, 'EU Democracy Promotion'.
103. Freyburg *et al* 'EU Promotion of Democratic Governance'.
104. The present paper does not allow to make inferences about the magnitude of external actors' influence. While they may have a reinforcing effect, it is beyond the scope of the paper to measure these effects.

Notes on contributor

Anne Wetzel is post-doctoral researcher at the Centre for EU Studies, Ghent University, Belgium. Her research focuses on the EU's external relations, including democracy promotion and the EU in international institutions.

Bibliography

Advisory Committee on Fisheries and Aquaculture (ACFA). *ACFA Opinion on the Commission Green Paper Concerning the Reform of the CFP* (*COM*(2009)163). EP(09)158 final. 9 December 2009.
Andrés Viñas, David. *EU's Democracy Promotion Policy in the Mediterranean: Squaring the Stability-Democracy Circle?* Working Paper of Observatorio of European Foreign Policy 80, 2009.
Beetham, David. *Democracy and Human Rights*. Cambridge: Polity Press, 1999.

Bernauer, Thomas. *Genes, Trade, and Regulation. The Seeds of Conflict in Food Biotechnology.* Princeton: Princeton University Press, 2003.

Bienen, Derk, Corinna Freund and Volker Rittberger. 'Societal Interests, Policy Networks and Foreign Policy: An Outline of Utilitarian-Liberal Foreign Policy Theory'. *Tübinger Arbeitspapiere zur Internationalen Politik und Friedensforschung* 34 (2000).

Borg, Joe. 'A Partner in Global Fisheries and Beyond: The European Union's Drive for the Sustainable Management of Our Oceans and Seas', Address at Shanghai Fishery University on 10.11.2007.

Churchill, Robin and Daniel Owen. *The EC Common Fisheries Policy.* Oxford: Oxford University Press, 2010.

Council of the European Union. (2001). 'General Affairs Council Conclusions on Human Rights and Democratisation in Third Countries'. 10228/01 (Presse 250-G). 25 June 2001.

Council of the European Union.'Council Regulation (EC) No 2371/2002 of 20 December 2002 on the Conservation and Sustainable Exploitation of Fisheries Resources under the Common Fisheries Policy'. *Official Journal of the European Communities* L 358 (31.12.2002): 59–80.

Council of the European Union. (2004). 'Fisheries Partnership Agreements with Third Countries – Council Conclusions'. 11234/2/04 REV 2 (Presse 221), C/04/221. 19 July 2004.

Council of the European Union. (2005). 'Note from Council Secretariat to Council. Adoption of a Council Decision Concerning the Participation of the European Community in Negotiations on Genetically Modified Organisms under the Convention on Access to Information, Public Participation in Decision-Making and Access to Justice in Environmental Matters, including the Second Meeting of the Parties (Almaty, Kazakhstan, 25-27 May 2005)'. 6889/05 RESTREINT UE. 3 March 2005.

Council of the European Union. 'Council Regulation (EC) No 861/2006 of 22 May 2006 Establishing Community Financial Measures for the Implementation of the Common Fisheries Policy and in the Area of the Law of the Sea'. *Official Journal of the European Union* L 160 (14.06.2006): 1–11.

Council of the European Union. 'Council Conclusions on Democracy Support in the EU's External Relations'. 2974th External Relations Council Meeting. 17 November 2009.

Crawford, Gordon.'The European Union and Democracy Promotion in Africa: The Case of Ghana'. *The European Journal of Development Research* 17(4) (2005): 571–600.

Dür, Andreas (2008). 'Bringing Economic Interests Back Into the Study of EU Trade Policy-Making'. *British Journal of Politics & International Relations* 10(1) (2008): 27–45.

Elgström, O. 'Trade and Aid? The Negotiated Construction of EU Policy on Economic Partnership Agreements'. *International Politics* 46(4) (2009): 451–468.

European Commission. 'Communication from the Commission to the Council and the European Parliament. The European Union's Role in Promoting Human Rights and Democratisation in Third Countries'. *COM*(2001) 252 final. 8 May 2001.

European Commission. 'Communication from the Commission on an Integrated Framework for Fisheries Partnership Agreements with Third Countries'. *COM*(2002) 637 final. 23 December 2002.

European Commission. '*Innovation and Competitiveness in European Biotechnology*'. Brussels: Enterprise Directorate-General: Enterprise Papers, no. 7. 2002.

European Commission. 'Report from the Commission to the European Parliament, the Council and the European Economic and Social Committee – Life Sciences and Biotechnology – A Strategy for Europe – Second Progress Report and Future Orientations'. *COM*(2004)250 final. 7 April 2004.

European Commission. 'Communication from the Commission: European Neighbourhood Policy. Strategy Paper'. *COM*(2004) 373 final. 12 May 2004.

European Commission. 'Communication from the Commission: Governance in the European Consensus on Development. Towards a Harmonised Approach within the European Union'. *COM*(2006) 421 final. 30 August 2006.

European Commission. 'Commission Staff Working Paper Accompanying the Commission Working Paper 'EU Report on Policy Coherence for Development''. *SEC*(2007) 1202. 20 September 2007.

European Commission. '*European Neighbourhood and Partnership Instrument. ENPI Eastern Regional Indicative Programme 2007–2010*'. 2007.

European Commission. '*Commission Working Document. Reflections on further Reform of the Common Fisheries Policy*'. 17 September 2008.

European Commission. *The Common Fisheries Policy. A User's guide*. Luxembourg: Office for Official Publications of the European Communities, 2009.

European Commission and Council of the European Union – General Secretariat. 'Joint Paper on Democracy Building in EU External Relations'. *SEC*(2009) 1095 final. 27 July 2009.

European Commission/Cape Verde. *Accord de Partenariat dans le Secteur de la Pêche, 1ère Commission Mixte – Procès Verbal*. 18–19 June 2009.

European Commission/Comoros. *Accord de Partenariat dans le Secteur de la Pêche, 2ième Commission Mixte – Procès Verbal*. 17–18 September 2008.

European Commission/Greenland. *Fisheries Partnership Agreement, Joint Committee Meeting – Minutes*. 25 November 2008.

European Commission/Greenland. (2009). *Fisheries Partnership Agreement, Joint Committee Meeting – Minutes*. 18 March 2009.

European Commission/Guinea Bissau. *Accord de Partenariat dans le Secteur de la Pêche, 1ère Commission Mixte – Procès Verbal*. 3–4 July 2008.

European Commission/Guinea Bissau. *Accord de pêche CE/Guinée-Bissau 2007–2011, Matrice de l'Appui au Secteur de la Pêche – Années 2008–2011*. 2008.

European Commission/Guinea Bissau. *Accord de Partenariat dans le Secteur de la Pêche, Commission Mixte – Procès Verbal*. 11–12 March 2010.

European Commission/Ivory Coast. *Accord de Partenariat dans le Secteur de la Pêche, 1ère Commission Mixte – Procès Verbal*. 17–18 July 2008.

European Commission/Ivory Coast. *Accord de Partenariat dans le Secteur de la Pêche, 2ème Commission Mixte – Procès Verbal*. 28–29 May 2009.

European Commission/Madagascar. *Accord de Partenariat dans le Secteur de la Pêche, 2ième Commission Mixte – Procès Verbal*. 14–15 April 2008.

European Commission/Mauritania. *Rapport de la Seconde Réunion du Comité Scientifique Conjoint RIM-UE*. 8–10 October 2008.

European Commission/Mauritania. *Accord de Partenariat dans le Secteur de la Pêche. Résumé du Procès Verbal de la Commission Mixte*. 22–25 March 2010.

European Commission/Morocco. *Procès Verbal de la Quatrième Commission Mixte de l'Accord de Partenariat dans le Secteur de la Pêche*. 1–3 April 2009.

European Commission/Morocco. *Procès verbal de la cinquième Commission Mixte de l'Accord de Partenariat dans le Secteur de la Pêche*. 2–3 February 2010.

European Commission/Mozambique. *Fisheries Partnership Agreement, Minutes of the First Joint Committee*. 6 November 2008.

European Commission/São Tomé et Príncipe. *Procès Verbal de la 1ère Commission Mixte de l'Accord de Partenariat de Pêche*. 8–9 February 2007.

European Commission/Seychelles. *Fisheries Partnership Agreement, Joint Committee – Agreed Minutes*. 5–6 February 2009.

European Commission/Seychelles. *Fisheries Partnership Agreement, Joint Committee – Agreed Minutes*. 12 January 2009.

European Eco-Forum and other Civil Society organizations of the UN-ECE region. '*The Almaty Action Statement. Statement of the European Eco-Forum and Other Civil Society Organizations of the UN-ECE Region*'. 23 May 2005.

European Parliament. *Report on the Commission Communication on an Integrated Framework for Fisheries Partnership Agreements with Third Countries (COM*(2002) 637) – (2003/2034(INI))'. A5-0303/2003 final. 11 September 2003.

European Parliament and Council of the European Union. 'Directive 2000/60/EC of 23 October 2000 Establishing a Framework for Community Action in the Field of Water Policy. *Official Journal of the European Communities* L 327 (22.12.2000): 1–72.

European Parliament and Council of the European Union. 'Directive 2001/18/EC of 12 March 2001 on the Deliberate Release into the Environment of Genetically Modified Organisms and Repealing Council Directive 90/220/EEC'. *Official Journal of the European Communities* L 106 (17.04.2001): 1–38.

European Parliament and Council of the European Union. 'Decision No. 1600/2002/EC of 22 July 2002 Laying down the Sixth Community Environment Action Programme'. *Official Journal of the European Communities* L 242 (10.09.2002): 1–15.

European Parliament and Council of the European Union. 'Directive 2003/35/EC of 26 May 2003 Providing for Public Participation in Respect of the Drawing up of Certain Plans and Programmes Relating to the Environment and Amending with Regard to Public Participation and Access to Justice Council Directives 85/337/EEC and 96/61/EC'. *Official Journal of the European Union* L 156 (25.06.2003): 17–24.

European Parliament and Council of the European Union. 'Regulation EC No 1829/2003 of 22 September 2003 on Genetically Modified Food and Feed.' *Official Journal of the European Union* L 268 (18.10.2003): 1–23.

Europêche and COGECA. *Position by Europêche and COGECA on the Green Paper Presented by the Commission on the Future of the Common Fisheries Policy.* CP(01)75F1-EP(01)33. 12 July 2001.

Europêche and COGECA. *Answers to the Questions in the Green Paper on the Reform of the Common Fisheries Policy.* EP(09)89final/SP(09)3074:5. 14 October 2009.

Falkner, Robert. (2007). 'The Political Economy of 'Normative Power' Europe: EU Environmental Leadership in International Biotechnology Regulation'. *Journal of European Public Policy* 14(4) (2007): 507–26.

Falkner, Robert. *Business Power and Conflict in International Environmental Politics.* New York: Palgrave Macmillan, 2008.

Freyburg, Tina, Sandra Lavenex, Frank Schimmelfennig, Tatiana Skripka, and Anne Wetzel. 'EU Promotion of Democratic Governance in the Neighbourhood'. *Journal of European Public Policy* 16(6) (2009): 916–34.

Freyburg, Tina, Sandra Lavenex, Frank Schimmelfennig, Tatiana Skripka, and Anne Wetzel. 'Democracy Promotion Through Functional Cooperation? The Case of the European Neighbourhood Policy'. *Democratization*, this issue.

Freyburg, T., Tatiana Skripka, and Anne Wetzel. 'Democracy between the Lines? EU Promotion of Democratic Governance via Sector-Specific Co-Operation'. Zurich: *NCCR Working Paper 5*. 2007.

Friedrich, Dawid 'Old Wine in New Bottles? The Actual and Potential Contribution of Civil Society Organisations to Democratic Governance in Europe'. Oslo: *RECON Online Working Paper 2007/08*. 2007.

Friends of the Earth Europe. *Too Close for Comfort. The Relationship between the Biotech Industry and the European Commission. An Analysis.* Brussels. 2007.

George, Alexander. L. and Andrew Bennett. *Case Studies and Theory Development in the Social Sciences.* Cambridge, MA, London: MIT Press, 2005.

Gorez, Béatrice. *The Future of Fisheries Partnership Agreements in the Context of the Common Fisheries Policy Reform.* Presentation to the European Parliament Development Committee. 2 September 2009.

Held, David. *Models of Democracy.* 3rd ed. Cambridge: Polity, 2006.

Higgins, Holly. *Romania. Planting Seeds. Romanian Legislation for GMO Seeds.* USDA – Foreign Agricultural Service. GAIN Report #RO0005. 28 February 2000.

Hontelez, John. *Letter to the Environment Ministers of the EU Member States and Accession Countries Concerning the Aarhus Convention and Public Participation in Decision Making on GMOs.* 18 September 2003.

Hudson, Alan. 'Case Study of the Fisheries Partnership Agreements'. In *Policy Coherence for Development in the EU. Council Strategies for the Way Forward*, ed. Louise van Schaik et al. Brussels: Centre for European Policy Studies, 2006, 124–9.

Jünemann, Annette. 'From the Bottom to the Top: Civil Society and Transnational NGOs in the Euro-Mediterranean Partnership'. *Democratization* 9(1) (2002): 87–105.

Jünemann, Annette and Michèle Knodt. 'Explaining EU Instruments and Strategies of EU Democracy Promotion. Concluding Remarks'. In *Externe Demokratieförderung durch die Europäische Union*, ed. Annette Jünemann and Michèle Knodt. Baden-Baden: Nomos, 2007, 353–69.

Jünemann, Annette (2009). 'Externe Demokratieförderung im südlichen Mittelmeerraum: Ein rollentheoretischer Erklärungsansatz für die Kluft zwischen Anspruch und Wirklichkeit in den EU-Außenbeziehungen'. In *Der Nahe Osten im Umbruch. Zwischen Transformation und Autoritarismus*, ed. Martin Beck, Cilja Harders, Annette Jünemann and Stephan Stetter. Wiesbaden: VS Verlag, 151–74.

Kaufmann, Daniel, Aart Kraay, and Massimo Mastruzzi. *Aggregate and Individual Governance Indicators 1996–2008.* The World Bank Policy Research Working Paper 4978 (2009).

King, Gary, Robert Owen Keohane, and Sidney Verba. *Designing Social Inquiry: Scientific Inference in Qualitative Research.* Princeton: Princeton University Press, 1994.

Kochenov, Dimitry. 'Behind the Copenhagen Façade. The Meaning and Structure of the Copenhagen Political Criterion of Democracy and the Rule of Law'. *European Integration Online Papers* 8(10) (2004), http://eiop.or.at/eiop/pdf/2004-010.pdf (acessed June 15, 2011).

Kruszewska, Iza. 'Der Wilde Osten. Zur Einführung der Gentechnik in Mittel- und Osteuropa'. *Politische Ökologie* (2003): 81–2.

Lavenex, Sandra. 'EU External Governance in 'Wider Europe''. *Journal of European Public Policy* 11(4) (2004): 680–700.

Lavenex, Sandra. 'A Governance Perspective on the European Neighbourhood Policy: Integration Beyond Conditionality?' *Journal of European Public Policy* 15(6) (2008): 938–55.

Lequesne, Christian. *The Politics of Fisheries in the European Union.* Manchester: Manchester University Press, 2004.

Lequesne, Christian. 'Fisheries Policy. Letting the Little Ones Go?' In *Policy-Making in the European Union*, ed. Helen Wallace, William Wallace and Mark. A. Pollack. Oxford: Oxford University Press, 2005, 353–76.

Maier, Sylvia and Frank Schimmelfennig. 'Shared Values: Democracy and Human Rights'. In *Governing Europe's Neighbourhood: Partners or Periphery?*, ed. Katja Weber, Michael E. Smith and Michael Baun. Manchester: Manchester University Press, 2007, 39–57.

Martin, Lloyd. 'Position Paper by the International Private Sector on its Role in the Reform of Water and Wastewater Utilities in Eastern Europe, Caucasus and Central Asia' In *Financing Water Supply and Sanitation in Eastern Europe, Caucasus and Central Asia.* Paris: Organisation for Economic Co-operation and Development, 2006, 221–31.

Moravcsik, Andrew. 'Taking Preferences Seriously: A Liberal Theory of International Politics'. *International Organization* 51(4) (1997): 513–53.

Mott MacDonald. *Water Governance in the Western EECCA Countries*. TACIS/2008/137-153 (EC), Inception Report – Final. 2008.

Olsen, Gorm Rye. 'Promotion of Democracy as a Foreign Policy Instrument of 'Europe': Limits to International Idealism'. *Democratization* 7(2) (2000): 142–67.

Olsen, Gorm Rye. 'The European Union: An Ad Hoc Policy with a Low Priority'. In *Exporting Democracy. Rhetoric vs. Reality*, ed. Peter J. Schraeder. Boulder: Lynne Rienner, 2002, 131–45.

Orbie, Jan. 'Civilian Power Europe. Review of the Original and Current Debates'. *Cooperation and Conflict* 41(1) (2006): 123–28.

Page, Ben and Maria Kaika. 'The EU Water Framework Directive. Part 2. Policy Innovation and the Shifting Choreography of Governance'. *European Environment* 13 (2003): 328–43.

Partzsch, Lena (2009). 'European Union Water Policy: To Transition or Not to Transition? Coalitions as Key'. In *Water Policy Entrepreneurs. A Research Companion to Water Transitions Around the Globe*, ed. Dave Huitema and Sander Meijerink. Cheltenham: Edward Elgar, 2009, 237–49.

Pollack, Mark. A. and Gregory C. Shaffer. C. *When Cooperation Fails: The International Law and Politics of Genetically Modified Foods*. Oxford: Oxford University Press, 2009.

Powel, Brieg Tomos. 'A Clash of Norms: Normative Power and EU Democracy Promotion in Tunisia'. *Democratization* 16(1) (2009): 193–214.

Ramani, Shyama. 'Creating Incentives: A Comparison of Government Strategies in India and France'. *Biotechnology and Development Monitor* 26 (1996): 18–21.

Rosendal, G. Kristin. 'Governing GMOs in the EU: a Deviant Case of Environmental Policy-Making?' *Global Environmental Politics* 5(1) (2005): 82–104.

Schimmelfennig, Frank. 'The Community Trap: Liberal Norms, Rhetorical Action, and the Eastern Enlargement of the European Union'. *International Organization* 55(1) (2001): 47–80.

Schimmelfennig, Frank. 'Europeanization Beyond Europe'. *Living Reviews in European Governance*, 4(3):15 17.12.2009, http://europeangovernance.livingreviews.org/Articles/lreg-2009-3/ (accessed June 15, 2011).

Schimmelfennig, Frank and Hanno Scholtz. 'EU Democracy Promotion in the European Neighborhood. Political Conditionality, Economic Development and Transnational Exchange'. *European Union Politics* 9(2) (2008): 187–215.

Schmidt, Manfred G. *Demokratietheorien*, 4th ed. Wiesbaden: Verlag für Sozialwissenschaften, 2008.

Schmitter, Philippe. C. Participation in Governance Arrangements: Is There a Reason to Expect it Will Achieve "Sustainable and Innovative Policies in a Multi-Level Context"?' In *Participatory Governance. Political and Societal Implications*, ed. Jürgen R. Grote and Bernard Gbikpi. Opladen: Leske+Budrich, 2002, 51–69.

Schraeder, Peter. J. 'The State of the Art in International Democracy Promotion: Results of a Joint European-North American Research Network'. *Democratization* 10(2) (2003): 21–44.

Silina, Mara and John Hontelez. 'Why the EU Needs to Take the Aarhus Convention More Seriously!' *Metamorphosis* (37) (2005): 1–2.

Smith, Karen. E. *European Union Foreign Policy in a Changing World*. Cambridge: Polity, 2008.

Snyder, Jack. *From Voting to Violence: Democratization and Nationalist Conflict*. New York: Norton, 2000.

UNECE. *Report of the Second Meeting of the Working Group on Genetically Modified Organisms*. MP.PP/AC.2/2003/4. Geneva. 2003.

USDA. *GAIN Report Ukraine*. No. UP1029. 7 December 2010.

Val Giddings, L. *Letter to the Aarhus Convention Secretariat*. 10 June 2003.

van Hoof, Luc and Jan van Tatenhove. 'EU Marine Policy on the Move: The Tension Between Fisheries and Maritime Policy'. *Marine Policy* 33(4) (2009): 726–32.

Verba, S. *Small Groups and Political Behavior*. Princeton: Princeton University Press, 1961.

Verba, Sidney. 'Democratic Participation'. *The Annals of the American Academy of Political and Social Science* 373(1) (1967): 53–78.

Verschueren, Christian. *Letter to the Aarhus Convention Secretariat*. CV/ml/04-0153. 4 February 2004.

Warkotsch, Alexander. 'Non-Compliance and Instrumental Variation in EU Democracy Promotion'. *Journal of European Public Policy* 15(2) (2008): 227–45.

West African Artisanal Fisheries' Organisations Representatives. *Nouakchott Declaration of West Africa Artisanal Fisheries Sector Organisations*. Nouakchott. 11 November 2009.

Yin, Robert K. *Case Study Research: Design and Methods*. Thousand Oaks, London, New Delhi: Sage, 2003.

Youngs, Richard. 'The European Union and Democracy Promotion in the Mediterranean: A New or Disingenuous Strategy?' In *The European Union and Democracy Promotion. The Case of North Africa*, ed. Richard Youngs and Richard Gillespie. London: Frank Cass, 2002, 40–62.

Zoeller, R. 'CEE's Experimental Fields'. *Finance New Europe*, November 2006.

Transgovernmental networks as catalysts for democratic change? EU functional cooperation with Arab authoritarian regimes and socialization of involved state officials into democratic governance

Tina Freyburg

Centre for Comparative and International Studies (CIS), ETH Zurich, Switzerland

With the European Neighbourhood Policy, the European Union (EU) intensified functional cooperation in a wide range of sectors. This contribution investigates whether this kind of transnational exchange can trigger subtle processes of democratization. It argues that third state officials become acquainted with democratic governance by participating in transgovernmental policy networks implementing functional cooperation between state administrations of established democracies and authoritarian regimes. In this vein, it enriches the governance model of democracy promotion by adding a new level, the micro-level of democratic socialization. Empirically, the argument is tested taking two Twinning projects that the EU has set up in Morocco, that is, the projects on competition policy and on the environment. The conclusion is that in some non-politicized policy fields, such as the environment, EU transgovernmental policy networks can successfully yield processes of democratic socialization in the context of a stable authoritarian regime, like that in Morocco.

Introduction

External efforts to democratize authoritarian regimes with a functioning strong statehood are ultimately confronted with one inherent problem: Why should the ruling political elite agree with and adopt reforms that affect its core practices of power preservation? Why should it be willing to commit what amounts to political and economic suicide by enacting *true* democratic changes? All instruments and strategies adopted by external actors directly to promote democracy, such as democratic assistance, political dialogue and conditionality – apart from intervention by force – require the (at least tacit) consent of the regime members. Straightforward attempts at openly promoting democratic norms and practices in stable

117

authoritarian contexts are likely condemned to produce at best window-dressing reforms. The ruling elite may agree to establish formally democratic institutions, yet without granting them any real content that would impact upon their political and economic power. Ultimately, it is hard to think of any incentive that would be strong enough to make a rational elite engage in such a potentially dangerous endeavour if it rules a stable and effective authoritarian regime. Hence, if external efforts at inducing democratic norms and practices are to bear fruit, an indirect, gradual approach appears to be more suitable to transfer democratic features 'through the backdoor' of activities not aimed to promote democratic rules in the first place. This approach is based on subtle processes of democratization.

This contribution aims to explore these subtle processes of democratization that are possibly a by-product of external activities undertaken for purposes other than democratization. It investigates to what extent functional cooperation with authoritarian regimes influences the attitudes of the administrative staff towards democratic rules and practices of decision-making, even if this has (hitherto) not translated into effective change of administrative governance, let alone regime change.

State officials employed by authoritarian regimes are a relevant target group for scrutinizing as to whether functional cooperation with authoritarian regimes is able to create democratic stakeholders in a non-democratic polity. Although the long-term effects are difficult to estimate, it can be reasoned that a reform-minded bureaucracy may signify a problem for the maintenance of an authoritarian regime, in particular, if democratization is promoted and happening at the level of the regime. This might be especially true in Arab authoritarian regimes, most notably in bureaucratic monarchies such as Morocco which attach great importance to state bureaucracy for the maintenance and stability of the regime.[1] As Max Weber wrote, '*Herrschaft ist im Alltag primär: Verwaltung*' ('Everyday rule is primarily administration').[2] Evidently, in any political system, administrative staff have a particular importance in policy-making as they are the body entrusted with carrying out government decisions. In effect, as government in action, state officials formulate and implement policy. In contrast to the political elite and diplomats, they represent that part of the public sector with which citizens have contact and thus help shape citizens' perceptions as to how a political system functions.[3] Moreover, state officials themselves constitute a significant social group. In the Arab world, they generally represent a large proportion of the educated population and comprise a major component of the (emerging) middle class,[4] factors commonly seen as social conditions or 'requisites' supporting democratization as a bottom-up process.[5]

An understanding of the attitudes towards appropriate governance of state officials who exercise everyday rule and how these attitudes are shaped by transnational influences is thus crucial in assessing external influences on authoritarian regimes. Surprisingly, the democratization literature typically ignores this arena.[6] It broadly acknowledges that in order to be fruitful, democratic reforms at the polity level require state officials familiar with democratic modes of governance. Otherwise, democratization processes risk resulting in 'enlightened dictatorship' that circumvents rather than allowing effective democratic control by the citizens when used by specific classes and oligarchies to control political power and sustain ineffective, corrupt regimes.[7] Yet, this literature body largely neglects to actually devote attention to the understandings of appropriate governance within public administrations.

In the context of this special issue, the present study examines the governance model of external democracy promotion at a novel level, the micro-level of attitude change through social interaction. According to the governance model, norms and practices of democratic administrative governance are transferred indirectly, as a side-effect of joint problem-solving in functional cooperation. Freyburg *et al.* demonstrate that albeit functional cooperation may help implant provisions of democratic governance in domestic legislation of authoritarian regimes, these provisions are generally not applied in administrative decision-making.[8]

By taking a micro-perspective of attitude change, this contribution seeks to shed light on the question of the discrepancy between formal change (legislative adoption) and change in practice (application of these legal provisions). A high degree of appraisal of democratic governance among the administrative staff suggests that these state officials may nevertheless have become acquainted with democratic governance through social interaction with bureaucrats employed by established democracies. Consequently, the study's results may provide hints as to whether this discrepancy between form and practice can be explained by disapproval of the administrative staff or whether it is more likely due to other factors such as insufficient capacities, the stickiness of established authoritarian routines or hesitations in view of likely repressive consequences.

In the first section, I theoretically embed this study's argument of democratic socialization through functional cooperation in the analytical framework of this special issue. In the subsequent section, the methodology is specified. In the third section, empirical evidence for the argument based on the analysis of original survey data is provided. Empirically, to investigate the democratizing impact of functional cooperation, I explore the effect of participation in a specific type of transgovernmental policy networks, notably EU's Twinning programme, on the attitudes towards democratic governance of Moroccan state officials. The results support the argument that functional cooperation with authoritarian regimes can yield subtle processes of democratic socialization that have hitherto been disregarded.

Transgovernmental networks and socialization into democratic governance. The theoretical argument

Domestic processes of democratization can be induced and supported from the outside by a variety of foreign policies and transnational influences. If one focuses on the promotion and stabilization of transformation processes with civilian means, the democracy promotion efforts of the European Union (EU) present a particularly prominent example.[9] In light of the limits of straightforward democracy promotion policies in authoritarian contexts as outlined in the introductory contribution in this special issue,[10] democratization scholars specify indirect approaches as to how democratic principles and practices can be transferred into non-democratic regimes without being openly suggestive of undermining the regimes' political and economic power basis. These approaches view democratization not as a result of various instruments and strategies intentionally used by external norm- or policy-entrepreneurs. Instead, they build on subtle mechanisms of norm transfer that do not require a policy actively promoting democratic principles and practices.

An innovative approach is presented by the governance model that acknowledges the democratizing potential of transgovernmental cooperation at the level of policy sectors.[11] In this perspective, norms and practices of democratic administrative governance are transferred indirectly, as a side-effect of joint problem-solving. This contribution aims to examine this governance model of external democracy promotion from a micro-perspective, notably by focusing on socialization into democratic governance of state officials who participated in transgovernmental policy networks.

Transgovernmental policy networks as catalysts for democratic change

The European Neighbourhood Policy (ENP) presents a prime example of a reform policy that seeks to approximate legal and administrative standards in neighbouring countries to those of the Union as a means of managing interdependence and fostering integration below membership at the level of sectors. This policy is translated into action by transgovernmental policy networks, described as 'pattern[s] of regular and purposive relations among like government units working across borders that divide countries from another and that demarcate the "domestic" from the "international" sphere'.[12] These networks are initiated at the intermediate level between government and society and operate among sub-units of governments 'when they act relatively autonomously from higher authority in international politics'.[13]

Transgovernmental policy networks constitute a site of socialization, as they bring together specialists from the administrations of both EU member states and neighbouring countries in order to implement policy solutions and carry out legal requirements that approximate legal and administrative standards in the ENP countries to those of the Union. Given that the rules to be transferred were developed for advanced democracies, they logically embody elements of democratic governance. In this respect, cooperation is not only about acquiring policy solutions and enacting legal requirements, but also about introducing new governance patterns. Moreover, since the European specialists are professionally socialized in a democratic polity, they apply and impart democratic governance when serving as experts abroad. As part of their advisory service, they address issues suppressed in domestic discourse such as the participation of non-state actors in administrative decision-making and the availability of information to the public. In this vein, their counterparts may possibly become familiarized with practices of administrative governance in democracies and can be introduced to democratic principles of governance unknown under authoritarian ruling. The information made available in transgovernmental networks allows them to contrast European democratic modes of governance with domestic authoritarian rule. As a consequence, state officials may seek to engage in individual and collective strategies to implement democratic governance styles within state administration and expedite regime-level democratization processes in the long run.

Socialization into democratic governance

In this study, democratic socialization is defined as being present to the degree that individuals change their attitude towards democratic governance due to experiences made in policy networks that are set up and implemented by established democracies.[14] Attitudes are understood as 'evaluative dispositions' that are learnt and can be altered through either communication with others or direct personal experiences.[15] They encompass affective (i.e. emotion-based) and cognitive (i.e. belief-based) components.[16] Attitude change thus not only refers to affective change as increased agreement and support, where actors ultimately internalize democratic modes of governance and define them as appropriate in specific situations, but also covers influences at the level of cognition. Actors may acquire knowledge about democratic governance leading to a change in their 'factual beliefs', that is, their knowledge about the meaning, prerequisites, performance and other attributes of democratic as appropriate governance. Although it is important analytically to distinguish between affective and cognitive components, a difference in the outcome is not discernible for this study. Since norms of democratic governance present rather abstract norms, which are unlikely supported (and reported) without being understood, I assume that, first, affective attitude change presumes prior cognitive processes and, second, that individuals' attitude towards democratic governance can to a large extent be summarized as a one-dimensional attitude.

While participation in transgovernmental policy networks may indeed shape state officials' attitudes towards democratic governance, it does not necessarily impact on their behaviour. Behaviour and behavioural intentions are treated as potential consequences rather than as integral components of attitude change itself. Factors such as hesitations due to likely repressive consequences can hinder the actual application of democratic governance in practice. In order to uncover subtle effects of EU functional cooperation at the level of attitudes that are not necessarily expressed in actual behaviour, this contribution seeks to directly measure attitudes rather than deriving them from behaviour.

The notion of democratic governance corresponds to the manifestation of democratic principles in administrative decision-making.[17] For the purpose of assessing state officials' attitudes towards democratic modes of decision-making, a multidimensional concept of democratic governance is used. Democratic govern-ance may vary in quality along three dimensions: transparency, accountability and participation.[18] Transparency is about the provision of and access to various kinds of information for the general public.[19] Accountability at the administrative level refers to the obligation for officials to justify the use of resources and the achieve-ment of outcomes towards citizens and independent third parties and the establish-ment and application of procedures for administrative review, including the possibility of sanctions in case of infringement.[20] Finally, participation largely cor-responds to the key feature of the conventional understanding of democracy at the level of the nation-state.[21] Transferred to administrative governance, participation means that all willing members of the public should have an equal and effective opportunity to make their interests and concerns known, thereby shaping the outcome of the decisions. Although the margins between these dimensions are sometimes blurred, they are analysed individually. This allows for the exploration of whether functional cooperation is more likely to influence the attitude towards some dimensions of democratic governance than towards others.

Democratic modes of governance imply changing the culture of administrative rules and practices in authoritarian regimes where 'bureaucracy has been reduced to a service tool of political leaders rather than a professional institution with special skills for independent analysis and action'.[22] As a strategy to prevent or react to political unrest and, in the long-run, potential regime crisis triggered by dis-contented citizens, 'modern' authoritarian regimes often seek to address social grievances. Albeit such responsiveness might involve some consultation measures of concerned people at the local level, it can hardly qualify as democratic openness to participation. Rather than a 'vehicle for the transmission of propaganda',[23] which is an attempt made to shape political discourses by improving state–society relations, participation demands the involvement of a plurality of diverse non-state actors and the consideration of their views in administrative decision-making, even if they challenge the regime's preferred policy. Transparency directly contradicts the fundamental secrecy of authoritarian regimes where information may be an official's only asset. Finally, accountability poses difficulties for the rigid structure of political authority, as it obliges state administration to public dis-closure and justification of decisions and their making.

To measure the attitudes towards democratic governance of Moroccan state officials, I constructed a closed-end questionnaire. Given the lack of similar surveys, the creation of democratic governance items is crucial for developing suit-able questions. I operationalized the three theoretically derived dimensions of democratic governance – transparency, accountability and participation – with issue indicators pertaining to various aspects of administrative decision-making. I thereby drew on conceptual work on public administration (reform) and linkage of (good) governance and development.[24] All items are measured using a five-point Likert scale on agreement responses. To minimize the risk of response tendencies, I randomly distributed the statement items in 2 out of 36 different sets of questions and formulated both positively and negatively oriented statements on democratic governance.[25]

I applied an exploratory factor analysis (EFA) in order to identify which of the statement items are most suitable for measuring the dependent variables, notably attitudes towards democratic governance in its three dimensions and the overall concept.[26] EFA enabled me to create scales with high internal consistency, as corroborated by each scale's internal reliability. It is run only on the positively oriented items. Due to a non-response rate of about 10% to the three negatively oriented items, their number of missing values is comparatively high. Their incorporation would have disproportionally decreased the number of cases and thus would have led to a substantial loss of information on the regular items. Table 1 shows factor loadings (Est.) of the positively oriented items, with those of at least 0.40 printed in bold; it displays the exact wordings of the items as they appear in the questionnaire.

Incorporation of both negatively and positively oriented agreement items validates the measurement of attitude towards democratic governance. Agreeing with positively framed democratic items is assumed to be 'easier' and more justifiable for state officials employed in an authoritarian regime that declares itself a 'modern' state than explicitly rejecting their logical opposites that refer to the still prevailing authoritarian culture. Based on this reasoning, I developed scales for each of the dimensions that aggregate the positively oriented items identified by the EFA as crucial for the respective factor (factor loading ≥ 0.40) and the theoretically corresponding negatively oriented item. Scales for the individual dimensions were constructed by adding values of individual items and dividing the sum by the number of items for each dimension. The overall concept of democratic governance was measured by the mean of the three individual scales.[27]

The first factor – participation – is traditionally perceived as the involvement of people in processes of policy-making (item 3). In this sense, participation does not only require that state officials seek to guarantee citizens' knowledge about current governmental decisions in order to enable meaningful participation (item 2). It first and foremost presumes that state officials are willing to admit non-state actors representing all relevant interests to their decision-making processes (item 1). The negatively oriented item referring to public participation addresses the authoritarian claim of unlimited approval whereupon state officials 'should always seek to bring the public into accordance with governmental policy'. This item reverses the direction of influence – citizens' views should not shape but are to be brought in line with governmental policies. Transparency as access to information for citizens means that governance-related information about administrative procedures is provided (item 4) and that up-to-date and comprehensive information that is actually demanded is available (item 6). The negatively transparency item directly challenges the democratic principle that information of interest to the general public should be accessible to citizens. In line with authoritarian thinking it states: 'A civil servant should ensure that information held by the public authority remains in the hands of the government only'. Finally, accountability

Table 1. Three dimensions of attitude towards democratic governance.

Indicators/items	Factors/dimensions						
	Participation		Transparency		Accountability		h^2
	Est.	S.E.	Est.	S.E.	Est.	S.E.	
1 'A civil servant should take into account the views and concerns of affected citizens before making decisions'	**0.981***	0.104	−0.050	0.035	−0.063*	0.027	0.873
2 'A civil servant should offer updated information on governmental policy'	**0.433**	0.168	0.051	0.127	0.250	0.178	0.386
3 'A civil servant should ensure that the citizens' views and concerns have an influence on shaping policies'	**0.644**	0.226	0.126	0.155	0.128	0.215	0.585
4 'A civil servant should work in a manner that is transparent and comprehensible for the general public'	0.119	0.198	**0.568**	0.186	0.242	0.217	0.476
5 'A civil servant should provide citizens with the possibility of advancing their views as an input for governmental decision-making'	0.299	0.196	**0.459**	0.147	0.261	0.179	0.542
6 'A civil servant should make information available to anyone requesting it'	−0.063	0.063	**0.878***	0.169	−0.134	0.128	0.762
7 'Monitoring by independent state institutions ensure the appropriateness and procedural correctness of bureaucratic acts'	−0.012	0.058	−0.068	0.094	**0.814***	0.203	0.653
8 'Possibilities for the general public and its associations to request scrutiny of the decision-making process and review of policies ensure the appropriateness and procedural correctness of bureaucratic acts'	0.028	0.169	0.001	0.106	**0.437***	0.176	0.205
Eigenvalues	1.498		0.868		3.316		
Variance explained (%)	18.73		10.85		41.45		

Note: Factor loading matrix. $N = 148$; Est. = factor loading (estimator), S.E. = standard error, h^2 = communality; factor loadings >0.40 are displayed in bold.
$*p \leq 0.05$; $**p \leq 0.01$; $***p \leq 0.001$.

refers to 'reviews [of] the expediency and procedural correctness of bureaucratic acts'.[28] This can be done either by means of independent state institutions ('horizontal accountability', item 7) or by possibilities for citizens and their associations to request scrutiny of administrative practices ('vertical accountability', item 8).[29] The negatively oriented accountability item addresses an attitude statement that distorts the meaning of accountability: 'Instructions of, and approval by, the higher authority ensures the appropriateness and procedural correctness of bureaucratic acts'.

The Twinning programme and democratic socialization in Morocco. Empirical analysis

The effect of functional cooperation with authoritarian regimes on the attitude towards democratic governance of involved state officials is examined by taking a most-likely case as an example: the EU Twinning programme in Morocco. With regard to the authoritarian regime to be selected, Morocco presents a most-likely case among the Arab countries for predominantly two reasons. First, the Arab world, in general, represents the 'largest block of countries under firmly and decidedly authoritarian rule'.[30] Among these countries, Morocco holds the first rank as the politically most liberalized country in the region. Across the three mostly used indicators, notably Freedom House, Polity IV and the World Bank Governance Indicators, Morocco appears to particularly qualify as 'liberalized autocracy'[31] with a mixture of 'guided pluralism, controlled elections and selective repression' that allows to expect a minimum degree of openness.[32] Second, concerning the influence of the EU as the selected external actor, Morocco was among the first Southern neighbouring countries to sign the ENP Action Plan and to initiate Twinning projects. Since October 2008, it has been enjoying a privileged status (*statut avancé*) within the ENP that increases functional cooperation.[33]

With regard to functional cooperation, the reason for choosing the Twinning programme as a most-likely case among the existing EU transgovernmental policy networks is again twofold. First, the Twinning programme presents an instrument created to offer assistance in those areas that are usually exclusive preserve of government. It is a tool for cooperation between a sub-unit of public administration in a neighbouring country and the equivalent institution in an EU member state: a team of European experts, usually one or two long-term and up to 30 short-term experts, relocate their offices to ENP country administrations in order to help the beneficiary departments in seeking an effective response to policy problems through training and reorganization as well as by drafting laws and regulations modelled after the EU *acquis*. Given that the *acquis* often embeds rules relating to transparency, participation or accountability, the policy solutions offered thus incorporate elements of democratic governance. Second, Twinning projects are based on intensive working relations on a day-to-day basis between European and neighbourhood country officials for a considerable period of time. This not only helps to build relationships based on trust and mutual understanding,[34] but may also help familiarize state officials with democratic administrative practices, since the European experts apply and demand democratic administrative governance.

The socializing potential of the Twinning programme is acknowledged by both policy and scholarly work. For instance, the EU itself stresses in the context of the 2004 enlargement round that '[t]wo of the most important, non-measurable but visible results of twinning are network building and change of attitudes and behaviour'[35] and consequent 'change [of] administrative cultures'.[36] This study seeks to investigate whether such appreciation of Twinning projects as generating change in administrative governance can be supported by a more systematic analysis.

The case selection means that if participation in transgovernmental networks impacts on the attitudes of state officials in neighbouring authoritarian regimes, then we should be able to detect such an effect in the case of EU Twinning projects in Morocco. In turn, in the case of a negative finding, it is acceptable to conclude that functional cooperation will show no significant effect if it is implemented by less institutionalized networks, which are located in politically less liberalized countries.

Two Moroccan Twinning projects were selected in policy fields that differ with regard to the degree of politicization, namely the Twinning project 'Coordinated Management of the Environment and the Harmonization of National Environmental Legislation' (MA04/AA/EN03) and the Twinning project 'Support for the Strengthening of the Competition Authorities' (MA06/AA/FI08). Although transgovernmental policy networks generally operate without much publicity and are relatively unaffected by the turbulences of political disputes,[37] they are still embedded in politics and affected by political considerations.

Politicized policy fields are generally characterized by a hierarchical leadership style[38] and the tendency to employ state officials who particularly adhere to authoritarian modes of decision-making. Studies on the role of bureaucracy in transitions from authoritarianism reveal that in politicized contexts, state officials regard transnational exchange with suspicion.[39] I, therefore, expect that if inter-administrative cooperation occurs in less politicized settings, interaction among the participants is more intense and trustworthy,[40] which, in turn, makes attitude change towards democratic governance more likely.

Interviews with Moroccan state officials, journalists and non-governmental activists as well as representatives of international organizations, EU member states and the Delegation of the European Commission helped to classify the degree of politicization of the policy issues under study as high, medium or low. 'Indicators for lower degree of politicization are, for example, that media coverage is more pluralized and sectoral cooperation is less impeded by political considerations. Touching upon internally sensitive issues such as corruption, patronage and the entwinement of private business with governmental responsibilities, competition policy in Morocco can be treated as highly politicized. Despite the conflicts of interest between pure environmental goals and economic development objectives, in particular, tourism and agriculture, and sectoral elite corruption making the implementation of environmental issues quite politically costly, the degree of politicization of environmental matters is rather low compared with competition matters. In the field of environment, media coverage is more pluralized and transgovernmental cooperation is less impeded by political considerations. Drawing on this reasoning, it is expected that the Twinning project on the environment shows a higher potential for democratic socialization than the Twinning project on competition policy.

The expected effect of politicization on democratic socialization reflects the results on the democratization effect of functional cooperation via legislation in the study undertaken by Freyburg et al,[41] where the two policy fields present contrasting cases with regard to the success of EU democratic governance promotion in Morocco. Whereas the adoption of provisions of democratic governance is weak in the field of competition, it is medium to strong in the field of environment. Moreover, we can observe at least some applications of democratic, mostly transparent, modes of governance in day-to-day administrative decision-making in the field of environment.[42] To what extent is this difference in the effect of norm transfer via legislation echoed if one looks at the impact functional cooperation may have on attitudes towards democratic governance of state officials? In addition to the effect of politicization, according to the literature on socialization in international institutions, it can be expected that if few beneficiary departments are involved ('size') and external experts stay for a long period of time ('duration'), interaction among the participants is more intense and trustworthy, which is supposed to make attitude change towards democratic governance more likely.[43]

The attitudes of Moroccan state officials towards democratic governance

To detect whether participation in a Twinning project positively impacts on the attitudes of state officials, I applied a quasi-experimental 'static group comparison'[44] design. To this end, I conducted a survey among state officials working in various ministries in Morocco. The respondents were selected by a theoretically controlled cluster sampling: all officials working in particular departments of certain ministries were invited to fill in the questionnaire.[45] The departments have been chosen so to equally cover two groups of officials: officials who participated in the selected Twinning project ($N = 32$ for the environment project; $N = 10$ for the competition project) and officials who are employed in a thematically related department in a ministry not targeted by a Twinning project ($N = 26$ and 12, respectively). Their attitudes towards democratic governance were statistically compared at a single point in time. The difference in attitude between these two groups is ascribed to the effects of participation while explicitly controlling for relevant properties of the state officials.[46] All respondents are officials at the intermediate level of administrative hierarchy and thus belong to that part of state administration that is evolving towards modernization.[47] Personal distribution of the questionnaire on site enabled a response rate of approximately 96%; nearly all officials available during a period of three months in summer 2008 responded.[48]

Drawing on the literature on transnational influences, this study also controls for potential differences in attitude between the experimental and the control groups that result from the properties of the state officials, notably their usage of foreign media for political information and stays abroad in established democracies.[49] Both transnational influences are expected to have a positive impact on attitudes towards democratic governance. Moreover, state officials were compared as regards socio-demographic features such as age and gender. It is expected that if a state official is younger and has thus spent more years of professional service under the present regime of the 'new' King Mohammed VI than under the previous regime ruled by King Hassan II, the more likely it is that he or she appreciates democratic administrative decision-making. The political regime constructed by King Hassan II during his long reign (1961–1999) was characterized by 'control over both the technocratic state apparatus and the army and the police'.[50] With the ascension of Mohammed VI in 1999, a new spirit of political, social and economic reform entered the country, while, at the same time, the actual potential for meaningful democratic change remained limited.[51] In a similar way, it is expected that female officials are more open towards democratic governance, since women generally support political modernization and democratization more strongly than men; they expect to personally benefit in terms of more rights and freedom.[52]

Several precautions were taken in the questionnaire design and survey setting in order to ensure that difference in attitude can be safely ascribed to the effect of participation in transgovernmental networks. First and most importantly, possible interfering effects of selective recruitment can be assumed to be marginal.[53] The survey among Moroccan state officials covered a question about the importance of certain factors for appointment as a participant in a Twinning project. The same question was included in a questionnaire filled in by European bureaucrats who served as Twinning experts in Morocco. The responses revealed that objective criteria are decisive, such as the field of responsibility in the department and professional performance rather than personal contacts and loyalties. Interviews with European and Moroccan Twinning participants, project leaders and experts corroborated this conclusion. In practice, however, almost every state official working in a beneficiary department was involved in at least one of the various activities.[54] Moreover, since there is no more than one Twinning project in any single subunit of public administration, overlapping effects of several Twinning projects can be excluded; the effect of cooperation programmes other than EU's Twinning programme is controlled.

Second, while the existence of preference falsification cannot be completely ruled out, it hardly signifies a problem for this study. I am not primarily interested in identifying the true understanding of appropriate governance among Moroccan state officials. Rather, I am concerned with estimating the difference in agreement with democratic governance between state officials who participated in transgovernmental networks and those who did not. It can generally be assumed that there is no systematic bias with regard to falsified preferences between these two groups. Yet, it is conceivable that network participants are more likely to agree with items commonly associated with European thinking and disagree with those that Europeans are assumed to dismiss. In this case, it can be argued that cognitive learning processes have taken place. As a consequence of their professional exchange with European bureaucrats, Moroccan officials might have learnt what kind of governance Europeans seem to acknowledge as appropriate administrative rules. Learning to 'talk the talk' is in essence a process of cognitive attitude change that can eventually trigger processes of habitualization and resolution of cognitive dissonance.[55]

The distribution of the outcome variables is shown in Figure 1.[56] The boxes show the middle values of the dependent variables (50% of the data) with the black line indicating the median value, while the ends of the vertical lines ('whiskers') stretch to the greatest and lowest values of these variables. Since a few outliers are present, as indicated by the circles, the whiskers extend to a maximum of 1.5 times the inter-quartile range.

A cursory glance suggests that administrative cooperation does have an effect on the attitudes towards democratic governance of involved third state officials:

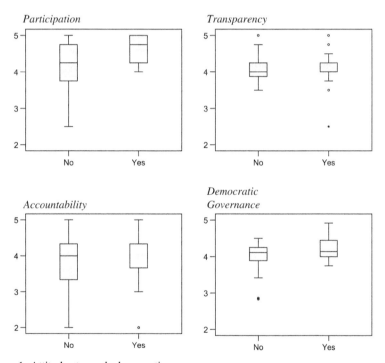

Figure 1. Attitudes towards democratic governance.
Note: Scores display attitude towards democratic governance overall, and in its three dimensions, values range between 1 (non-democratic) and 5 (democratic); $N = 38$ (control group, 'No') and 42 (experimental group, 'Yes'), cases with missing values excluded list wise. For transparency and accountability, the median lines of the 'yes' groups coincide with the ground lines of the respective boxes.

overall, the middle values are situated higher for the experimental group ('Yes') than for the control group ('No'). Whereas this effect is clearly visible with regard to the dimension of participation, it is less observable with regard to transparency (mean = 4.1; median = 4.0 for both groups) and accountability (mean = 3.84 (experimental group) and 3.82 (control group); median = 3.67 (experimental group) and 4.0 (control group)). Moreover, the attitudes of officials who were involved in a policy network have converged; boxes and 'whiskers' of the experimental group are smaller, which indicates that the values are less diverse. Generally noticeable is that both groups show a remarkable high degree of agreement with the attitude statements of democratic governance, given that the respondents are state officials employed by an authoritarian regime hitherto reluctant to any noteworthy political liberalization.

The democratizing potential of the Twinning programme in Morocco

To what extent is the observed difference in attitude towards democratic governance between participants and non-participants significant? And to what extent does the effect vary between individual projects? I used the Kruskal–Wallis test, a non-parametric analogue of a one-way analysis of variance (ANOVA) statistical procedure, which takes account of small n-samples and does not require the normality assumption.[57] Participation in a Twinning project, this contribution's key variable, is operationalized as a dichotomous variable measuring whether the individual state official participated in activities of such a project or not. I conducted the tests separately for the two selected Twinning projects in order to detect any likely differences in shaping the attitudes of participating officials towards democratic governance. For each project, four separate tests were applied, one per dimension plus the overall concept of democratic governance. The results of these eight Kruskal–Wallis tests are presented in Table 2.

The Kruskal–Wallis tests produced two main results. First, whereas we can find a significant difference in attitudes towards democratic governance between participating and non-participating officials in the case of the Twinning project on the environment, the analyses revealed no significant evidence for such an effect in the case of the Twinning project on competition matters. Second, the significant effect of the environmental Twinning project is limited to the subdimension of participation (large effect with $r = 0.054$) and the overall concept of democratic governance (medium effect with $r = 0.032$). The tests clearly showed no significant effect on the attitudes towards accountability.[58] This is plausible because in contrast to the competition project, the Twinning project on the environment attaches particular importance to the establishment of 'procedures concerning access to information and public participation'.[59] It even aims at establishing a 'démocratie environnementale'[60] based on the involvement of the public in decision-making on environmental matters.

As the generally high appreciation of participation in Figure 1 reveals, it seems as if state officials agree with the participatory modes of governance that enable

Table 2.   Democratic socialization in selected Twinning projects.

	Participation		Transparency		Accountability		Democratic governance	
	Env.	Comp.	Env.	Comp.	Env.	Comp.	Env.	Comp.
Participants	31.87	10.19	26.23	10.67	23.52	9.60	23.97	8.14
	(27)	(8)	(24)	(9)	(22)	(10)	(18)	(7)
Non-participants	16.57	10.71	21.67	11.25	24.42	9.38	16.60	7.88
	(22)	(12)	(23)	(12)	(25)	(8)	(21)	(8)
χ^2	14.516	0.039	1.409	0.052	0.052	0.008	4.068	0.013
p-value	**0.000**	0.844	0.235	0.820	0.820	0.928	**0.044**	0.908
N total	49	20	47	21	47	18	39	15

Note: Mean rank displayed with the number of cases in the parentheses, cases with missing values excluded case by case; df = 1; Env. = Twinning project on the environment, Comp. = Twinning project on competition matters; p-value ≤ 0.05 in bold.

decisions close to the concerns and interests of the people as, by definition, participatory governance obliges state officials to ensure citizens' influence on shaping policies. By contrast, accountability is hardly appreciated by the state officials as indicated by the relatively low mean values in Figure 1. This is not surprising since accountable governance is not only the most unfamiliar principle of democratic governance for state officials in authoritarian regimes and, therefore, probably the most difficult to fully comprehend, but it also affects the direct control of the state officials' acts more than the other two principles and thus bothers them more individually.[61]

To what extent can network properties shed light on the differences in the democratizing potential of the individual projects? And to what extent can the difference in attitude be ascribed to the fact of having participated in the project rather than be explained by the more general properties of the individual state officials? Non-parametric Kruskal–Wallis tests comparing the mean ranks for the four relevant properties of the state officials, notably stay abroad in an established democracy, usage of foreign media for political information, age measured as time served under the previous regime of King Hassan II ('generation') and gender,[62] displayed no significant differences between officials belonging to the experimental group and those present in the control group. As shown in Table 3, state officials who participated in one of the two Twinning projects did not possess characteristics that were substantially different from those of their colleagues who have not participated.

Yet, whereas differences in the properties of the state officials cannot explain the different impact, a glance at the properties of the two networks, notably their size, duration and the degree of politicization of the respective policy field, reveals possible explanations. A brief comparison of the two selected projects supports the expectation that the degree of politicization matters with regard to the potential for democratic socialization that a Twinning project can develop.

Table 3. Differences in the properties of state officials.

	Stay abroad	Foreign media	Generation	Gender
Twinning project on the environment	0.839 (0.360)	3.484 (0.062)	1.792 (0.181)	2.750 (0.097)
N	55	53	57	58
Twinning project on competition policy	2.973 (0.085)	1.116 (0.291)	0.700 (0.403)	0.146 (0.703)
N	22	20	22	22

Note: Chi-square displayed with p-value in the parentheses, cases with missing values excluded case by case; df $= 1$.

The environmental project shows a generally better performance in yielding attitude change towards democratic governance on the side of its participants than the competition project that takes place in a policy field characterized by a higher degree of politicization. However, it cannot be precluded that the length of exposure does matter, too. At the time of this study, the competition project had only lasted 9 months, whereas the environmental project had already been completed after 19 months' duration. It warrants further study whether duration is a decisive factor for socialization. On the basis of this study, it can be suggested that the size of the network does not constitute an important factor in terms of democratic socialization. The competition project encompasses only one department and can thus be judged as rather small; the environmental project, in turn, consists of five departments but all within the same ministry. Apparently, the small number of beneficiary departments could not compensate for the disadvantages in terms of politicization and duration that the project on competition policy has to face. These interpretations are, however, only tentative and need to be investigated more rigorously.

Conclusion

To what extent can processes of democratic change be externally encouraged in authoritarian contexts? The theoretical and empirical literature on the impact of external efforts to promote democratic norms is rather sceptical towards this question. Its assessment might, however, be biased in that most studies concentrate on the effect of direct strategies of democracy promotion at the level of the state (government). Their results show that explicit and straightforward democracy promotion policies, notably political conditionality ('leverage') and democratic assistance ('linkage'), are unlikely to yield processes of democratization in stable authoritarian regimes.

This contribution took a different approach by acknowledging that most of the present authoritarian regimes have agreed to functional cooperation with established democracies. It investigated the potential of inter-administrative cooperation to trigger processes of democratic socialization by taking two EU–Moroccan

Twinning projects on environmental and competition matters as examples. More precisely, it sought to detect whether joint problem-solving and social interaction between European experts and their Moroccan counterparts positively shape the attitudes towards democratic governance of the latter in the context of these programmes.

This study's results show that in the programmes studied, under the surface of stable authoritarian regimes seemingly immutable from the outside, transnational influences such as functional cooperation not only can leave their imprints in domestic law codes,[63] but can also positively shape the attitudes of state officials towards democratic governance. Moroccan state officials who participated in the Twinning project on the environment showed a significantly more positive attitude towards democratic governance than their non-participating colleagues, which cannot be ascribed to relevant alternative differences between these two groups of state officials. An optimistic reading of this finding tentatively advances the conclusion that the discrepancy between legal adoption and application in practice of democratic governance in non-politicized fields identified by Freyburg *et al.* in this issue might be less the result of disapproval among administrative staff than of alternative explanations such as lacking administrative capacities, time and/or fear in view of likely repressive consequences. Clearly, however, this question deserves additional research.

This study endeavours to be a stepping stone for future research. It provides a first analysis of the democratization potential of functional cooperation, a cooperation that is, in most cases, 'actively sought by regimes that see them as unthreatening and offering additional resources to boost policy-implementation capacity'.[64] The subtle processes of democratization generated by functional cooperation deserve further exploration. First, it appears that a low degree of politicization of the policy issues facilitates democratic socialization. It needs to be explored more rigorously to what extent the degree of politicization affects the effectiveness of functional cooperation as a catalyst of democratic attitudinal change. It would be interesting to see to what extent a higher degree of politicization can be compensated by network properties such as density and length of social interaction. Second, it warrants further study under what conditions a positive attitude towards democratic governance will translate into daily administrative practices. It remains to be seen whether (and if so, how and under what conditions) such democratic administrative governance will ultimately spill over into the general polity by unfolding dynamics that promote democratization rather than stabilization of the entire political system. An evaluation of the effectiveness of functional cooperation as a strategy to transfer democratic norms will crucially depend on the applied understanding of democratic change. If the criteria are gentle processes of political liberalization and governance reform, the assessment will certainly be more positive than that with regard to a wholesale overthrow of the political regime.[65] Importantly, however, when intentionally used for political purposes, functional cooperation risks losing its political innocence and potential to initiate subtle processes of democratization.

Acknowledgements

This contribution is based on research that won the European Union Studies Association (EUSA) 2011 Award for the Best Conference Paper, the International Studies Association (ISA) 2010 Carl Beck Award and the European Consortium for Political Research (ECPR) 2010 Best Graduate Student Paper Award of its Standing Group on International Relations (SGIR). Many people offered helpful comments and advice in the course of this study. I cordially thank, in particular, Stefanie Bailer, Martin Beck, Sandra Lavenex, Elham Manea, Frank Schimmelfennig and Rebecca Welge. I also thank the anonymous reviewers and the editors of *Democratization* for their careful reading and valuable remarks. I express my gratitude to the numerous European and Moroccan officials who enabled this study and to Naima Qadimi and Elisa Fornale with whom the survey became an enjoyable adventure. I thank the staff of the Foundation Friedrich Ebert in Rabat for their hospitality. Financial support from the Swiss National Science Foundation (SNSF) in the framework of the National Centre for Competence in Research (NCCR), Challenges to Democracy in the twenty-first century, is gratefully acknowledged.

Notes

1. Pawelka, 'Der Staat im Vorderen Orient', 432.
2. Weber, *Wirtschaft und Gesellschaft*, 126.
3. Baker, *Transitions from Authoritarianism*, 4; Berger, *Bureaucracy and Society*, 5.
4. Zerhouni, 'Morocco', 61.
5. Lipset, *Political Man*.
6. The actors-centred literature on democratization and regime transformation generally considers either elites ('evolution') or masses ('revolution') as relevant actors for democratic change. Other potential actors such as administrations are rather seen as moderating factors for liberalization or as necessary preconditions for consolidation, which are not further explored; see, e.g. Merkel, *Systemtransformation*, 111–8; O'Donnell and Schmitter, *Transitions from Authoritarian Rule*.
7. Baker, *Transitions from Authoritarianism*, 5; Jreisat, 'The Arab World'.
8. Freyburg *et al.*, 'EU Promotion of Democratic Governance'; 'Democracy Promotion'.
9. Kopstein, 'Transatlantic Divide'; Youngs, 'Ten Years On'. Externally initiated transition through coercion, notably military intervention, follows a substantially different dynamic, see Beetham, 'Democratization by Force'; Merkel, 'Democracy through War?'.
10. Lavenex and Schimmelfennig, 'Models of Democracy Promotion'.
11. Freyburg *et al.*, 'EU Promotion of Democratic Governance'.
12. Slaughter, 'Government Networks', 14; see also Lavenex, 'A Governance Perspective'.
13. Keohane and Nye, 'Transgovernmental Relations', 41.
14. For a discussion of the definitions of socialization in international relations and EU studies, see, in particular, Beyers, 'Conceptual and Methodological Challenges'; Checkel, 'International Institutions and Socialization in Europe'; Johnston, 'International Institutions as Social Environment'; Pollack, 'Exhausted Research Program'.
15. Perloff, *Dynamics of Persuasion*, 36–41.
16. Zimbardo and Leippe, *Psychology of Attitude Change*, 31; cf. Eagly and Chaiken, *Psychology of Attitude Change*; Olson and Zanna, 'Attitudes and Attitude Change'; Verplanken *et al.*, 'Components of Attitude'.
17. See footnote 11.
18. Freyburg *et al.* 'Democracy between the Lines?'; cf. Bovens, 'New Forms of Accountability'; Hyden *et al., Making Sense of Governance*; Brinkerhoff, 'Democratic Governance'.

19. Héritier, 'Composite Democracy', 819.
20. Grant and Keohane, 'Accountability and Abuses of Power', 29; Diamond *et al.* 'Introduction', 3.
21. Dahl, *Polyarchy*; Verba, *Democratic Participation*.
22. Jreisat, 'The Arab World', 417.
23. Göbel and Lambach, '(In-)Stability of Authoritarian Regimes', 3; cf. Brumberg, 'Democratization in the Arab World?'.
24. Baker, *Transitions from Authoritarianism*; Berger, *Bureaucracy and Society;* Hyden *et al.*, *Making Sense of Governance*; Page, *Political Authority.*
25. The two sets of questions are introduced as follows: 'There are different understandings of what determines the appropriateness and procedural correctness of bureaucratic acts in public administration. To what extent do you personally agree that the following items serve this function?' (items 7 + 8)/'There are different opinions as to what it takes to be a "good" civil servant. To what extent to you personally agree or disagree that a civil servant should have the following qualities?' (items 1–6).
26. The EFA is done using the robust mean and variance-adjusted weighted least squares (WLSMV) extraction procedure and the oblique rotation method Oblimin. Details on the EFA including model fit are given in the online appendix, available at: [http://www.eup.ethz.ch/people/freyburg].
27. The point estimate for the scale reliability (ρ) of participation is 0.79 (three items), of accountability 0.58 (two items) and of transparency 0.75 (three items), if Raykov's confirmatory FA-based method is applied. This approach is not only insensitive to violation of normality assumption but also presents a more accurate estimate of the reliability of multi-items measures than the usual Cronbach's alpha, though the value of the expressions is identical (cf. Raykov, 'Reliability if Deleted'; Sijtsma, 'On the Use'). Cronbach's alpha of participation is 0.68, of accountability 0.38 and of transparency 0.46. Given the exploratory character of this study, its objective (attitudes and preferences) and the small number of items per scale, the reliability of the individual scales is still acceptable if the theoretically corresponding negatively oriented item is added to each scale (cf. John and Benet-Martínez, 'Measurement': 346). Since these items could not be introduced in the EFA (see FN 30), Cronbach's alpha had to be used instead of the more reliable approach of Raykov. Cronbach's alpha is 0.61 for participation, 0.14 for accountability and 0.30 for transparency.
28. Schedler, 'Conceptualizing Accountability': 28.
29. For a note on unidimensionality and correlation between the factors, see the online appendix.
30. Burnell and Schlumberger, 'Promoting Autocracy', 2.
31. Brumberg, 'Democratization in the Arab World?'.
32. Al-Arkoubi and McCourt, 'Politics of HRM', 983; Mohamedou, 'Rise and Fall of Democratization', 211.
33. For example, Bicchi, 'The Impact of the ENP', 214.
34. Kelley, 'New Wine', 39–40; Tulmets, 'Open Method of Coordination', 82.
35. European Court of Auditors, 'Special Report no. 6/2003'.
36. European Commission, 'PHARE Ex-Post Evaluation', 141; 'Second Generation Twinning', 7; cf. Beer, *Ideen auf Reisen*, 168; Cooper and Johansen, 'Evaluation of Completed Twinning Projects', 6–7; Papadimitriou and Phinnemore, 'Exporting Europeanization', 631.
37. Pollack, 'Exhausted Research Program', 906; Slaughter, 'Government Networks', 200–2.
38. Waever, 'Securitization and Desecuritization'; Potter, 'Issue Area and Foreign Policy Analysis', 410.

39. Baker, 'Transitions from Authoritarianism', see, in particular, the introduction to this edited volume.
40. Checkel, 'Going Native', 210; Marsden, 'Network Data'; Slaughter, *A New World Order*, 198–200; van Waarden, 'Types of Policy Networks'.
41. Freyburg *et al.*, 'Democratic Governance Promotion'. I tried to include the Twinning light project on migration entitled 'Strengthening of the Operational Capacity of the Auxiliary Forces and of the High-Level Management in the context of Border Surveillance as a Means of Preventing Illegal Immigration' (MA05/AA/JH04-TL). Unfortunately, however, I was unable to get access to the Moroccan Ministry of Interior in order to conduct the survey among the relevant state officials.
42. Freyburg *et al.*, 'EU Promotion of Democratic Governance', 927; 'Democracy Promotion'.
43. Albeit all democratic governance provisions to be transferred are incorporated in the EU *acquis*, their actual meaning is specified by the external experts, which might be influenced by their national administrative styles. The Twinning project on competition matters is led by the German Federal Ministry of Economics and Technology and the *Bundeskartellamt*, the independent competition authority. The Twinning project on the environment is managed by the Italian Ministry for the Environment and Territory in cooperation with the Austrian Federal Environment Agency. In this article, however, a common non-formalized European system of governance is assumed that is based on a shared understanding of key democratic features in administrative governance, Bouckaert 'Administrative Convergence'.
44. Campbell and Stanley, *Experimental and Quasi-Experimental Design*, 12.
45. Due to this specific and limited nature of the target group, the questionnaire was cognitively pre-tested by knowledgeable experts, notably psychologists and political scientists specialized in Arab authoritarian regimes, and colleagues with Arab migratory background.
46. Halaby, 'Panel Models', 509–12.
47. Al-Arkoubi and McCourt, 'The Politics of HRM': 987.
48. Due to the opportunity to leave inconvenient questions blank, guaranteed anonymity and the persuasive approach taken, outright refusal was almost absent. Only one official flatly refused to fill in the questionnaire; fewer than five officials could not be reached because of professional commitments abroad or holidays. It is difficult to test sample bias conclusively because socio-demographic data on state officials in Morocco are not available. Distribution of the sample is available upon request. Respondents could choose the language of communication (French or Arabic). I did not leave the questionnaire with the officials.
49. Atkinson, 'Does Soft Power Matter?'; Kern and Hainmueller, 'Opium for the Masses'; Nye, *Soft Power*; Pérez-Armendáriz and Crow, 'Do Migrants Remit Democracy?'; Wejnert, 'Diffusion', 56; Whitehead, 'Three International Dimensions', 6–8.
50. Desrues and Moyano 'Social Change', 21.
51. Campbell, 'Morocco in Transition'; Zerhouni, 'Morocco'.
52. Hegasy, 'Young Authority', 31.
53. Hooghe, 'Several Roads'; Pollack, 'Exhausted Research Program'; Kerr, 'Changing Attitudes'.
54. Consequently, only a few officials were able to experience an indirect socialization effect of functional cooperation due to exchange with immediate colleagues involved in a Twinning project.
55. For conceptualization of these secondary mechanisms, see, in particular, Risse 'Neofunctionalism' and Zürn and Checkel 'Getting Socialized'.
56. For descriptive statistics, see Table A1 in the online appendix.
57. Further information on the Kruskal–Wallis test is provided in the online appendix.

58. The Kruskal–Wallis test does not provide information on the direction of the effect. That participation in the environmental project has a positive effect on the attitudes of state officials towards democratic governance can be inferred from the descriptive statistics given in the appendix. The democratizing trend of the environmental project is further supported by a positive standardized Jonckheere–Terpstra test statistics above the threshold of 1.65, more precisely $z = 3.810$ (participation) and $z = 2.017$ (democratic governance), for the environmental project. There is a lot of confidence that the significant effect produced by the Kruskal–Wallis test is genuine: the confidence interval range for participation is 0.000 and for democratic governance is 0.009, and thus, it does not cross the boundary of 0.05. Moreover, if one repeats the analysis with a Welch's ANOVA, which is robust to heteroscedasticity, and with a usual one-way ANOVA to test for differences between group means, similar results are produced by both tests (see Table A2 in the online appendix).
59. European Commission, 'EU/Morocco Action Plan', 36.
60. Final Twinning Report, MA04/AA/EN03, 18 November 2007.
61. For a more detailed analysis of the attitudes towards democratic governance of state officials in Morocco, see Freyburg, 'Demokratisierung durch Zusammenarbeit?'.
62. The sample covers 18 female state officials in the environmental group, of which 7 participated in the Twinning project, and 12 female state officials participated in the competition group, of which 5 participated in the project.
63. Freyburg et al., 'Democratic Governance Promotion'.
64. Youngs 'Democracy Promotion as External Governance?', 898.
65. Youngs 'Democracy Promotion as External Governance?', 902.

Notes on contributor

Tina Freyburg is a postdoctoral researcher and lecturer in the European Politics team of the Centre for Comparative and International Studies at ETH Zurich. Her main research interest is in International Relations and EU Studies. Current research projects focus on international democracy promotion, notably on socialization into democratic governance through transnational exchange in authoritarian contexts and the impact of EU political conditionality under difficult conditions.

Bibliography

Al-Arkoubi, Khadija, and Willy McCourt. 'The Politics of HRM: Waiting for Godot in the Moroccan Civil Service'. *International Journal of Human Resource Management* 15, no. 6 (2004): 978–95.

Atkinson, Carol. 'Does Soft Power Matter? A Comparative Analysis of Student Exchange Programs 1980–2006'. *Foreign Policy Analysis* 6, no. 1 (2010): 1–22.

Baker, Randall, ed. *Transitions from Authoritarianism. The Role of the Bureaucracy* London: Praeger, 2002.

Beer, Doris. *Ideen auf Reisen. Institutionentransfer in der Politikberatung für die Transformationsländer.* Baden-Baden: Nomos, 2006.

Beetham, David. 'The Contradictions of Democratization by Force: The Case of Iraq'. *Democratization* 16, no. 3 (2009): 443–54.

Berger, Morroe. *Bureaucracy and Society in Modern Egypt: A Study of the Higher Civil Service.* Princeton, NJ: Princeton University Press, 1957.

Beyers, Jan. 'Conceptual and Methodological Challenges in the Study of European Socialization'. *Journal of European Public Policy* 17, no. 6 (2010): 909–20.

Bicchi, Federica. 'The Impact of the ENP on EU-North Africa Relations: The Good, the Bad and the Ugly'. In *The European Neighbourhood Policy in Perspective. Context, Implementation and Impact*, ed. Richard G. Whitman and Stefan Wolff, 206–22. Basingstoke: Palgrave Macmillan, 2010.

Bouckaert, Geert. 'Administrative Convergence in the EU: Some Conclusions for CEECs'. In *East-West Co-operation in Public Sector Reform*, ed. Frits van den Berg, György Jenei, and Lance T. Leloup, 59–68. Amsterdam: IOS Press, 2002.

Bovens, Mark. 'New Forms of Accountability and EU-Governance'. *Comparative European Politics* 5, no. 1 (2007): 104–20.

Brinkerhoff, Derick W. 'Democratic Governance and Sectoral Policy Reform: Tracing Linkages and Exploring Synergies'. *World Development* 28, no. 4 (2000): 601–15.

Brumberg, Daniel. 'Democratization in the Arab World? The Trap of Liberalized Autocracy'. *Journal of Democracy* 13, no. 4 (2002): 56–68.

Burnell, Peter, and Oliver Schlumberger. 'Promoting Democracy – Promoting Autocracy? International Politics and National Political Regimes'. *Contemporary Politics* 16, no. 1 (2010): 1–15.

Campbell, Donald T., and Julian C. Stanley. *Experimental and Quasi-Experimental Designs for Research*. Chicago: Rand McNally, 1966.

Campbell, Patricia J. 'Morocco in Transition: Overcoming the Democratic and Human Rights Legacy of King Hassan II'. *African Studies Quarterly* 7, no. 1 (2003), http://web.africa.ufl.edu/asq/v7/v7i1a4.htm (last accessed June 3, 2011)

Checkel, Jeffrey T. '"Going Native" in Europe? Theorizing Social Interaction in European Institutions'. *Comparative Political Studies* 36, nos. 1/2 (2003): 209–31.

Checkel, Jeffrey T. 'International Institutions and Socialization in Europe: Introduction and Framework'. *International Organization* 59, no. 4 (2005): 801–26.

Cooper, Chris, and Mikael Johansen. *An Evaluation of Completed Twinning Projects. A Report Presented to the National Contact Points' Meeting*, January 30–31, 2003 (Brussels, 2003). http://ec.europa.eu/enlargement/pdf/financial_assistance/phare/phare_ex_post_twining_en.pdf.' last (accessed June 3, 2011).

Dahl, Robert A. *Polyarchy: Participation and Opposition*. New Haven: Yale University Press, 1971.

Desrues, Thierry and Eduardo Moyano. 'Social Change and Political Transition in Morocco'. *Mediterranean Politics* 6, no. 1 (2001): 21–47.

Diamond, Larry, Marc F. Plattner, and Andreas Schedler. 'Introduction'. In *The Self-Restraining State. Power and Accountability in New Democracies*, eds. Andreas Schedler, Larry Diamond, and Marc F. Plattner, 1–10. Boulder, CO: Lynne Rienner, 1999.

Eagly, Alice H., and Shelly Chaiken. *The Psychology of Attitude Change*. San Diego: Harcourt Brace Janovich, 1992.

European Commission. *PHARE Ex-Post Evaluation of Country Support Implemented from 1997-98 to 2000-1*, Consolidated Background Report (Brussels, 2003).

European Commission. *Second Generation Twinning – Preliminary Findings. Interim Evaluation of Phare Support Allocated in 1999–2002 and Implemented until November 2003*, Thematic Evaluation Report (Brussels, 2004).

European Commission. '*EU/Morocco Action Plan*', Annex to Proposal for a Decision on the position to be adopted by the European Community and its Member States [...] on the implementation of the EU-Morocco Action Plan, COM(2004) 788 final (Brussels. 2004).

European Court of Auditors. 'Special Report n° 6/2003 Concerning Twinning as a Main Instrument to Support Institution-building in Candidate Countries, Together with the Commission's Replies', *Official Journal* C167 (2003): 21–45.

Freyburg, Tina. 'Demokratisierung durch Zusammenarbeit? Funktionale Kooperation mit autoritären Regimen und Sozialisation in demokratischem Regieren'. *Zeitschrift für Internationale Beziehungen* 18, no. 1 (2011): 546.

Freyburg, Tina, Sandra Lavenex, Frank Schimmelfennig, Tatiana Skripka, and Anne Wetzel. 'Democracy Promotion Through Functional Cooperation? The Case of the European Neighbourhood Policy'. *Democratization* 18, no. 4 (2011): 1026–54.

Freyburg, Tina, Sandra Lavenex, Frank Schimmelfennig, Tatiana Skripka, and Anne Wetzel. 'EU Promotion of Democratic Governance in the Neighbourhood'. *Journal of European Public Policy* 16, no. 6 (2009): 916–34.

Freyburg, Tina, Tatiana Skripka, and Anne Wetzel. 'Democracy between the Lines? EU Promotion of Democratic Governance via Sector-Specific Co-operation'. NCCR Democracy Working Paper No. 5 (2007), Zurich.

Göbel, Christian and Daniel Lambach 'Accounting for the (In-)Stability of Authoritarian Regimes: Evidence from East Asia and Sub-Saharan Africa'. Paper presented at the APSA Annual Meeting, Toronto, Canada, September 2–6, 2009.

Grant, Ruth W., and Robert O. Keohane. 'Accountability and Abuses of Power in World Politics'. *American Political Science Review* 99, no. 1 (2005): 29–43.

Halaby, Charles N. 'Panel Models in Sociological Research: Theory into Practice'. *Annual Review of Sociology* 30, no. 1 (2004): 507–44.

Hegasy, Sonja. 'Young Authority: Quantitative and Qualitative Insights into Youth, Youth Culture, and State Power in Contemporary Morocco'. *The Journal of North African Studies* 12, no. 1 (2007): 19–36.

Héritier, Adrienne. 'Composite Democracy in Europe: The Role of Transparency and Access to Information'. *Journal of European Public Policy* 10, no. 5 (2003): 814–33.

Hooghe, Liesbet. 'Several Roads Lead to International Norms, but Few via International Socialization: A Case Study of the European Commission'. *International Organization* 59, no. 4 (2005): 861–98.

Hyden, Goran, Julius Court, and Kenneth Mease. *Making Sense of Governance: Empirical Evidence from Sixteen Developing Countries*. Boulder, CO: Lynne Rienner, 2004.

John, Oliver P., and Veronica Benet-Martínez. 'Measurement: Reliability, Construct Validation, and Scale Construction'. In *Handbook of Research Methods in Social and Personality Psychology*, ed. Harry T. Reis, and Charles M. Jud, 339–69. Cambridge: Cambridge University Press, 2000.

Johnston, Alastair Iain. 'Treating International Institutions as Social Environments'. *International Studies Quarterly* 45, no. 4 (2001): 487–515.

Jreisat, Jamil E. 'The Arab World. Reform or Stalemate'. *Journal of Asian and African Studies* 41, nos. 5/6 (2006): 411–37.

Kelley, Judith. 'New Wine in Old Wineskins: Promoting Political Reforms through the New European Neighbourhood Policy'. *Journal of Common Market Studies* 44, no. 1 (2006): 29–55.

Keohane, Robert O., and Joseph S. Nye. 'Transgovernmental Relations and International Organizations'. *World Politics* 27, no. 1 (1974): 39–62.

Kern, Holger Lutz, and Jens Hainmueller. 'Opium for the Masses: How Foreign Media Can Stabilize Authoritarian Regimes'. *Political Analysis* 17 (2009): 377–99.

Kerr, Henry H. 'Changing Attitudes through International Participation: European Parliamentarians and Integration'. *International Organization* 27, no. 1 (1973): 45–83.

Kopstein, Jeffrey. 'The Transatlantic Divide over Democracy Promotion'. *The Washington Quarterly* 29, no. 2 (2006): 85–98.

Lavenex, Sandra. 'A Governance Perspective on the European Neighbourhood Policy: Integration Beyond Conditionality?'. *Journal of European Public Policy* 15, no. 6 (2008): 938–55.

Lavenex, Sandra, and Frank Schimmelfennig. 'Models of EU Democracy Promotion: Leverage, Linkage, and Governance'. *Democratization*, this issue.

Lipset, Seymour Martin. *Political Man. The Social Bases of Politics*. Baltimore: John Hopkins University Press, 1981.

Marsden, Peter V. 'Network Data and Measurement'. *Annual Review of Sociology* 16 (1990): 435–63.

Merkel, Wolfgang. *Systemtransformation. Eine Einführung in die Theorie und Empirie der Transformationsforschung.* Opladen: Leske+Budrich, 1999.

Merkel, Wolfgang. 'Democracy through War?'. *Democratization* 15, no. 3 (2008): 487–508.

Mohamedou, Mohammad-Mahmoud. 'The Rise and Fall of Democratization in the Maghreb'. In *Middle East and North Africa: Governance, Democratization, Human Rights*, ed. Paul J. Magnarella, 209–39. Aldershot: Ashgate, 1999.

Nye, Joseph S. *Soft Power: The Means to Success in World Politics.* New York: Public Affairs, 2004.

O'Donnell, Guillermo, and Philippe Schmitter, ed. *Transitions from Authoritarian Rule: Tentative Conclusions about Uncertain Democracies* Baltimore: Johns Hopkins University Press, 1986.

Olson, James M., and Mark P. Zanna. 'Attitudes and Attitude Change'. *Annual Review of Psychology* 44 (1993): 117–54.

Page, Edward C. *Political Authority and Bureaucratic Power. A Comparative Analysis.* Brighton: Wheatsheaf Books, 1985.

Papadimitriou, Dimitris, and David Phinnemore. 'Exporting Europeanization to the Wider Europe: The Twinning Exercise and Administrative Reform in the Candidate Countries and Beyond'. *Southeast European and Black Sea Studies* 3, no. 2 (2003): 1–22.

Pawelka, Peter. 'Der Staat im Vorderen Orient: Über die Demokratie-Resistenz in einer Globalisierten Welt'. *Leviathan* 30, no. 4 (2002): 432–54.

Pérez-Armendáriz, Clarisa, and David Crow. 'Do Migrants Remit Democracy? International Migration, Political Beliefs, and Behavior in Mexico'. *Comparative Political Studies* 43, no. 1 (2010): 119–48.

Perloff, Richard M. *The Dynamics of Persuasion. Communication and Attitudes in the 21st Century.* Mahwah: Lawrence Erlbaum Ass, 2003.

Pollack, Mark A. 'Constructivism, Social Psychology, and Elite Attitude Change. Lessons from an Exhausted Research Program'. Paper presented at the biennial conference of Europeanists, Baltimore, MD, United States of America, February 26–March 1, 1998.

Potter, William C. 'Issue Area and Foreign Policy Analysis'. *International Organization* 34, no. 3 (1980): 405–27.

Raykov, Tenko. 'Reliability if Deleted, not "Alpha if Deleted": Evaluation of Scale Reliability Following Component Deletion'. *British Journal of Mathematical and Statistical Psychology* 60 (2007): 201–16.

Risse, Thomas. 'Neofunctionalism, European Identity, and the Puzzles of European Integration'. *Journal of European Public Policy* 12, no. 2 (2005): 291–309.

Schedler, Andreas. 'Conceptualizing Accountability'. In *The Self-Restraining State: Power and Accountability in New Democracies*, ed. Andreas Schedler, Larry Diamond, and Marc F. Plattner, 13–28. Boulder, CO: Lynne Rienner, 1999.

Sijtsma, Klaas. 'On the Use, the Misuse, and the Very Limited Usefulness of Cronbach's Alpha'. *Psychometrika* 74, no. 1 (2009): 107–20.

Slaughter, Anne-Marie. 'Government Networks: The Heart of the Liberal Democratic Order'. In *Democratic Governance and International Law*, ed. Gregory H. Fox, and Brad R. Roth, 199–235. Cambridge: Cambridge University Press, 2000.

Slaughter, Anne-Marie. *A New World Order.* Princeton, NJ: Princeton University Press, 2004.

Tulmets, Elsa. 'The Introduction of the Open Method of Coordination in the European Enlargement Policy: Analysing the Impact of the New PHARE/Twinning Instrument'. *European Political Economy Review* 3, no. 1 (2005): 54–90.

Van Waarden, Frans. 'Dimensions and Types of Policy Networks'. *European Journal of Political Research* 21 (1992): 29–52.

Verba, Sidney. 'Democratic Participation'. *Annals of the American Academy of Political and Social Science* 373, no. 2 (1967): 53–78.

Verplanken, Bas, Godelieve Hofstee, and Heidi J.W. Janssen. 'Accessibility of Affective versus Cognitive Components of Attitude'. *European Journal of Social Psychology* 28 (1998): 23–35.

Waever, Ole. 'Securitization and Desecuritization'. In *On Security*, ed. Ronnie D. Lipschutz, 46–86. New York: Columbia University Press, 1995.

Weber, Max. *Wirtschaft und Gesellschaft*. 5th ed. Tübingen: J.C.B. Mohr, 1972.

Wejnert, Barbara. 'Diffusion, Development, and Democracy 1800–1999'. *American Sociological Review* 70, no. 1 (2005): 53–81.

Whitehead, Laurence. 'Three International Dimensions of Democratization'. In *The International Dimensions of Democratization: Europe and the Americas*, ed. Laurence Whitehead, 3–25. Oxford: Oxford University Press, 1996.

Youngs, Richard. 'European Union Democracy Promotion Policies: Ten Years On'. *European Foreign Affairs Review* 6 (2001): 355–73.

Youngs, Richard. 'Democracy Promotion as External Governance?'. *Journal of European Public Policy* 16, no. 6 (2009): 895–915.

Zerhouni, Saloua. 'Morocco: Reconciling Continuity and Change'. In *Arab Elites. Negotiating the Politics of Change*, ed. Volker Perthes, 61–85. Boulder, CO: Lynne Rienner Publ., 2004.

Zimbardo, Philip G., and Michael R. Leippe. *The Psychology of Attitude Change and Social Influence*. New York: McGraw-Hill, 1991.

Zürn, Michael, and Jeffrey T. Checkel. 'Getting Socialized to Build Bridges: Constructivism and Rationalism, Europe and the Nation-State'. *International Organization* 59, no. 4 (2005): 1045–79.

Democracy promotion through functional cooperation? The case of the European Neighbourhood Policy

Tina Freyburg[a], Sandra Lavenex[b], Frank Schimmelfennig[a], Tatiana Skripka[c] and Anne Wetzel[d]

[a]Centre for Comparative and International Studies (CIS), ETH Zurich, Switzerland; [b]Institute of Political Science, University of Lucerne, Switzerland; [c]KFG 'The Transformative Power of Europe', Free University of Berlin, Germany; [d]Centre for EU Studies, Ghent University, Belgium

This contribution explores whether and under what conditions functional sectoral cooperation between the EU and the countries of the European Neighbourhood Policy (ENP) promotes democratic governance. In an analysis of four countries (Jordan, Moldova, Morocco, and Ukraine) and three fields of cooperation (competition, environment, and migration policy), we show that country properties such as the degree of political liberalization, membership aspirations, and geographic region do not explain differences in democratic governance. Rather, sectoral conditions such as the codification of democratic governance rules, the institutionalization of functional cooperation, interdependence, and adoption costs matter most for the success of democratic governance promotion. We further reveal a notable discrepancy between adoption and application of democratic governance in the selected ENP countries that has not been remedied in the first five years of the ENP.

Introduction

The European Neighbourhood Policy (ENP) is a strategy for the progressive approximation of non-member states to the European Union's *acquis communautaire* through their association with the EU.[1] The fact that the relations with the neighbouring countries are based on the EU's system of rules and regulations opens new perspectives for the study of democracy promotion. Having been designed by and for democratic states, these rules often embody norms related to transparency, participation, or accountability that cannot be taken for granted in (semi-)authoritarian states or countries in transition.[2] In this contribution, we explore the governance model of democracy promotion outlined in the introduction to this Special Issue[3] and ask how far and under which conditions the EU is effective in transferring such embedded democratic governance norms to the ENP countries.

One of the main challenges facing the effectiveness of the ENP is posed by the strong heterogeneity of countries to which it applies. While the ENP was originally conceived for the Eastern neighbours of the EU, it was soon expanded to encompass the Southern neighbouring countries as well. The expediency of this decision has always been disputed. Some scholars maintain that the Council 'put[s] apples and pears (Eastern Europe and Southern non-Europe) in the same policy basket', with problematic consequences for implementation.[4] The ENP's Eastern and Southern dimensions are said to 'pull in different directions' because the policy unites countries with opposed membership opportunities under one framework.[5] Although the ENP has never offered a membership perspective, it has been acknowledged from the very beginning that the 'prospect of accession to the EU' is the main difference between the Eastern and Southern neighbourhood.[6]

The Eastern European countries, such as Moldova and Ukraine that have expressed a strong membership aspiration, and, despite the EU's understanding that the ENP should be an alternative to membership, see the ENP as a first step towards accession and try to redefine it accordingly.[7] EU actors recognize the membership aspiration of Moldova and tacitly acknowledge the membership perspective for Ukraine.[8] Thus, although there is no direct membership incentive, we may expect the EU to possess a certain 'leverage' towards the Eastern European countries, inciting them to engage in political reforms in order to gain an officially favourable long-term accession perspective.[9]

The situation is completely different for the Southern neighbours, which do not aspire for membership and for which the ENP does not offer strong incentives for implementation of the agreed commitments.[10] Thus, the prospects of policy change are expected to be much smaller for the Southern neighbours than for the Eastern. This should in particular be the case with regard to governance reforms that transcend the level of pure technical convergence to EU standards. Here, a clear dividing line can be expected between transfer of democratic governance in the East and in the South.

From a governance perspective to democracy promotion, not only the choice of target countries but also the composition of policy sectors covered by the ENP exacerbates its heterogeneity. As a 'composite policy',[11] the ENP combines overarching foreign policy goals with functional, sectoral cooperation across the spectrum of the EU's *acquis communautaire*, from commercial to environmental or migration policy. While we expect this *acquis* to generally incorporate certain democratic governance norms, their concrete manifestation varies from one policy sector to another, as do the institutional modes of cooperation between the EU and the ENP countries in the various sectors.[12] This variation as well as diverging patterns of interdependence and cost/benefit constellations related to the different policy sectors are, like the country-specific variables mentioned above, expected to impact on the effectiveness of EU rule transfer.

In this contribution, we assess the relevance of country- and sector-related variables for the effectiveness of EU democratic governance promotion in relation to four countries (Moldova and Ukraine to the East, Jordan and Morocco to the South) and in three policy sectors (competition: state aid, environmental: water governance, and migration policy: asylum). The analysis is primarily based on 199 semi-structured interviews conducted in 2007–2009 with governmental and non-governmental actors in the four countries and with Commission officials and complemented by information drawn from the relevant official documents and reports.

The analysis shows that the general country-specific factors (region, membership aspirations, and political liberalization) do not explain variation in the adoption of democratic governance rules. Rather, democratic governance promotion follows a sectoral logic. In the issue areas we studied, diverse combinations of favourable sector properties (codification of democratic governance, institutionalized functional cooperation, interdependence with the EU, and low adoption costs) led the ENP countries to adopt democratic governance rules. The application of these rules, however, has so far been weak. Whereas our study demonstrates that the promotion of democratic governance does indeed work independently of general political conditions and relations, its effectiveness is limited.

Democratic governance

In contrast to the traditional understanding of democratization that focuses on changes in state institutions, the governance approach concentrates on changes in governance rules and practices within individual policy sectors. We define our dependent variable as the transfer of democratic governance rules measured at the level of policy sectors and distinguish between formal rule adoption in domestic legislation and rule application in administrative practices. According to the governance model, changes in both rule adoption and application occur as a consequence of third countries' approximation to the EU *acquis* as well as experience of democratic policy-making gained by policy-makers and experts in the ENP states in interaction with their counterparts in the EU.[13]

We speak of democratic governance rather than democracy in order to capture democratization at the sectoral level and distinguish it from democratic developments at the polity level. Our notion of democratic governance is based on an understanding of democracy defined according to its underlying principles rather than specific institutions embodying them. Since democratic principles are applicable to all situations in which collectively binding decisions are taken,[14] they can be translated into sectoral policy-making. Democratic sectoral governance may thus be achieved by incorporating democratic principles into administrative rules and practices even within a non-democratic polity. We define sectoral governance with reference to 'how the rules of the political game are managed'.[15] In this sense, democratic governance is similar to good governance.[16] The latter, however, refers mainly to the effectiveness of governance and need not be democratic.

Our concept of democratic governance consists of three dimensions: transparency, accountability, and participation.[17] *Transparency* refers both to access to issue-specific data and to governmental provision of information about decision-making. *Accountability* concerns public officials' obligation to justify their decisions and actions, the possibility of appealing, and sanctioning over misconduct. We distinguish between horizontal accountability that refers to 'all acts of accountability that take place between independent state agencies',[18] such as investigating committees, ombudsmen, and anticorruption bodies, and vertical accountability that emphasizes the obligation for public officials to justify their decisions. Finally, *participation* denotes non-electoral forms of participation such as involvement of non-state actors in administrative decision- and policy-making.[19] These democratic principles are incorporated – but not 'labelled overtly as democracy-focused'[20] – in EU sectoral *acquis* and policy programmes towards the neighbouring states. They may take different forms in different sectors.

It should be noted that an increase in democratic governance cannot be a real substitute for democratic transformation proper and that rules pertaining, e.g. to transparency provisions in environmental legislation or to independent judicial review in asylum policy are only small drops in the ocean of institutional provisions constituting a democratic order. What is more, some of these provisions may, as with asylum policy, represent low minimum standards from the perspective of liberal democracies. Nevertheless, implementation even of minimum standards regarding citizens' access to information, participation in administrative processes, or the accountability of administrative decisions 'requires a process of transformation in those countries where such traditions are lacking',[21] and may constitute one step within a broader democratization of state and society.

Determinants of democratic governance transfer

The governance model suggests that the transfer of democratic governance provisions to ENP countries will be influenced by both country-specific properties and sector-related variables. The following sections discuss the two sets of explanatory factors in detail. Table 1 summarizes country and sectoral properties.

Impact of country properties

We identify two main country properties that may have an impact on democratic governance transfer: membership aspiration and political liberalization. Studies have shown that a certain degree of prior *political liberalization* is needed in order to effectively foster domestic democratization processes.[22] For instance, the existence of an active civil society and decentralized decision-making structures is required so that sub-governmental administration officers implement the provisions on participation as one of the aspects of democratic governance. In relation to

Table 1. Operationalization of explanatory variables.

Variables		Operationalization
Country properties		
Membership aspiration	Present	ENP country aspires joining the EU
	Absent	ENP country is not interested in joining the EU
Political liberalization	Present	Medium level of citizen participation and political freedoms
	Absent	Low level of citizen participation and political freedoms
Sector properties		
Codification	Strong	Democratic governance elements are incorporated in and specified by both EU *acquis* and international rules
	Medium	Democratic governance elements are incorporated in and specified by EU *acquis* or international rules
	Weak	Democratic governance elements are incorporated in EU *acquis* or international rules but require further specification
Costs of rule adoption	High	Rule adoption diminishes the government's domestic power base
	Medium	Rule adoption diminishes the power base of the sectoral authorities
	Low	Rule adoption has marginal consequences for the power of the government and the sectoral authorities
Institution-alization	Strong	Existence of both bilateral and EU-controlled regional fora dealing with the relevant rules
	Medium	Only EU–third-country bilateral fora dealing with the relevant rules
	Weak	Only third countries' fora, not controlled by the EU
Interdependence	Strong	ENP state perceives to be more or equally dependent on the EU in solving its sectoral problems
	Medium	ENP state perceives to be less dependent on the EU than *vice versa* or more dependent on other external actors than the EU in solving its sectoral problems
	Weak	No reliance on the EU in solving sectoral problems

democratic governance, a minimal degree of political liberalization may serve as a precondition for establishing horizontal transgovernmental ties of functional cooperation between public officials in an ENP state and their EU counterparts.

Incentives offered by the EU to the ENP countries range from enhanced cooperation on economic issues, including a stake in the internal market, to sectoral enticements, such as favourable visa regimes. In this, the ENP largely resembles the enlargement strategy.[23] Although the ENP lacks the biggest incentive the EU can offer, a membership perspective, several ENP states aspire joining the EU nevertheless. Such *membership aspiration* might have an impact on rule adoption because of the perceived low credibility of the EU's refusal to open accession negotiations. Some ENP countries are 'not taking no for an answer' and therefore 'may go ahead with adoption of EU standards'.[24]

We hypothesize that the effectiveness of democratic governance transfer increases (H1) the more the ENP state strives for EU membership irrespective of actual offer, and (H2) the higher the degree of political liberalization of this state is.

Impact of sectoral properties

The governance model of external democracy promotion follows an institutionalist perspective, according to which the properties of cooperation in sectors have an impact on rule transfer. We identify four sectoral properties as relevant for democratic governance promotion: codification of democratic governance provisions, costs associated with the adoption of democratic governance rules for country elites, institutionalization of transgovernmental cooperation in a particular sector, and sectoral interdependence.

Codification is about the incorporation of democratic governance provisions in the EU *acquis* and/or international conventions and rule determinacy. The expected impact of this variable is based on the observation that 'the way in which EU rules are communicated and transferred to the non-member states'[25] influences the likelihood of being adopted by them. We expect that adoption is more likely, if (i) democratic-governance provisions are perceived as being legitimate by virtue of incorporation in both EU *acquis* and international conventions[26] and (ii) they are clear and precise enough to qualify as templates without considerable adaptation to the context of third countries.[27] High sectoral *adoption costs* occur if adoption of democratic governance provisions is expected to diminish the government's domestic power base.[28] Medium adoption costs occur when the power base of sectoral authorities is diminished but the central government is not directly affected.

Institutionalization concerns formalized transgovernmental policy cooperation between the EU and ENP states. We expect that the more the institutionalized sector-specific policy cooperation with the EU is, the more likely the third countries are to adopt EU democratic governance provisions. Enhanced transgovernmental cooperation exposes sectoral officials to the practices of democratic governance, thus facilitating rule adoption. In weakly institutionalized sectors, only regional frameworks of cooperation without EU engagement exist. Medium institutionalization characterizes bilateral channels of policy cooperation with the EU. Strongly institutionalized sectors enjoy formalized transgovernmental cooperation in both bilateral and EU-controlled regional fora.

Finally, *interdependence* refers to a cooperating party's conviction that sector-specific problems can be solved in collaboration with the EU rather than domestically or in collaboration with other external parties.[29] As a form of external governance, the ENP can be understood as the EU's strategy of managing interdependence with its neighbouring countries. Following the power-based explanation of external governance, we expect that EU democratic governance promotion through the ENP is more likely to have an impact when EU–third country relations are asymmetric in favour of the EU.[30] At the same time, the impact of democratic governance promotion is constrained when the target country is facing strong interdependence with another third country[31]. We adopt the concept of sectoral interdependence from Keohane and Nye who argue that 'patterns of outcomes and distinctive political processes are likely to vary from one set of issues to another'.[32]

We hypothesize that (H3) the stronger the codification is and (H4) the more an ENP state is involved in transgovernmental networks, the higher the likelihood of successful rule transfer is. The positive impact of cooperation in transgovernmental networks, however, may be offset by other sector-specific factors. The relevant hypotheses are: (H5) the higher the expected adoption costs of the third country are and (H6) the less sectoral interdependence favours the EU, the less likely EU rule transfer is.

Democratic governance promotion in the neighbourhood

The remainder of the contribution presents the results of our empirical analysis of functional cooperation between the EU and four ENP countries in three policy sectors. We start with the impact of country properties on rule adoption and substantiate the selection of countries chosen for the case studies. We then turn to the sectoral perspective and introduce our choice of policy sectors. The hypotheses regarding the impact of sectoral variables on democratic-governance promotion are discussed for each sector. Next follows the presentation of our findings on rule adoption and application in the selected countries and policy sectors. We conclude with a comparative analysis of the impact of country- and sector-related characteristics on democratic governance promotion in the EU neighbourhood.

Country-specific factors in the EU neighbourhood

For our empirical study, we selected four ENP countries, two from the Eastern (Moldova and Ukraine) and two from the Southern neighbourhood of the EU (Morocco and Jordan). These countries are among the most active and advanced participants in the ENP and are characterized as 'willing partners'[33]. At least until the 2011 revolutions, within their respective regions, these countries were the most politically liberalized. At the same time, Moldova and Ukraine enjoy substantially higher levels of *political liberalization* than Jordan and Morocco. The 2008 'Voice and Accountability' Governance indicator assigned Moldova a liberalization score of -0.27 and Ukraine a score of -0.03, both of which we regard as medium. For Jordan and Morocco, the scores were -0.71 and -0.70, respectively, which we can characterize as low.[34]

As regards *membership aspiration*, there is, again, a clear difference between the Eastern and Southern neighbours. Whereas the former seek to join the EU eventually, the latter are not pursuing the strategy of integration with the EU. Moldova and Ukraine, as Eastern European countries, are in geographical terms eligible for EU membership. Despite the fact that the EU has so far failed to offer such a perspective, both countries aspire to join the EU.[35] Moldova set up a National Commission for European Integration that elaborated and submitted to the European Commission the Concept of the Integration of Moldova into the EU. Moreover, it transformed the Foreign Ministry into the Ministry of Foreign Affairs and European Integration. As for Ukraine, in January 2005, newly elected President Yushchenko declared Ukraine's membership in the EU as a strategic goal. In contrast, neither Jordan nor Morocco wants to join the EU. In 1987, Morocco sought membership in the European Economic Community, but predominantly for economic reasons. Today, the ENP offers Morocco a stake in the EU internal market without political-institutional integration, which is a very attractive option for the country.[36]

Based on our hypotheses H1 and H2, we expect that Moldova and Ukraine will be more likely to adopt democratic governance provisions than Jordan and Morocco, since they enjoy higher degree of political liberalization and aspire to EU membership. If in our empirical analysis we do not find supportive evidence for these hypotheses, the relevance of country-specific explanatory factors will be challenged.

Sector-specific factors in the EU neighbourhood

The selection of the three sectors – environment, competition, and migration – was guided by the strength of codified democratic-governance provisions. In the field of environment, *codification* is strong, because both EU environmental *acquis* and international conventions provide the most developed democratic governance templates. On the issue of water management, a number of EU directives, including the 2000 Water Framework Directive, provide a strong *acquis*, complemented and reinforced by the Aarhus Convention of 1998. For competition policy, codification of democratic governance is weak: *acquis* provisions are tailored to EU institutions and are not suitable for third countries. While in the EU, the European Commission acts as an implementing authority, it is independent national bodies that have to deal with the issue of state aid in non-EU states.[37] Moreover, EU provisions on state aid are not backed by international agreements. Finally, asylum policy in the migration sector is moderately codified. Democratic-governance provisions are relatively strong, but they mainly originate in international conventions and are hardly present in the EU *acquis*.

Whereas codification is the same for all countries in one sector, the remaining three sectoral variables – institutionalization, interdependence, and costs of rule adoption – may vary across countries. In the field of 'competition', *institutionalization* of cooperation with the EU is moderate in all four countries. In Moldova, the issue of state aid is regularly discussed in the subcommittee on financial, economic, and statistical issues. A similar bilateral subcommittee deals with the issue in Ukraine. Although no further specific institutional arrangements exist in either country, expert cooperation on legislative issues proceeds on an *ad hoc*, but relatively regular basis. In both countries, the EU is actively present as an advisor at all stages of policy elaboration, particularly through Technical Assistance to the Commonwealth of Independent States projects and Technical Assistance and Information Exchange seminars. Likewise, in Morocco, the state aid issue receives attention in the context of the ongoing Twinning project that focuses on daily competition practices. In Jordan, too, the EU used to be actively present as an advisor at various stages of legislative process, in particular in the framework of the Euro-Jordanian Action for the Development of Enterprise programme (EJADA), which was active in 2000–2006, and a Twinning project monitoring the implementation of legislation, which largely failed. Presently, the issue is rarely addressed in the relevant subcommittee.

Interdependence is high except in EU–Jordan relations. The EU is a major trade partner for all four countries and alignment with EU competition rules is highly relevant for improving their access to EU markets. Whereas trade relations with Moldova, Morocco, and Ukraine are asymmetric in favour of the EU and not balanced by other partners, Jordan preserves official neutrality in its cooperation with Europe, the USA, and the conservative Gulf States.[38]

Costs of rule adoption in the competition sector are uniformly high. In all four countries, the issue of state aid is highly sensitive in domestic politics due to the vested interests of political and business elites and unwillingness of the state to give up its power to intervene in business practices.

Environment

In the field of water management, the two Eastern and two Southern ENP countries also display similar values on sectoral properties. Cooperation with the EU is strongly *institutionalized* in all four cases. Moldova and Ukraine are part of several EU-led frameworks of cooperation on water, particularly the Eastern Europe, Caucasus and Central Asia component of the EU Water Initiative (EUWI), including national dialogue, and the EU-sponsored Danube–Black Sea Task Force (DABLAS). Jordan and Morocco take part the Mediterranean component of the EUWI and were members of the Short- and Medium-Term Priority Environmental Action Programme. At the bilateral level, a large project on water − *Al-Meyyah* − is financially supported by the EU and implemented by the predominantly EU-funded Programme Management Unit within the Jordanian Ministry of Water. Jordan also benefited from the LIFE 99/00 project 'environmental law enforcement' supporting changes in the environment protection law, and Morocco took part in the Twinning project on harmonization of environmental legislation.

Interdependence with the EU is high for Moldova, Morocco, and Ukraine, and medium for Jordan. As a downstream country at the Danube's estuary, Moldova theoretically has a stronger interest in cooperating with the EU than *vice versa*. At the same time, given the inherently transboundary nature of water-related problems, the EU is one of the main drivers and financiers of environmental cooperation in the region. Ukraine/Morocco and the EU are mutually dependent on cooperation on solving problems with local water and in the context of the Black Sea and the Mediterranean Sea, respectively. Ukraine's aim of approximation to the EU's water *acquis* makes the EU the main external partner, although the country also collaborates with the United Nations Development Programme and Russia, with which the country shares river basins. Dealing with water scarcity, Jordan relies on a number of external cooperation partners, which makes it less dependent on the EU. Besides the EU, it cooperates with the German technical cooperation agency Gesellschaft für Technische Zusammenarbeit, the Japan International Cooperation Agency, and the United States Agency for International Development.

Adoption costs in the environmental sector are medium in all countries. In Moldova, the issue of water governance is not politically sensitive at the domestic level, but there is reluctance of sectoral policy-makers to implement the rules of democratic governance due to fear of power and information loss. Similarly, in Ukraine, '[c]orruption and mismanagement are among the main factors that have an adverse impact on access to environmental information'.[39] Introduction of democratic governance rules is associated with a loss of discretion and private benefits for sectoral officials. Likewise, in Jordan and Morocco, sectoral elite corruption hinders sustainable water management as these elites perceive this as conflicting with economic development and its water-intensive investments. In both countries, economic development is often prioritized over environmental considerations, in particular as regards tourism and agriculture.

Migration

With respect to asylum policy, Moldova, Morocco, and Ukraine enjoy the same sectoral properties. Jordan, however, stands apart due to its exceptional exposure to consistent migratory waves since the outset of the Arab-Israeli conflict.[40] *Institutionalization* of policy cooperation with the EU is stronger in Eastern Europe than with Morocco, where we attribute a medium value, and Jordan where it is low. In Moldova and Ukraine, cooperation on asylum policy is regionally well institutionalized through the Söderköping and Budapest processes, networks where information and best practices of EU asylum policy are shared. Moreover, Moldova and Ukraine cooperate with the EU's agency for the management of cooperation at the external borders FRONTEX . In this framework, border guard experts from the EU member states liaise with their counterparts from third countries. Specialized training of Moldovan border guard and migration officers is also undertaken by the International Organization for Migration Moldova. In Ukraine, cooperation on migration has been based on separate Action Plans since 2001 and proceeds in addition through subcommittee and scoreboard meetings. EU–Morocco cooperation on asylum is formalized as a working party as part of the Association Agreement. Yet, interviews with the responsible officials in the

EU's Rabat delegation revealed that cooperation is mainly informal due to Morocco's reluctance. EU's engagement in asylum policy in Jordan consists only of limited financial support of the United Nations High Commissioner for Refugees (UNHCR), as part of the joint financial and technical assistance to third countries in the areas of migration and asylum (AENEAS) project on the resettlement of Iraqi refugees. There is no actual policy cooperation.

Interdependence is medium in the EU's asylum cooperation with Moldova, Morocco, and Ukraine. Moldova is a transit country for migration flows into the EU, which makes the EU interested in establishing an adequate asylum system in Moldova. However, large-scale labour migration of Moldovan citizens to the EU endangers the country's socio-economic development. Therefore, Moldova is willing to make concessions to the EU on these issues.[41] Likewise in Ukraine, another transit country: limited capacity of the Ukrainian Migration Services to handle asylum issues[42] makes them dependent on external support. Morocco is currently a transit country for incoming migration flows in the EU. The number of asylum seekers in Morocco itself is, however, likely to increase due to more adequate protection and more restrictive EU regulations. Interdependence is therefore considered medium. Jordan and the EU do not depend on each other in solving asylum-related issues.

Sectoral *adoption costs* for the asylum policy are medium in all four countries. In Moldova, asylum policy is structurally and politically under-prioritized due to perceived non-importance, compared with problems caused by outward migration, such as trafficking in human beings. Furthermore, there is reluctance of police-trained policy officers to implement a human-rights-oriented approach to asylum, largely resting on democratic governance provisions. In Ukraine, granting asylum to refugees and taking back irregular migrants might be more unpopular than costly because foreigners are often seen as being the root of problems such as violence and illnesses.[43] Furthermore, the establishment of a central agency dealing with asylum and migration issues that would make procedures more transparent and enhance accountability has been delayed for many years among others because of several agencies' fears of loss of resources.[44] Disputes about the creation of the State Migration Service eventually led to the collapse of the Ukrainian asylum system in 2009. Asylum presents a politically very sensitive topic in Jordan, in particular because of its large share of Palestinian refugees and the proximity to other persistent conflicts regions such as Iraq. Access to the 1951 United Nations Convention or enacting national law that respond to the international standards is perceived as being too costly by the current government. In Morocco, migration is seen as the issue of internal security. The Ministry of Interior, responsible for migration and asylum policy, is unlikely to even partially transfer its power to non-state actors such as the UNHCR.[45]

Based on our hypotheses H3 and H4, we expect higher values of codification and institutionalization to be associated with a higher likelihood of successful rule transfer. In line with H5 and H6, we further expect that the positive impact of cooperation in transgovernmental networks might be impaired by high adoption costs and weak sectoral interdependence.

Democratic governance in the EU neighbourhood

Eastern neighbourhood I: Moldova

In all three sectors, Moldova has reached a medium level of rule adoption. Moreover, prepared legislation will, if adopted, significantly strengthen democratic governance provisions, thus targeting high degree of rule adoption in the future. Relatively successful rule adoption is, however, not matched by rule application that remains weak.

In the field of *competition*, the Law on the Protection of Competition 1103-XIV of 2000 set out a general framework and established a legal basis for an independent competition authority, the National Agency for the Protection of Competition (NAPC). The law, however, did not enter into force until 2007.[46] Progress in the implementation of the law and the inception of the NAPC was triggered by the EU.[47] The newly established NAPC, with participation of EU-affiliated experts, drafted an amended competition law that passed a concordance check for compatibility with EU directives at the Centre for Harmonization of Legislation. The law received a parliamentary approval in 2008, but was vetoed by the president. Currently, a new competition law is under preparation at the NAPC, to be finalized by 2011.[48] In 2008, a draft of a new law on state aid compatible with EU practices was prepared by the NAPC in consultation with international experts. It is expected to introduce the principles of transparency and accountability into Moldovan legislation on state aid by affording the NAPC with broad competences in receiving information about aid from all state agencies, investigate possible violations, approve sanctions and apply to court. However, the law is still under governmental examination.[49]

Moldova was one of the first countries to ratify the Aarhus Convention on Access to Information, Public Participation in Decision-making and Access to Justice in *Environmental* Matters in 1999. The 2000 Law on Access to Information 982-XIV translated the provisions of the Convention into domestic legislation, not only with respect to environmental issues, but also for all governmental policy-making. However, 'the requirements of the Aarhus Convention continue not to be fully incorporated into [environmental] legislation'.[50] Furthermore, the observance of the Convention's provisions remains problematic. While the EU notices some progress in Moldova's efforts at increasing transparency of environmental issues,[51] better openness seems to be a goal in itself and does not serve improving accountability. There is little, if any, participation of the public in legislative and policy-making processes in Moldova. For instance, whereas engagement of non-state actors and stakeholders in frameworks such as the DABLAS is provided by Moldovan policy-makers as an example of public participation, no comparable scheme exists for national policy programmes. The main law regulating water resources in Moldova, the Water Code 1532 from 1993, having survived several amendments, did not acquire the provisions reflecting Moldova's obligations under the Aarhus Convention, as well as those reflected in the ENP Action Plan. A new law on water is currently being drafted by the Ministry of Ecology and Natural Resources to enable the application of the EU directive regulating water management policy. Among others, the proposed law contains provisions on public participation in policy-making (Art. 94).

The preamble to the Law on the Status of Refugees 1286-XV from 2002 explicitly states that the law is to bring domestic legislation on *asylum* in line with internationally recognized standards. The ENP Action Plan encourages further efforts in this direction (Art. 46). Already the first ENP progress report acknowledged substantial progress.[52] The recent amendments to the law established the main principles of a human rights approach to refugees and asylum seekers, exhaustively covering the application of the principles of transparency, accountability and participation, such as fair consideration of applications for asylum, provision of exhaustive information about procedures, possibilities for appeal and contacting the UNHCR representative. Yet, the implementation of legislation commended by the EU is a major problem. The main concern is the non-application of the human-rights approach by the Moldovan migration and border control authorities. These principles are almost exclusively implemented by international organizations, such as the IOM and the UNHCR, and Moldovan non-governmental organizations (NGOs) supporting refugees and asylum seekers. Moldova has no national centre for temporary accommodation of irregular migrants, asylum seekers and refugees. The Centre for Illegal Migrants built by the IOM in 2008 and financed particularly through EU programmes was not operational, for the absence of a normative framework in legislation, until June 2009.

Eastern neighbourhood II: Ukraine

Ukraine displays similar developments as Moldova with regard to the transfer of EU rules of democratic governance, both with regard to rule adoption, where it even slightly lags behind Moldova, and rule application.

As to *competition*, there have been several setbacks regarding the legislative approximation to EU rules on state aid. In 2004, a draft law which was closely modelled on EU *acquis* provisions was rejected by the Parliament.[53] In 2007, the drafted Law on Protection of Economic Competition No. 3263, which had been amended with the aim of introducing provisions on state aid control, also failed in Parliament. Without an appropriate legal framework, the Ukrainian competition authority 'is not provided with the adequate authority required for the independent supervisory authority to exercise the control on state aid'.[54] The present system of granting aid is thus not transparent. Participation and accountability are low. Until the expiration of the Action Plan, no progress has been achieved in the field of state aid.[55]

Ukrainian *environmental* legislation has included provisions on access to environmental information, participation and accountability for many years. Scholars acknowledged a decade ago that '[a]lmost all laws connected with environmental protection and natural resources usage contain the principles of public participation in environmental decision making and other citizens' rights'.[56] After Ukraine became a member of the Aarhus Convention, several laws have been amended accordingly, although some shortcomings remain. Regarding the legislation referring to water issues, the Water Code No. 213/95-VR from 1995 and the law 'On Drinking Water and Drinking Water Supply' 2918-III from 2002 incorporate democratic governance provisions of the EU Water Framework Directive.[57] The result of reforms in the sphere of environmental and in particular water governance can be described as mixed. On the one hand, there are some positive judgements regarding progress in public involvement and access to environmental information.[58] For example, NGOs were involved in the drafting of the Drinking Water Programme of Ukraine for 2006–2020.[59] On the other hand, this does not mean that the situation is satisfactory. Despite the quite developed legislation, implementation remains 'sporadic'.[60] Access to justice is guaranteed by the law but in practice remains a problem.

Migration and asylum policy in Ukraine is strongly based on the Law on Refugees 2557-III from 2001. This law has some major shortcomings, especially with respect to the accelerated asylum procedure because this provision is often used to reject claims without substantive investigation. Furthermore, there are limitations to transparency and participation, since '[i]t does not provide access for legal specialists of NGOs or UNHCR to refugees' individual files, or for refugees to have legal representation during refugee status determination (RSD) interviews with the Migration Services'.[61] These legal shortcomings have implications for rule application. UNHCR concluded that the 2005 amendments to the Refugee Law resulted in more arbitrary rejections. When applications are rejected as 'manifestly unfounded', reasons are not provided in the written notifications (accountability). UNHCR also faces problems of getting access to the files of asylum seekers (transparency).[62] Similarly, lawyers from relevant NGOs have difficulty to meet detained asylum seekers (participation). The latter, in turn, often do not receive adequate information by officials about the RSD procedure.[63] At the same time, the creation of a consultative Civil Council at the State Committee for Nationalities and Religion as the responsible authority in 2008 led only to a temporary increase of participation. Consultations stopped in 2009. In 2010, the European Commission diagnosed the collapse of the Ukrainian asylum system: 'there is no longer any entity competent to take binding decisions in asylum matters'.[64]

Southern neighbourhood I: Jordan

Jordan has made very limited progress with democratic governance rule adoption and application, compared to Moldova, Morocco, and Ukraine. Draft legislation can be expected to make changes in the competition and environmental sectors, provided it is adopted. Given the absence of legal provisions, it is not surprising that rule application is low. It took Jordan two failed attempts in 1996 and 1998 until the *Competition* law No. 33 was finally adopted in 2004. The law established the Committee for Competition Matters, which – headed by the responsible minister – is a merely consultative body. Its members include representatives of regulators, consumer organizations, and experts on competition in specific sectors, which are, however, selected according to obscure rules (participation). The Competition Directorate embedded within the Ministry of Industry and Trade is also not a separate autonomous entity. The revision of the law, which is under preparation, would transform it into an 'independent' Commission, i.e. the judicial procedure would no longer be mediated by the minister. However, the 2004 law grants any legal person the right to directly address the court (Art. 17A). It further states that the Directorate must publish an announcement regarding any petition, though at the expense of the applicant, and the decision in two daily newspapers (transparency; Art. 10D, 11B). This announcement 'shall' include an invitation to any interested party to present its opinion (participation). The competition law, however, does not present any progress in the specific issue of state aid.[65] Implementation of the 2004 law's provisions suffers mainly from the lack of independence of the body tasked with administration, the lack of adequate knowledge among lawyers, judges, and prosecutors, and the power of big companies that dictate their own terms.[66] Only few cases were referred to the courts by the Directorate since 2004 but no decisions were hitherto taken (accountability).[67] There is strong opposition among the ruling elite to establish the Directorate as a separate autonomous commission. As to state aid, the data collected under the budget law continue to fall short of international standards in terms of transparency, disclosure, and comprehensiveness.[68]

Although a number of *environmental* laws exist and water issues are salient in water-scarce Jordan, preparation of legislation on water *per se* started with the new water strategy officially endorsed in 2009. Primary legislation is hitherto a by-law issued under the 1995 Environment Protection Law (and its amendments 2003 and 2006), which does not contain any governance provisions. Still, some improvements of access to information and participation can be observed.[69] For instance, the water strategy states that the 'development of appropriate legislation will require regular and systematic consultation with a diversity of stakeholders and water users'.[70] Until now no (independent) authority exists that supervises water management (accountability). Generally, many by-laws implementing the adopted laws are missing and informal networks based on family ties jeopardize rules on sound water management. Responsibilities overlap between water institutions and procedures of accountability do not exist. A top-down approach is applied: stakeholders are normally not involved in decision-making (participation) and the right to information is confused with education and awareness campaigns.[71] The horizontal 2008 access to information law is too restrictive to be effective.[72]

Due to its exposure to consistent *migratory* waves since the outset of the Arab-Israeli conflict (see, e.g. Note 38), Jordan has not endorsed the 1951 UN convention on refugees and the 1967 protocol. The asylum procedure is deferred to the UNHCR which operates on the basis of the 1998 Memorandum of Understanding (MoU), and predominantly concerns Iraqi refugees and excludes Palestinians.[73] Although Article 21 of the 1952 Jordanian constitution guaranteed the right to asylum for political refugees, the Law on Residence and Foreigner Affairs No. 24 from 1973 does not include any provisions on asylum. Deportees can demand judicial review of their decision before court based on law 19 of 1992 on the high court of justice and the MoU, but only few do so and if, it is very unlikely to succeed (accountability). The MoU is not respected by the Jordanian government. Iraqis are regularly deported, independently of whether they are registered by the UNHCR or not, and are often already rejected at the frontiers without giving them the opportunity to make refugee claims.[74]

Southern neighbourhood II: Morocco

Although belonging to the EU's Southern neighbourhood, Morocco stands farther apart from Jordan than from Moldova or Ukraine with regard to rule adoption. In fact, Moldova, Morocco, and Ukraine display the same medium level of demo-cratic-governance rule adoption. Likewise, Morocco displays the same 'gap' between formal adoption of democratic governance provisions and their implementation as the Eastern neighbours. As to *competition* policy, Morocco does not yet possess a noteworthy state aid control regime. The legal basis of its competition policy is the 1999 Law 06-99 on Freedom of Prices and Compe-tition. The Prime Minister is the sole authority that may issue rulings on anti-com-petitive practices. His decisions can, however, be challenged before an administrative court (accountability). The Competition Council may give the Prime Minister non-binding advisory opinions on all draft legislation concerning state aid allocation (Art. 16). Nominated by the King, the Council president enjoys direct royal backing, which makes it a less reliant authority.[75] In order to introduce true participation, the revised competition law elaborated as part of a Twinning project foresees that Council and government need to consult interested parties before taking decisions. The revised law also improved provisions on transpar-ency. The competition law is only partially implemented. The Competition Council has been activated in January 2009, but it is still far away from being an independent authority with decision competencies. Progress in transparency is limited to provision of information on the total amount and the distribution of aid in form of annual reports to the Commission.[76] The revised law leaves pub-lication of decisions at the authority's discretion, but grants access to the records. As for participation, even the General Confederation of Moroccan Enterprises is only occasionally consulted by the government, usually after the decision has been made.

EU influence on the creation of a Law on Access to *Environmental* Information (transparency), as well as on policy-specific laws, such as the modification and implementation of the 1995 Law 10-95 on Water is high, in particular as a result of the Twinning project's focus on legal harmonization. With the establishment of the Water and Climate Council, the creation of water basin agencies – local 'petits parliaments de l'eau'[77]– and the development of contractualization,[78] Morocco has developed a participative, consultative and decentralized approach to water management. The 2003 Law on Environmental Impact Studies 12-03 guarantees public access to environmental information (transparency) and the right to appeal (accountability). Still, Morocco's environmental legislation shows several shortcomings. Authorities are not obliged to communicate their decisions, and claimants of appeals do not participate in juridical procedures.[79] As regards participation, the 1995 Law establishes the Supreme Council on Water and Climate, a consultative and non-permanent institution consisting of scientific experts and association representatives and serving as a platform for exchange of ideas.[80] Although the transfer of democratic governance elements to Moroccan environmental legislation has been quite successful, these are hardly applied. Administrative structures, such as the Water Council, are 'empty',[81] and legislation is rarely addressed by implementing decrees. The Law on Access to Environmental Legislation has hitherto not been ratified by the parliament. Participation of non-state actors in environmental decision-making is ceremonial, since they are invited only after the decisions are taken. Information offered to the public takes the form of pre-arranged reports on the state of the environment and public awareness campaigns (transparency).[82]

The legal basis of the Moroccan *asylum policy* is the 1957 'Decree on the Modalities of the Application of the Convention Relating to the Status of Refugees of 1951' (2-57-1256). However, it is not enforced due to the disregard of the legal supremacy of international law.[83] The 2003 Law 02-03 on the Entry and Stay of Foreigners acknowledges the primacy of international Conventions signed by Morocco. Importantly, it also introduces a few articles on refugees and asylum seekers that follow democratic norms and that have been incorporated as response to EU demands.[84] In case of refusal of asylum application, it obliges the authorities to explain their decision (accountability) and inform asylum seekers of their rights (transparency), provide access to a lawyer, and allow contesting the decision before an administrative court. However, it does not specify participation of other relevant actors. Furthermore, the law considerably strengthens the administration's discretionary use of power.[85] The application of the 2003 Law is problematic since without implementing decrees, it did not fully enter into force. Further, Morocco has no national centre for temporary accommodation of illegal migrants, asylum seekers and refugees. To compensate for this, the Moroccan Human Rights Organization opened the Reception and Legal Centre for Refugees. Its effect remains marginal, however, because lawyers and judges are not familiar with international standards and deportations proceed too fast for any juridical procedure to take place.

Table 2.   Country characteristics and democratic governance.

	Eastern neighbourhood		Southern neighbourhood	
	Moldova	Ukraine	Jordan	Morocco
Country properties				
Membership aspiration	$+$	$+$	$-$	$-$
Political liberalization	$+$	$+$	$-$	$-$
Democratic governance				
Adoption	$+/- (+)$	$+/-$	$- (+/-)$	$+/- (+)$
Application	$-$	$-$	$-$	$-$

Notes: Values: high or present, $+$; medium, $+/-$; low or absent, $-$. Values in brackets correspond to draft legislation.

Determinants and success of democratic governance transfer: comparative analysis

The most striking general finding of our analysis is the ambiguous impact of EU democratic governance promotion (Table 3). On the one hand, there is not a single case of strong application of EU democratic governance rules in the sample, and there are only two cases out of 12 in which some application has taken place. On the other hand, EU policies have a clear impact on the legislative adoption of democratic governance norms. While there has only been one case of strong compliance (Moldovan migration policy), in a clear majority of cases (9 out of 12), some adoption has taken place or is currently on the way. Given that our sample comprises the most favourable ENP countries, we cannot expect EU democratic governance promotion to work better elsewhere. But the variation in rule adoption is worth analysing further.

Our analysis does not support the East–South divide argument. Country properties indicate a clear dividing line between the Eastern and Southern neighbours of the EU: the former should be more successful in adopting and implementing democratic governance rules than the latter. Yet, as our discussion above showed, patterns in both rule adoption and rule application are quite similar across the four countries. Country properties, therefore, do not provide a satisfactory explanation for democratic governance transfer. To demonstrate this finding, we aggregate in Table 2 values for democratic governance in the three sectors under study into one average per country, based on our sectoral findings given in Table 3.

Regarding sector-specific factors, Table 3 shows that the transfer of democratic-governance provisions into domestic legislation of the selected ENP states follows a sectoral dynamic. A comparative analysis reveals that – with the exception of migration policy in Jordan – the selected sectors show similar properties across the four countries. Half of the cases show the same constellation of sectoral conditions and outcomes both in the presence and in the absence of membership aspirations and moderate political liberalization. This finding further undermines

DEMOCRACY PROMOTION IN THE EU'S NEIGHBOURHOOD

Table 3. Sectoral characteristics and democratic governance.

	Eastern neighbourhood		Southern neighbourhood	
	Moldova	Ukraine	Jordan	Morocco
Competition				
Sector properties				
Codification	−	−	−	−
Institutionalization	+/−	+/−	+/−	+/−
Interdependence	+	+	+/−	+
Costs	−	−	−	−
Democratic governance				
Adoption	− (+)	−	− (+/−)	−
Application	−	−	−	−
Environment				
Sector properties				
Codification	+	+	+	+
Institutionalization	+	+	+	+
Interdependence	+	+	+/−	+
Costs	+/−	+/−	+/−	+/−
Democratic governance				
Adoption	+/− (+)	+/−	− (+/−)	+/− (+)
Application	+/−	+/−	−	−
Migration				
Sector properties				
Codification	+/−	+/−	+/−	+/−
Institutionalization	+	+	−	+/−
Interdependence	+/−	+/−	−	+/−
Costs	+/−	+/−	+/−	+/−
Democratic governance				
Adoption	+	+/−	−	+/−
Application	−	−	−	−

Notes: Values: high or present, +; medium, +/−; low or absent, −. Values in brackets correspond to draft legislation. Note that the signs for 'costs' have been reversed for better comparison: high costs, here −, have a negative impact on adoption.

the East–South divide argument and refutes hypotheses H1 and H2 on the impact of country characteristics.

In contrast, hypotheses H3–H6 find general support for the proposition that sectoral properties affect democratic governance rule adoption. Our analysis generally demonstrates that democratic governance transfer is the more successful, the more strongly its provisions are codified in the sectoral *acquis*, the more institutionalized cooperation between the EU and ENP states is, the more interdependent the parties are, and, finally, the lower adoption costs are for national governments and sectoral authorities. Whenever all four sectoral conditions are at least moderately favourable (medium or high values), which happens to be the case in seven out of our 12 cases, legislation stipulating democratic governance is either adopted or under way. In contrast, none of the sectoral conditions is individually sufficient or necessary (see Table 4).

Conclusions

This contribution explored the democratizing potential of transgovernmental sectoral cooperation between the EU and four of its neighbours to the East and South. We argued that the governance model of external democracy promotion, which foresees the transfer of democratic rules and principles as part of policy-problem solutions, is an indirect strategy of fostering democratization in such countries, which resist direct democracy promotion efforts from the outside. We compared democratic governance rule transfer between two countries in the Eastern neighbourhood of the EU (Moldova and Ukraine) and a pair of states in the Southern neighbourhood (Jordan and Morocco) and explored country- and sector-related factors that are likely to facilitate or obstruct successful promotion of democratic governance.

Contrary to the East–South divide argument, we found similar patterns of rule adoption and rule application in all four countries. Both in the East and in the South, we detected a clear discrepancy between rule adoption and rule application: Whereas the EU has been fairly successful in inducing the four ENP countries to adopt legislation in line with democratic governance provisions, these provisions have – at least so far – generally not been implemented.

These commonalities between the Eastern and the Southern neighbours undermine the theoretical expectation about the influence of country characteristics on democratic governance transfer. In contrast, the influence of sector-specific properties is generally supported by the evidence. The absence of high adoption costs, and at least moderate interdependence, codification, and institutionalization, could be associated with actual or potential rule adoption. To predict rule adoption with high confidence, however, all conditions had to be jointly at least moderately favourable.

Can we generalize our results to the rest of the ENP countries? Although low liberalization and the absence of membership aspiration do not seem to present an obstacle to the transfer of *acquis*-based democratic governance elements, the importance of country-related factors cannot be completely ruled out. First, the selected countries comprised the politically most liberal countries in the respective regions at the time of research. While the difference in political liberalization did not matter for this sample, even weaker liberalization in the other ENP countries may well undermine far-reaching cooperation. Furthermore, changes in government, such as those recently experienced in Moldova and Ukraine, may yield not only retrogressions in levels of political liberalization but also a turn away from an EU focus and, despite the relative autonomy of sectoral cooperation dynamics, also declining levels of approximation to EU rules. Second, the comparatively less successful rule transfer in the case of Jordan appears to demonstrate the significance of proximity: Jordan's geographic position leads to less

Table 4. Data and truth table.

	Membership aspiration	Political liberalization	Codification	Institutionalization	Interdependence	Costs	Adoption
MOL COM	1	1	0	1	1	0	1
MOL ENV	1	1	1	1	1	1	1
MOL MIG	1	1	1	1	1	1	1
UKR COM	1	1	0	1	1	0	0
UKR ENV	1	1	1	1	1	1	1
UKR MIG	1	1	0	1	1	1	1
JOR COM	0	0	0	1	1	0	1
JOR ENV	0	0	1	1	1	1	1
JOR MIG	0	0	0	0	0	1	0
MOR COM	0	0	0	1	1	0	0
MOR ENV	0	0	1	1	1	1	1
MOR MIG	0	0	1	1	1	1	1

Memasp	Pollib	Cod	Inst	Interd	Cost	N	Adoption
1	1	1	1	1	1	4	1
1	1	0	1	1	0	2	0/1
0	0	1	1	1	1	3	1
0	0	0	0	0	1	1	0
0	0	1	1	1	1	2	0/1

Notes: The data are arranged as a 'truth table'; that is, each conditional configuration (combination of values of the independent variables) present in the data set is represented in one row together with the associated ('truth') value of the dependent variable 'adoption'. Conditions coded as present (1) when at least medium value in favour of adoption. Adoption coded as present (1) when at least medium and legislation under way.

interdependence with the EU and a less exclusive focus on the EU as a cooperation partner than in the closer neighbours. Liberalization and proximity can be expected to shape the degree of cooperation in general. On the basis of our findings, it can, however, be reasoned that if cooperation is agreed, the extent to which it influences the likelihood of successful promotion of democratic governance depends again on sectoral properties.

In sum, we maintain that the governance model has some potential for encouraging democratic developments in countries where more direct forms of external democracy promotion fail. The analysis clearly shows that democratic governance promotion is a separate model of democracy promotion that functions to some extent independently of general political conditions in the EU's neighbouring countries.

But were the EU to succeed in prompting democratic governance in its neighbouring states, would democratic governance trigger democratization at the polity level? The relationship between democratic governance and democracy is not necessarily bidirectional. On the one hand, empirical studies confirm that democracy is positively associated with democratic governance.[86] First, strong democratic institutions have a constraining effect on corruption and discretionary power of government officials. Second, they ensure the functioning of free media that have a supervisory function over governmental action, thus improving democratic accountability and transparency of policy-making.

On the other hand, there is no conclusive evidence that strong democratic governance in policy sectors leads necessarily to democratization of political institutions. Three scenarios are possible. First, in a neutral 'de-coupling' scenario, legislation containing democratic governance rules may simply remain a dead letter.[87] Governments adopt these rules in order to increase their legitimacy with the EU and other organizations and reap the benefits of international cooperation but will not apply them in practice if they harm vested political, administrative, or economic interests or if implementation is costly. At best, such a strategy of democratic governance promotion might lead to hybrid regimes through 'grafting "modern" liberal forms of governance in certain spheres onto essentially authoritarian structures'.[88] This is the most probable short-term scenario emerging from our case studies. Second, in the negative scenario, external actors may even risk undermining the prospects for further democratic reforms, stabilizing non-democratic political systems and eventually creating the so-called enlightened dictatorships.

Finally, viewed from a more optimistic and long-term perspective, the adoption of the principles of transparency, accountability and participation in sectoral legislation may, if properly applied, be one step in the mobilization of a more vivid civil society and a stronger societal control of state power, both of which would constitute important preconditions for democracy proper. We therefore conclude that while democratic governance is unlikely to – by itself – engender systemic change, it nevertheless plays an important role in preparing the legal and bureaucratic basis upon which eventual transitions towards a new democratic order can draw.

Acknowledgements

This contribution won the International Geneva Award of the Swiss Network of International Studies (SNIS), which is given to publications that are particularly relevant for International Organizations. This contribution presents the results of a project on 'Promoting Democracy in the EU's Neighbourhood' led by Sandra Lavenex and Frank Schimmelfennig within the Swiss National Centre for Competence in Research (NCCR) 'Challenges to Democracy in the 21st Century'. Financial support by the Swiss National Science Foundation (SNSF) is gratefully acknowledged. We would like to thank EU officials, representatives of international organizations, and Jordanian, Moldovan, Moroccan, and Ukrainian officials and civil society activists who provided the information for our empirical study. We also owe thanks for helpful comments to our two external reviewers, Michael Blauberger, participants of the 2009 special-issue workshop in Zurich, and to the discussant Rachel Vanderhill and audience at the ISA 2010 convention in New Orleans.

Notes

1. Lavenex, 'EU External Governance'; Lavenex, 'A Governance Perspective'; Magen, 'Transformative Engagement'.
2. Freyburg et al., 'EU Promotion of Democratic Governance'; Freyburg, Skripka, and Wetzel, 'Democracy between the Lines'.
3. Lavenex and Schimmelfennig, 'Models of EU Democracy Promotion'.
4. Missiroli, 'The ENP Three Years on', 1–2.
5. Sasse, 'The European Neighbourhood Policy', 297.
6. Patten and Solana, 'Wider Europe'.
7. Sasse, 'The European Neighbourhood Policy', 306.
8. European Commission/Moldova, 'EU-Moldova Action Plan', 2; Council of the EU, 'EU/Republic of Moldova Cooperation Council'; Sasse, 'The European Neighbourhood Policy', 308; Bürger, 'Implementing the Neighbourhood Policy', 172.
9. Casier, 'The EU's Two-Track Approach'.
10. E.g. Whitman and Wolff, 'Much ado about Nothing?', 12–13.
11. Sedelmeier, 'The European Neighbourhood Policy'.
12. Lavenex, Lehmkuhl, and Wichmann, 'Modes of External Governance'.
13. On democratic governance promotion via social interaction, see Freyburg 'Transgovernmental Networks'.
14. Beetham, Democracy and Human Rights, 4–5.
15. Hyden, Court, and Mease, Making Sense of Governance, 2.
16. Kaufmann, Kraay, and Mastruzzi, 'Governance Matters VI'.
17. Freyburg, Skripka, and Wetzel, 'Democracy between the Lines'.
18. Schedler, 'Conceptualizing Accountability', 25.
19. Cf. the concept of 'stakeholder democracy' in Matten and Crane, 'Stakeholder Democracy'.
20. Youngs, The European Union and the Promotion of Democracy, 363.
21. Zaharchenko and Goldenman, 'Accountability in Governance', 232.
22. Schimmelfennig and Sedelmeier, 'Governance by Conditionality', 669.
23. Kelley, 'New Wine in Old Wineskins'.
24. Emerson, Noutcheva, and Popescu, 'European Neighbourhood Policy', 10.
25. Schimmelfennig and Sedelmeier, 'Introduction', 18; cf. Franck, Legitimacy Among Nations.
26. Simmons, 'Compliance', 87.
27. Chayes and Handler Chayes, 'On Compliance', 188–92; Franck, Legitimacy among Nations, 38, 52–83.

28. Schimmelfennig, Engert, and Knobel, 'EU Political Conditionality', 31.
29. Dimitrova and Dragneva, 'Constraining External Governance'.
30. Lavenex and Schimmelfennig, 'EU Rules', 803–4.
31. Dimitrova and Dragneva, 'Constraining External Governance'.
32. Keohane and Nye, *Power and Interdependence*, 30–1.
33. Emerson, Noutcheva, and Popescu, 'European Neighbourhood Policy'.
34. Available at http://info.worldbank.org/governance/wgi/index.asp (accessed August 30, 2010).
35. European Commission, *ENP Country Report Moldova 2004*, 5.
36. Kelley, 'New Wine in Old Wineskins', 51; Del Sarto and Schumacher, 'From EMP to ENP'.
37. For a discussion of the particularities of transfer of EU state aid rules beyond Europe, see Blauberger and Krämer, 'European Competition'.
38. Bouillon, 'Walking the Tightrope', 17.
39. Article 19 and EcoPravo Kyiv, 'For Internal Use Only', 65.
40. E.g. Olwan, 'Iraqi Refugees in Jordan'.
41. European Community/Moldova, 'Agreement on the Facilitation of the Issuance of Visas'. 10 October 2007.
42. UNHCR, 'UNHCR Position'.
43. Zimmer, 'Ein ständiges Kommen und Gehen', 45.
44. Institute for Public Policy, Institute for Development and Social Initiatives 'Viitorul', and International Centre for Policy Studies, 'Migration Trends', 44.
45. Freyburg, 'The Janus Face', 13.
46. Until the NAPC was established to implement the 2000 competition law, the State Antimonopoly Committee had been supervising competitive practices in the Moldovan economy according to the 1992 Law on Restrictions of Monopolistic Activities and Development of Competition.
47. European Commission, *Country Report Moldova 2004*, 2; *Progress Report on Moldova 2006*, 10.
48. European Commission, *ENP Progress Report Moldova 2010*, 12.
49. Ibid.
50. European Commission, *ENP Progress Report Moldova 2008*, 16.
51. European Commission, *ENP Progress Report Moldova 2008*, 15–6.
52. European Commission, *ENP Progress Report Moldova 2006*, 11.
53. Akhtyrko et al. 'Free trade', 17, 20.
54. ECORYS Nederland BV and CASE Ukraine, *Global Analysis Report*, 120.
55. European Commission, *ENP Progress Report Ukraine 2008*, 11; European Commission, *ENP Progress Report Ukraine 2009*, 12.
56. Skrylnikov and Tustanovska, 'Ukraine', 135.
57. Stashuk, A., *Garmonizacija prirodoohrannogo Zakonodatel'stva*, 48–9.
58. European Commission, *ENP Progress Report Ukraine 2006*, 15.
59. UNECE, *Environmental Performance Reviews: Ukraine*, 49.
60. Article 19 and EcoPravo Kyiv, 'For Internal Use Only', 49.
61. European Commission, *ENP Progress Report Ukraine 2008*, 13.
62. UNHCR, 'UNHCR Position', 6–7, 9, 11.
63. ECRE, *Country Reports 2007*, 65–6.
64. European Commission, *ENP Progress Report Ukraine 2010*, 13.
65. European Commission, *ENP Progress Report Jordan 2009*.
66. *Jordan Times*: 'Making a Monopoly' (Yusuf Mansur), 30.06.2009.
67. Nabulsi, 'Implementation', 18.
68. Oxford Analytica, *Jordan. Fiscal Transparency, Country Report 2005*, 236.
69. European Commission, *ENP Progress Report Jordan 2009*, 14–5.

70. Ministry of Water and Irrigation of Jordan, 'Water Strategy 2008-22 "Water for Life"', 2009.
71. Wardam, 'More Politics then Water', 104, 114; Saidam and Ibrahim, 'Institutional and Policy Framework', 38.
72. *Jordan Times*: 'Journalists Say Access to Information Law Hinders Press Freedoms', 24 June 2007.
73. Government of Jordan/UNHCR, 'Memorandum of Understanding'; *Jordan Times*: 'Jordan-UNHCR Agreement on Refugees Signed in lieu of International Treaties' (Amy Henderson), 15 April 1998.
74. Olwan, 'Iraqi Refugees', 8.
75. See El Mernissi, 'Le Conseil De La Concurrence', 246–8 ; *Telquel*: 'Conseil de Concurrence. Le Coup de Pouce royal" (Fahd Iraqi), no. 337, 2009.
76. European Commission, *ENP Progress Report Morocco 2008.*
77. Hatimy, 'Loi sur l'Eau', 107.
78. Agoumi and Debbarh, 'Ressources en Eau', 51.
79. Final Twinning Report MA04/AA/EN03 from 18 November 2007, provided by the Ministry of Energy, Environment and Water of Morocco.
80. Decree on the Composition and Functioning of the Water and Climate Council, 2-96-158, 20 November 1996.
81. Sadeq, *Du Droit de l'Eau.*
82. European Commission, *ENP Progress Report Morocco 2006.*
83. Elmadmad, *Asile et Réfugiés.*
84. *Telquel*: 'Le Maroc brade la Question des Immigrés' (Laetitia Grotti), no. 68, 2003.
85. Rbii, 'La Loi 02-03', 90–5.
86. Cf., Rivera-Batiz, 'Democracy, Governance'; Baker, *Transitions from Authoritarianism.*
87. Meyer and Rowman, 'Institutional Organizations', 57.
88. Holden, 'Hybrids', 466.

Notes on contributors

Tina Freyburg is post-doctoral researcher and lecturer at the Centre for Comparative and International Studies, ETH Zurich, Switzerland.

Sandra Lavenex is Professor of International Politics at the University of Lucerne, Switzerland.

Frank Schimmelfennig is Professor of European Politics at the ETH Zurich, Switzerland.

Tatiana Skripka is a post-doctoral research fellow, KFG 'Transformative Power of Europe', Free University of Berlin, Germany.

Anne Wetzel is a post-doctoral researcher at the Centre for EU Studies, Ghent University, Belgium.

Bibliography

Agoumi, Ali, and Abdelhafid Debbarh. 'Ressources en Eau et Bassins versants du Maroc: 50 Ans de Développement (1955–2005)'. *50 Ans de Développement Humains. Perspectives 2025.* 2006. http://www.rdh50.ma (last accessed June 3, 2011).
Article 19 and EcoPravo Kyiv. 'For Internal Use Only. Is post-Chornobyl Ukraine Ready for Access to Environmental Information?' London, 2008.
Baker, Randall, ed. *Transitions from Authoritarianism. The Role of the Bureaucracy.* London: Praeger, 2002.

Beetham, David. *Democracy and Human Rights*. Cambridge: Polity Press, 1999.
Blauberger, Michael, and Rike U. Krämer. 'European Competition vs. Global Competitiveness: Transferring EU Rules on State Aid and Public Procurement beyond Europe'. Centre for Competition Policy (CCP) Working Paper 10, 2010.
Bouillon, Markus. 'Walking the Tightrope. Jordanian Foreign Policy from the Gulf Crisis to the Peace Process and Beyond', in *Jordan in Transition 1990–2000*, ed. George Joffé. London: Hurst, 2002, 1–22.
Bürger, Judith. 'Implementing the Neighbourhood Policy in the East: The Case of Ukraine', in *Europe's Near Abroad. Promises and Prospects of the EU's Neighbourhood Policy*, ed. Dieter Mahncke and Sieglinde Gstöhl. Brussels: Peter Lang, 2008, 165–83.
Casier, Tom. 'The EU's Two-Track Approach to Democracy Promotion. The Case of Ukraine'. *Democratization* 18, no. 4 (2011): XX–XX.
Chayes, Abram, and Antonia Handler Chayes. 'On Compliance'. *International Organization* 47, no. 2 (1993): 175–205.
Council of the EU. 'EU/Republic of Moldova Cooperation Council', 17732/09, Presse 388, 21 December 2009.
Del Sarto, Raffaella A., and Tobias Schumacher. 'From EMP to ENP: What's at Stake with the European Neighbourhood Policy Towards the Southern Mediterranean?'. *European Foreign Affairs Review* 10, no. 1 (2005): 17–38.
Dimitrova, Antoaneta, and Rilka Dragneva. 'Constraining External Governance: Interdependence with Russia and the CIS as Limits to the EU's Rule Transfer in the Ukraine'. *Journal of European Public Policy* 16, no. 6 (2009): 853–72.
ECORYS Nederland BV and CASE Ukraine. *Global Analysis Report for the EU-Ukraine TSIA*, Ref: TRADE06/D01. Final Version. 30 August 2007.
ECRE. *Country Reports 2007. Belarus, Moldova, Russian Federation and Ukraine. Situation for Refugees, Asylum-Seekers and Internally Displaced Persons (IDPs)*, 2008. http://www.ecre.org/resources/Policy_papers/1222 (last accessed June 3, 2011).
Elmadmad, Khadija. *Asile et Réfugiés dans les Pays Afro-Arabes*. Casablanca: Eddif, 2002.
El Mernissi, Mohamed. 'Le Conseil de la Concurrence: Organe de Régulation de la Concurrence'. *Revue Marocaine de Droit et d'Economie du Développement* no. 49 (2004): 243–63.
Emerson, Michael, Gergana Noutcheva, and Nicu Popescu. 'European Neighbourhood Policy Two Years on: Time indeed for an "ENP Plus"'. Centre for European Policy Studies (CEPS) Policy Briefs, 126, 2007.
European Commission. *ENP Country Report Moldova*, SEC(2004)567, 12 May 2004.
European Commission. *ENP Progress Report Morocco*, SEC(2006)1511/2, 4 December 2006.
European Commission. *ENP Progress Report Moldova*, SEC(2006)1506/2, 4 December 2006.
European Commission. *ENP Progress Report Ukraine*, SEC (2006)1505/2, 4 December 2006.
European Commission. *ENP Progress Report Morocco*, SEC(2008)398, 3 April 2008.
European Commission. *ENP Progress Report Moldova*, SEC(2008)399, 3 April 2008.
European Commission. *ENP Progress Report Ukraine*, SEC (2008)402, 3 April 2008.
European Commission, ENP Progress Report Ukraine, SEC(2009)515/2, 23 April 2009.
European Commission. *ENP Progress Report Jordan*, SEC(2009)517/2, 23 April 2009.
European Commission. *ENP Progress Report Moldova*, SEC(2010) 523, 12 May 2010.
European Commission. *ENP Progress Report Ukraine*, SEC(2010) 524, 12 May 2010.
European Commission/Moldova. 'EU-Moldova Action Plan', 21 February 2005. http:// ec.europa.eu/world/enp/pdf/action_plans/moldova_enp_ap_final_en.pdf (last accessed June 3, 2011)

Franck, Thomas M. *The Power of Legitimacy among Nations*. Oxford: Oxford University Press, 1990.

Freyburg, Tina. 'Transgovernmental Networks as Catalysts for Democratic Change? EU Functional Cooperation and Socialization into Democratic Governance' *Democratization* 18, no. 4 (2011): 1001–1025.

Freyburg, Tina. 'The Janus Face of EU Migration Governance: Impairing democratic governance at home – improving it abroad?'. Paper presented at the joint conference of the Swiss, Austrian and German Political Science Associations, Basel, Switzerland, January 13–14, 2011.

Freyburg, Tina, Sandra Lavenex, Frank Schimmelfennig, Tatiana Skripka, and Anne Wetzel. 'EU Promotion of Democratic Governance in the Neighbourhood'. *Journal of European Public Policy* 16, no. 6 (2009): 916–34.

Freyburg, Tina, Tatiana Skripka, and Anne Wetzel. 'Democracy between the Lines? EU Promotion of Democratic Governance via Sector-Specific Co-operation'. NCCR Democracy Working Paper 5, 2007.

Government of Jordan/UNHCR. 'Memorandum of Understanding', *Jordanian Official Gazette* 4277, 3 May 1998.

Grotti, Laetitia, 'Le Maroc brade la Question des Immigrés', *Telquel*, no. 68, 2003.

Hatimy, Farid. 'Loi Sur L'eau: Aspects Innovants Et Acteurs Intervenants'. *Revue Marocaine d'Administration Locale et de Développement* 37 (2001): 69–112.

Henderson, Amy, 'Jordan-UNHCR Agreement on Refugees Signed in lieu of International Treaties, *Jordan Times*, April 15, 1998.

Holden, Patrick. 'Hybrids on the Rim? The European Union's Mediterranean Aid Policy'. *Democratization* 12, no. 4 (2005): 461–80.

Hyden, Goran, Julius Court, and Kenneth Mease. *Making Sense of Governance. Empirical Evidence from Sixteen Developing Countries*. Boulder: Lynne Rienner, 2004.

Institute for Public Policy, Institute for Development and Social Initiatives 'Viitorul', and International Centre for Policy Studies. *Migration Trends and Policies in the Black Sea Region: Cases of Moldova, Romania and Ukraine*. Kiev, 2008.

Iraqi, Fahd, 'Conseil de Concurrence. Le Coup de Pouce royal', Telquel, no. 337, 2009.

Jordan Times, 'Journalists Say Access to Information Law Hinders Press Freedoms', June 24, 2007.

Kaufmann, Daniel, Aart Kraay, and Massimo Mastruzzi. 'Governance Matters Vi: Governance Indicators for 1996–2007'. The World Bank Policy Research Working Paper 4954, 2007.

Kelley, Judith. 'New Wine in Old Wineskins: Promoting Political Reforms through the New European Neighbourhood Policy'. *Journal of Common Market Studies* 44, no. 1 (2006): 29–55.

Keohane, Robert, and Jospeh S. Nye. *Power and Interdependence*. Boston: Little, Brown and Co., 1989.

Lavenex, Sandra. 'EU External Governance in "Wider Europe"'. *Journal of European Public Policy* 11, no. 4 (2004): 688–708.

Lavenex, Sandra. 'A Governance Perspective on the European Neighbourhood Policy: Integration Beyond Conditionality?'. *Journal of European Public Policy* 15, no. 6 (2008): 938–55.

Lavenex, Sandra, Lehmkuhl, Dirk, and Nicole Wichmann. 'Modes of External Governance: A Cross-National and Cross-Sectoral Comparison'. *Journal of European Public Policy* 16, no. 6 (2009): 813–33.

Lavenex, Sandra, and Frank Schimmelfennig. 'EU Rules beyond EU Borders: Theorizing External Governance in European Politics'. *Journal of European Public Policy* 16, no. 6 (2009): 791–812.

Lavenex, Sandra, and Frank Schimmelfennig. 'Models of EU Democracy Promotion: From Leverage to Governance?'. *Democratization* 18, no. 4 (2011): 885–909.

Magen, Amichai. 'Transformative Engagement Through Law: The *Acquis Communautaire* as an Instrument of EU External Influence'. *European Journal of Law Reform* 9, no. 3 (2007): 361–92.

Matten, Dirk, and Andrew Crane. 'What is Stakeholder Democracy? Perspectives and Issues'. *Business Ethics* 14, no. 1 (2005): 107–22.

Meyer, J.W., and Rowan, B. 'Institutional Organizations: Formal Structure as Myth and Ceremony', in *The New Institutionalism in Organizational Analysis*, ed. W.W. Powell and P.J. DiMaggio. Chicago: University of Chicago Press, 2001, 41–62.

Ministry of Water and Irrigation of Jordan, *Water Strategy 2008-2022 'Water for Life'*, February 2009.

Missiroli, Antonio. '*The ENP Three Years On: Here From – and Where Next?*'. Brussels: European Policy Centre Policy Brief, 2007.

Nabulsi, Mohamed. 'Implementation of Jordan-EU Action Plan: A CSS Independent Evaluation 2008'. Amman: Centre for Strategic Studies at the University of Jordan, 2009.

Olwan, Mohammed. 'Iraqi Refugees in Jordan: Legal Perspective'. CARIM Analytic and Synthetic Notes 22, 2009.

Oxford Analytica. *Jordan. Fiscal Transparency. Country Report 2005*, 233–49. http://www.calpers.ca.gov/eip-docs/investments/assets/equities/international/permissible/jordan-fiscal-report.pdf (last accessed June 3, 2011).

Patten, Christopher, and Javier Solana. *Wider Europe*, 7 August 2002.

Rbii, Hamid. 'La Loi 02-03 relative à l'Entrée et au Séjour des Etrangers au Maroc, À l'Emigration et l'Immigration irrégulières: Contrôle des Flux migratoires et Droits des Etrangers'. *Centre d'Etudes des Mouvements Migratoires Maghrébins* 8 (2006): 88–122.

Rivera-Batiz, Francisco L. 'Democracy, Governance, and Economic Growth: Theory and Evidence'. *Review of Development Economics* 6, no. 2 (2002): 225–47.

Sadeq, Houria Tazi. *Du Droit de l'Eau au Droit à l'Eau au Maroc et Ailleurs*. Casablanca: EDDIF, 2006.

Saidam, Mohammed, and Mohammed Ibrahim. 'Institutional and Policy Framework. Analysis of Water Sector Jordan'. Policy paper of the Royal Scientific Society, 2006.

Sasse, Gwendolyn. 'The European Neighbourhood Policy: Conditionality Revisited for the EU's Eastern Neighbours'. *Europe-Asia Studies* 60, no. 2 (2008): 295–316.

Schedler, Andreas. 'Conceptualizing Accountability', in *The Self-Restraining State: Power and Accountability in New Democracies*, ed. Andreas Schedler, Larry Diamond, and Marc F. Plattner. Boulder: Lynne Rienner, 1999, 13–28.

Schimmelfennig, Frank, and Ulrich Sedelmeier. 'Governance by Conditionality: EU Rule Transfer to the Candidate Countries of Central and Eastern Europe'. *Journal of European Public Policy* 11, no. 4 (2004): 661–79.

Schimmelfennig, Frank, and Ulrich Sedelmeier. 'Introduction: Conceptualizing the Europeanization of Central and Eastern Europe', in *The Europeanization of Central and Eastern Europe*, ed. Schimmelfennig, Frank, and Ulrich Sedelmeier. Ithaca, NY: Cornell University Press, 2005, 1–28.

Schimmelfennig, Frank, Stefan Engert, and Heiko Knobel. 'The Impact of EU Political Conditionality', in *The Europeanization of Central and Eastern Europe*, ed. Frank Schimmelfennig, and Ulrich Sedelmeier. Ithaca, NY: Cornell University Press, 2005, 29–50.

Sedelmeier, Ulrich. 'The European Neighbourhood Policy: A Comment on Theory and Policy', in *Governing Europe's Neighbourhood: Partners or Periphery?* ed. Katja Weber, Michael E. Smith, and Michael Baun. Manchester: Manchester University Press, 2007, 195–208.

Simmons, Beth A. 'Compliance with International Agreements'. *Annual Review of Political Science* 1 (1998): 75–93.
Skrylnikov, Dmitriy, and Irina Tustanovska. 'Ukraine', in *Doors to Democracy. Current Trends and Practices in Public Participation in Environmental Decisionmaking in the Newly Independent States*, ed. Ecopravo-Lviv and the Regional Environmental Center for Central and Eastern Europe. Szentendre, 1998, 135–65.
Stashuk, A. *Garmonizacija prirodoohrannogo Zakonodatel'stva (Ukraina)*. Kiev, 2006.
UNECE. *Environmental Performance Reviews: Ukraine*, Second Review. New York, 2007.
UNHCR. 'UNHCR Position on the Situation of Asylum in Ukraine in the Context of Return of Asylum-Seekers'. 2007. http://www.unhcr.org/refworld/docid/472f43162.html (last accessed June 3, 2011).
Wardam, Batir. 'More Politics Then Water: Water Rights in Jordan', in *Water as a Human Right: The Understanding of Water in Arab Countries of the Middle East*, ed. Karen Assaf, Bayoumi Attia, Ali Darwish, Batir Wardam, and Simone Klawitter. Berlin: Heinrich-Böll-Foundation, 2004, 60–107.
Whitman, Richard G., and Stefan Wolff. 'Much Ado About Nothing? The European Neighbourhood Policy in Context', in *The European Neighbourhood Policy in Perspective. Context, Implementation, and Impact*, ed. Richard G. Whitman and Stefan Wolff. Houndmills, Basingstoke: Palgrave Macmillan, 2010, 3–26.
Yevhenia Akhtyrko, Oleksiy Blinov, Borys Bordiuh, Ildar Gazizullin, Oleksiy Kalachov, Oleksandr Liakh, Kateryna Maliuhina, et al. *Free Trade between Ukraine and the EU: An Impact Assessment*. Kiev: International Centre for Policy Studies, 2007).
Youngs, Richard. *The European Union and the Promotion of Democracy: Europe's Mediterranean and Asian Policies*. Oxford: Oxford University Press, 2001.
Zaharchenko, Tatiana R., and Gretta Goldenman. 'Accountability in Governance: The Challenge of Implementing the Aarhus Convention in Eastern Europe and Central Asia'. *International Environmental Agreements: Politics, Law and Economics* 4 (2004): 229–51.
Zimmer, Kerstin. 'Ein ständiges Kommen und Gehen. Die Rolle der Ukraine im europäischen Migrationssystem'. *Geographische Rundschau* 59, no. 12 (2007): 40–6.

Index

environmental policy 99–106: access to
environmental information 99–102,
149, 153–6, 158; Central and Eastern
Europe 96, 99, 153; competition
policy 127; cooperation 99–100, 102–
3, 105–6; costs of adoption 151;
European Neighbourhood Policy 144,
149, 150–1, 153, 156–8, 160; fisheries
18, 96, 98–9, 103–5, 106; genetically
modified organisms 18, 96, 98–102,
106; governance model 18; impact
assessments 99; Jordan 156; Moldova
153; Morocco 19, 126–7, 130, 132,
157–8; participation 99–106; sectoral
economic interests 96, 97–8; security
98; state officials in authoritarian
regimes, socialization of 19, 126–7,
130, 132; transparency 145; water
governance102–3,106, 144, 149–51
Erdoğan, Recep Tayyip 30, 31, 39
essential elements clauses 15
Euro-Mediterranean partnership (EMP)
(Barcelona Process) 48–50
European Convention on Human
Rights 35, 54
European Neighbourhood Policy (ENP)
142–64: access to environmental
information 149, 155–6,158;
accession/enlargement 76, 143–9, 162;
accountability 142–3, 152–8, 163;
application of rules 18, 144, 148, 161;
asylum policy 144, 149, 151–5, 157–9;
authoritarian regimes 15, 142–3, 163;
benchmarking 52, 55–62; Central and
Eastern Europe 17–18, 76–8, 83, 87,
99–103, 106, 143–4, 148–55, 159, 161;
civil society 145; codification 147–8,
149, 152–3, 160–2; competition 144,
149–50, 153, 156, 160;
cooperation 12–13, 15, 143–4, 147,
150–2, 160–3; cost-benefit analysis
143–4, 161; costs of adoption 147–53,
161–2; country properties 145–61;
decentralization 145; effectiveness
143–4, 147; environment 144, 149,
150–1, 153, 155–8, 160; functional
cooperation 143–4, 146, 148–61;
geographical position 161–3;
governance model 2, 3–4, 12, 16, 18,
144; human rights 154;
institutionalization 147, 149–50, 152–
3, 160–3; intensity of cooperation 15,
17, 56; interdependence 143–4, 147–
53, 161–2; Jordan 144, 148–52, 155–7,

159, 161–2 ; leverage model 4, 14–15,
17, 49, 143; Mediterranean/Southern
region 3–4, 15, 17, 49–50, 52, 55–63,
143–4, 148–61; migration policy 144,
149, 151–60; Moldova 143–4, 148–54,
159, 161; Morocco 144, 148–52, 157–
9; non-candidate countries 3, 14–15;
participation 142–3, 153–4, 157, 163;
political liberalization 144–5, 149,
159–61; positive conditionality 17, 49;
rule adoption 2, 12, 76, 142–61;
sectors 95, 98, 143–61; shared values
3, 15; state aid 144, 149–50, 153–4,
156–7; technical assistance 150, 152;
transgovernmental networks 12–13,
120, 161; transparency 142–3, 152–4,
157–8, 163; Turkey 3–4; twinning 150,
157; Ukraine 17–18, 76–8, 83, 87,
143–4, 148–55, 159, 161; water
governance 144, 149–51, 153–8 see
also action plans (ENP)
experts 120–1, 125, 128, 133, 150

Falkner, Robert 101
fisheries 18, 96, 98–9, 103–5, 106
formal democracy 17–18, 73–88
freedom of movement 26, 37–8
Freyburg, Tina 119, 127
functional cooperation: European
Neighbourhood Policy 143–4, 146,
148–61; sectoral economic interests
95, 105; state officials in authoritarian
regimes, socialization of 118–19, 121,
125, 127, 132–3

gender equality 32, 35, 42, 59, 61–2
genetically modified organisms (GMOs)
18, 96, 98–102, 106
geographical proximity 15, 16, 97, 98,
161–3
governance model of democracy
promotion 11–14: accountability 11–
12, 20, 145; administration, autonomy
and accessibility of 13–14, 16;
application of rules 18, 144; Central
and Eastern Europe 3–4, 18, 73;
channels of democracy promotion 6;
civil society 12, 13–14, 20;
codification 147, 149; competition
policy 18; costs of adoption 13, 18;
definition 2, 3; democracy, definition
of 144; determinants of transfer 145–
8; effectiveness 12–14, 18;
environmental policy 18; European

Related titles from Routledge

Defending Democracy and Securing Diversity

Edited by Christian Leuprecht

The chapters in this volume strive to enlighten the debate on democracy by laying out the concepts, clarifying theoretical issues, and providing empirical evidence. The case studies draw on Canada, Guyana, the Netherlands, South Africa, and the United Kingdom. They examine ethno-cultural, gender, and sexual-minority diversity in a variety of missions, including Bosnia-Herzegovina and Afghanistan. Although scholarly in nature, the book is readily accessible to professionals and practitioners alike.

This book was published as a special issue of *Commonwealth and Comparative Politics*.

Christian Leuprecht is associate professor of political science at the Royal Military College of Canada and cross-appointed to the School of Policy Studies and Department of Political Studies at Queen's University.

July 2010: 216 x 138mm, 256pp
Hb: 978-0-415-57649-9
£85 / $133

www.routledge.com/9780415587198

Related titles from Routledge

European Neighbourhood through Civil Society Networks?

Policies, Practices and Perceptions

Edited by James Wesley Scott and Ilkka Liikanen

This book has a dual objective: on the one hand, it focuses on the actual and potential roles of civil society in developing new forms of political, economic, and socio-cultural cooperation between the European Union and its neighbours. On the other hand, through this investigation of civil society networks we will contribute to debate on the EU's role as promoter of greater regional co-operation.

We ask whether the EU's promotion of cross-border co-operation (e.g. though the European Neighbourhood Policy) is empowering civil society within member states and in neighbouring countries such as Russia, Moldova, Turkey and Morocco.

James Wesley Scott is Professor of Geography in the Karelian Institute, University of Joensuu, Finland.

Ilkka Liikanen is Researcher in Comparative Historical Sociology, the Karelian Institute, University of Joensuu, Finland.

February 2011: 246 x 174: 136pp
Hb: 978-0-415-58719-8
£95 / $133

For more information and to order a copy visit
www.routledge.com/9780415587198

Available from all good bookshops

www.routledge.com/9780415594233

Related titles from Routledge

Promoting Party Politics in Emerging Democracies

Edited by Peter Burnell and Andre Gerrits

This book offers a critical and comparative examination of international support to political parties and party systems in emerging and prospective new democracies in several world regions. It combines the insights of a strong international grouping of leading academics and pioneering doctoral studies, and draws on extensive new field work inquiries. The wide-ranging coverage pools evidence from countries in Europe and Eurasia, Africa, East Asia and Central America. This book was published as a special issue of *Democratizations*.

Peter Burnell is a Professor in the Department of Politics and International Studies, University of Warwick, England.

Andre W. M. Gerrits is Jean Monnet Chair in European Studies at the University of Amsterdam and Senior Research Fellow at the Netherlands Institute of International Relations Clingendael, The Hague.

July 2011: 234 x 156: 256pp
Hb: 978-0-415-59423-3
£90 / $133

For more information and to order a copy visit
www.routledge.com/9780415594233

Available from all good bookshops